# Princess
# Mary

# Princess Mary

## The First Modern Princess

## Elisabeth Basford

### Foreword by Hugo Vickers

The History Press

*For J.D.*

First published 2021
Reprinted 2021

The History Press
97 St George's Place, Cheltenham,
Gloucestershire, GL50 3QB
www.thehistorypress.co.uk

British Library Cataloguing in Publication Data.
A catalogue record for this book is available from the British Library.

ISBN 978 0 7509 9261 9

Typesetting and origination by The History Press
Printed and bound in Great Britain by TJ Books Limited, Padstow, Cornwall.

# Contents

# Acknowledgements

There are many people who made the research and writing of this biography such a joyous experience and to them I am truly grateful. Every effort has been made to locate copyright holders and obtain permission to reproduce sources. For those sources where it has been difficult to trace the copyright holder of the work, I would be grateful for information. If any copyright holder would like an amendment to the acknowledgements, please notify me and I shall gladly update the next reprint. Sincerest apologies if I have omitted anyone from this list. Again, I would be happy to amend this in the next reprint.

My thanks go to the following for providing considerable research material. To Her Majesty Queen Elizabeth II for her gracious permission to study and reproduce Princess Mary's letters and Queen Mary's letters and diaries. To the Royal Archives at Windsor and especially to Julie Crocker, Lynette Beech and Colin Parish. If it had not been for Colin, I would never have made it up the steep incline to the Archives. To Mark and Clare Oglesby at Goldsborough Hall, who started me off on my journey and gave their time and considerable knowledge so generously. Goldsborough Hall is now as spectacular as it was in the time of Princess Mary and visiting the Hall inspired me greatly. To David Lascelles, 8th Earl of Harewood, and the Harewood House Trust, especially Rebecca Burton and Lindsey Porter for permissions and assistance in all things Harewood. To Tasha Swainston, archivist at the National Army Museum and Elizabeth Ennion-Smith, Pembroke College, University of Cambridge for enabling me to see so many of Mary's letters and for helping me to disprove another misconception concerning Mary. To Christopher Ussher, Princess Mary's godson, for personal insight. To the Royal Scots Regimental Office and Frank Gogos, curator at the Royal Newfoundland Regiment Museum for information concerning Mary as a colonel-in-chief. To Jane Rosen and Belinda Haley at the Imperial War Museum for so much information concerning the Princess Mary Tin and enabling me to hear Mary's voice for the first time. To Lord Middleton for permission to view a large number of letters from Princess Mary to Lord Middleton. To Gareth Williams, curator and head of learning at the Weston Park Foundation for being so generous with his knowledge and for providing many photographs. To Anne Williamson and John Gregory of the Henry Williamson Society for such benevolence. Rebecca Higgins at Special Collections, University of Leeds Library. University of Leeds Archive for sourcing information relating to Mary's patronage of the university and information regarding her patronages in the north of England. To Denise Summerton and Jayne Amat, Manuscripts and Special Collections, Nottingham University. To Guy Storrs, for permission to reproduce extracts from the Ronald Storrs archive and such a wonderful email correspondence. To L'Institut Pasteur for permissions relating to the Duke of Windsor.

In addition, I should like to thank the institutions who provided contemporary sources and information from their archives: Alan and Julie at the Special Collections Department, Toronto Reference Library; the Australian War Memorial; the Borthwick Institute for Archives, York; Danielle Triggs, West Yorkshire Archive Service, Leeds; Helen Clark, supervisor, East Riding Archives; Library and Archives, Canada; Nick Baldwin at Great Ormond Street Hospital NHS Foundation Trust; Aidan Haley, assistant archivist and librarian, Devonshire Collection Chatsworth; Lloyd Pocock from Ashstead Pottery; Lyndsey Hendry, Girlguiding UK; Newfoundland Museum; Portumna Castle; Public Record Office Northern Ireland; QARANC Association; Rebecca Jackson, Staffordshire and Stoke on Trent Archive Service; Wiltshire and

Swindon History Centre; the Memorial University of Newfoundland; Visit Portumna; West Yorkshire Leeds Archives; Ludgrove School.

Thanks to the British Newspaper Archive and in particular Eddie Bundy for permissions and proving to be such an invaluable source of factual information and to Tom at Back Issue Newspapers for providing copies of *The Times*.

For additional photographs: Bibelots London: Ephemera and Curiosities; the wonderful Barry Sullivan at D.C. Thomson; Royal Newfoundland Regiment Museum; Lee Turnbull; Victoria Ann Fletcher for her incredible image of Harewood.

Individuals who shared with me details of their personal archives so generously: Elaine Merckx at Wakefield Girls' High School; Joy Broughton at the Red Poll Cattle Society; Julia Knight at the Queen Mother's Clothing Guild.

For additional permissions: Katie Widdowson, assistant archives officer, UK Parliament, Westminster, London; Kate Symonds at the Wellcome Collection; Laura Lacey, rights and licensing executive, British Medical Journal; Megan McCooley, moving image archivist, Yorkshire Film Archive; Penguin Books; Renegade Productions; Orion Publishing Group; Jack Baker at Harper Collins Publishers; the Jack the Ripper Tour; the Witchita State University Digital Collection; the Girl Guiding movement; the Irish Wolfhound Society; Wakefield Publishing; BBC Sounds; JPI Media; Orion Publishing Group Ltd.

For details concerning personal items belonging to Princess Mary: Christies Auctioneers.

In the virtual world of social media: to all the followers of my blog *Write On Ejaleigh*, especially Messiah Kaeto. To the Facebook and Instagram followers of Princess Mary, Princess Royal. To Nash Rambler and the Esoteric Curiosa.

To Mary Mackie for her knowledge of PMRANS; Marlene A. Eilers Koenig for her encyclopaedic knowledge of European dynasties and Alexandra Churchill for her knowledge of George V as a father. To Milly Johnson for inspiration in my writing. To Nick Holland, a fellow writer and Brontë lover, who supported and encouraged me right from the very start of this process.

To The History Press, especially Christine McMorris and my editors, Simon Wright and Alex Waite; for helping me to tell Princess Mary's story.

An immense thank you to the wonderful royal biography community, who have welcomed me so warmly. My sincere thanks go especially to Christopher Warwick for his kind-heartedness, generosity and vast knowledge and for being such a wonderful and witty raconteur.

To my family and friends for understanding during this process, especially to Auntie Jenny for supporting me so much in my writing, William for his historical context knowledge and Sofia for all things social media and IT.

Thank you to Joanne Spick for sparking my love of royal history since 1982 and Derek Maberly for encouraging me to write this for thirty years.

To work colleagues, especially Catherine and Sue, for believing in me and for allowing me time off to research and write.

Thank you to Hugo Vickers for kindly writing a foreword and for assisting me so much in my research. For years I have admired you greatly and I am still so much in awe of you.

To my husband for all the jobs you did around the house, all the times you drove me to places and all the days you let me go into my own world to write.

Finally, this book is dedicated to my dad, who always answered every question I asked as a child, sat around waiting for me at every event, got himself into immense debt to ensure I was educated and more than anything else, encouraged me to write this book. Thank you, J.D.

*Elisabeth J. Basford, 2020*

# Foreword

At last a biography of Princess Mary, the Queen's aunt – and a good one. Until now, we have had to search for her in other books, perhaps the best account can be found in the memoirs of her son, Lord Harewood – *The Tongs and the Bones.* She was the daughter of George V and Queen Mary and sister to two kings. She has long deserved a full study and in Elisabeth Basford she has found a dedicated and sympathetic biographer, who has done her full justice.

In the early days of this reign, the Queen and Prince Philip had a young family and there were very few working members of the Royal Family, the others being the Queen Mother, Princess Margaret, the Duke and Duchess of Gloucester, and Princess Marina, with the young Duke of Kent and Princess Alexandra beginning to undertake royal duties. Princess Mary was a hard working member of this team, doing what the Royal Family do best – supporting the monarch and taking on the engagements she doesn't have time to fulfil. In this book, we see Princess Mary emerging from the confines of royal life as an immensely popular princess, nursing in the First World War, supporting the troops in whatever way she could, and her marriage to Viscount Lascelles, becoming Yorkshire's Princess – but this did not stop her travelling all over the world. She was well known in Canada and the Caribbean, and 17,000 children cheered her to the echo as she toured a racecourse in

Ibadan in an open Land Rover during an important visit to Nigeria in 1957, waving with the circular hand wave of Queen Mary. Princess Mary had to face many challenges in her life and Elisabeth Basford tackles these as well.

It is a particular pleasure for me to be asked to introduce this special book. Only now does it occur to me that the Princess Royal was the first member of the Royal Family I ever saw close to, as opposed to taking part in a distant ceremony. I was 8 years old and walking along Brompton Road with my mother. We saw a small crowd gathered outside Lord Roberts's Workshops, more or less opposite Harrods. It seems that the Princess paid them an annual visit each November and this I worked out was on 6 November 1959. Presently she came out and walked to her car. We got such a good view of her. I remember being sad when she died, relatively young, in 1965.

Now, at last, I have been able to read her whole story.

Hugo Vickers
October 2020

# Preface

On a magnificent spring morning in April 2011 Catherine Middleton, a commoner, processed down the aisle of Westminster Abbey in an Alexander McQueen dress of ivory satin and gazar silk, while the uplifting sound of Sir Hubert Parry's choral anthem 'I was glad' filled the nave. After the ceremony, and accompanied by a full peal of bells, she emerged radiantly from the abbey; a royal princess and a possible future queen. There was much joyous celebration, with over a million people lining the route from the abbey. As the new bride made her way on to the Buckingham Palace balcony she was seen to exclaim, 'Wow!' at her first glimpse of the crowds who had surged past the Queen Victoria Memorial in order to demonstrate their approval. The sun shone even brighter that day on the new golden couple, whom everyone believed would bring some much-needed fresh blood and humanity to the royal family. Hailed as the 'wedding of the century', here was the living embodiment of a fairy tale; a prince and future king had married a beautiful young woman for love, rather than any political or dynastic alliance. Catherine was a new breed of princess, for a modern age of monarchy.

Within a few weeks, Catherine had already begun her philanthropic work championing the causes most significant to her, such as vulnerable women and children, the homeless, mental health and addiction. In lieu of receiving gifts for their wedding, Catherine and William established the Royal Wedding Charity Fund to support their charities. Catherine is considered to be a down-to-earth princess who is strongly aware of social issues and takes a hands-on role in all her charity work, such as designing a garden for children at Chelsea to inspire families to go out-doors into nature, donating her hair to cancer victims as part of the Little Princess Trust, working as a 'secret' midwife in order to raise awareness of their work, speaking on a podcast of her own difficulties when first becoming a mother.

Some might believe that her behaviour as a princess is modelled greatly on her late mother-in-law, Diana, Princess of Wales. Certainly, Diana was not afraid to take on causes that were unpopular at the time, such as leprosy and HIV. Diana was far more tactile and involved in her royal duties and she was the first member of the royal family to shake hands with a sufferer of AIDS. We tend to believe that it was Diana who first ripped up the royal rule book that determined how a princess should behave in modern times. We could not be further from the truth.

When they married, both Diana and Catherine continued a royal bridal tradition of honouring the war dead by placing their bridal bou-quets on the Tomb of the Unknown Soldier in Westminster Abbey. In doing so, they were continuing a tradition started in 1922 by a royal bride who stopped during the ride back to her wedding breakfast at Buckingham Palace and laid a bouquet on the Cenotaph to honour the dead from the First World War. Her name was Princess Mary, and she was the only daughter of the present queen's grandfather, King George V, and his wife, Queen Mary.

Today Princess Mary remains relatively unknown. Few people know who she was or what she looked like and yet so many modern prin-cesses owe her a debt of gratitude for the way she paved for them in ensuring that a princess's life was not just about standing around look-ing pretty and organising social gatherings. Mary wanted to make a difference in her work and, more than anything, she wished to use her elevated position to help those who were less fortunate than herself. What makes this even more remarkable is that she was born during Queen Victoria's Diamond Jubilee in 1897, a time of deference to the crown and solemnity.

Princess Mary was Britain's first modern princess. This is evident from a glance at some of her most significant charitable achievements. During the First World War she visited hospitals and welfare organisations with her mother, Queen Mary. In particular, she was involved with charities supporting the wives and children of soldiers serving in France. She organised the Princess Mary Gift Fund during the First World War as a way of ensuring British troops and sailors received a Christmas gift. She worked in a canteen in a munitions factory in Hayes. But her main interest lay in nursing, especially the work of the Voluntary Aid Detachment (VAD). Mary trained to be a nurse and worked on a ward at Great Ormond Street Hospital.

Princess Mary was one of the hardest working members of the royal family. She was known as the 'Queen of the North', a title given because she lived at Harewood in Yorkshire and because the number of royal engagements that she undertook, mainly in the north of England, was monumental. In 1922 Mary married the much older heir to the Earldom of Harewood, Henry Lascelles. Mary spent over thirty years living at Harewood House in Yorkshire from 1930. Harewood is a magnificent stately home that houses many treasures including art from the Renaissance and Chippendale furniture, as well as landscapes designed by Capability Brown. Mary took a keen interest in the interior decoration and renovation of Harewood.

Yet Mary was the daughter of a king and the sister of two others, as well as being the aunt of the current queen, Elizabeth II. Mary held a unique position in many key events and meetings in twentieth-century royal history. She witnessed how George V had to adapt the monarchy to ensure its survival at a particularly turbulent time following the fall of the empires of his first cousins Nicholas II of Russia and Wilhelm II of Germany. Similarly, after the First World War, the monarchies of Austria, Greece and Spain fell to revolution and war. George V changed the name of the royal family to Windsor in 1917 as a result of anti-German public sentiment. He was the first monarch to give a Christmas speech in 1932. He understood the importance of being visible to his subjects and he established a standard of conduct for British royalty that reflected the upper middle class rather than the upper class.

Mary was the sister of Edward, Prince of Wales, later Edward VIII and ultimately the Duke of Windsor. As siblings they were very close. Mary saw at first hand the full implications and issues surrounding the abdication crisis of 1936. Mary was the first royal to visit Edward VIII in exile and would always spend time with him when he returned for brief periods to England. She was one of the first members of the royal family to meet the Duchess of Windsor, albeit not until 1953.

In history books and in most royal biographies, Mary appears only briefly. She usually merits little more than the odd page or footnote. In many cases this lack of coverage has led to many misconceptions. Only recently the film *Downtown Abbey* portrayed Mary as something of a forlorn and insipid woman, struggling within an unhappy arranged marriage. Other rumours abound: her childhood was unhappy and she refused to attend Princess Elizabeth's wedding because the Duke of Windsor was not invited. I find it unbelievable that someone who has contributed so much to the nation by her devotion to duty can be so easily overlooked and so misunderstood. My aim in writing this book is to redress this balance and to ensure we never forget the debt of gratitude that we owe to Princess Mary for redefining the role of a princess in the modern age.

# 1

# The Birth of a Princess

Heard from *Georgie* that May had given birth to a little girl, both doing well. It is strange that this child should be born on dear *Alice*'s birthday, … the last was on the anniversary of her death.[1]

Queen Victoria's diary, 25 April 1897

Princess Victoria Alexandra Alice Mary, known as Princess Mary, was born on 25 April 1897 at York Cottage on the Sandringham estate. She was the third child and only daughter of the then Duke and Duchess of York, who would later become George V and Queen Mary. Mary's father, Prince George, Duke of York, was the only surviving son of the direct heir to the throne, Edward, the Prince of Wales, and his wife Alexandra, the Princess of Wales, who would in 1901 become King Edward VII and Queen Alexandra. The year of Mary's birth was known more for the Jubilee celebrations of her great-grandmother, Queen Victoria, who by this time had been on the throne for a monumental sixty years. In 1897, the average life expectancy was a mere forty to forty-five years; thus Victoria had been monarch throughout most people's lives. Princess Mary would witness no fewer than six monarchs in her lifetime.

The United Kingdom of 1897 was a far cry from the realm Victoria had inherited in 1837. In the same way that our modern Elizabethan age has witnessed vast sociological, cultural, scientific, technological and political changes, Victoria's era was a time of radical advancements. The British Empire grew significantly during her reign and at its peak made up a quarter of the world's population. The Diamond Jubilee public holiday of 22 June brought hundreds of thousands of people to witness the royal parade and service of thanksgiving. 'The crowds were quite indescribable & their enthusiasm truly marvellous & deeply touching,' Victoria recorded in her diary.[2]

When she acceded to the throne Victoria's position was precarious, with only a handful of royal family members in the line of succession. However, by the end of her reign, Victoria was known as the 'Grandmother of Europe' having over thirty living adult grandchildren. She ensured not just the survival of her direct line but that of many European monarchies, including Norway, Denmark, Sweden and Spain. Even within her own family, Victoria was regarded 'as a divinity of whom even her own family stood in awe'.[3]

Princess Mary's mother was Princess Victoria Mary of Teck, known in the family as May. Princess May was the eldest child and only daughter of Princess Mary Adelaide of Cambridge and Francis, Duke of Teck. Francis was the child of a morganatic marriage (a marriage between two people of unequal social rank), meaning that he had no rights of succession to the Kingdom of Württemberg and was therefore a mere serene highness – though later HH The Duke of Teck. Finding a marriage partner for him had been difficult. Mary Adelaide of Cambridge was a granddaughter of George III, and for some time was in the direct line of succession. However, she also experienced similar difficulties in finding a marriage partner because of her colossal physical size. English historian and writer Janet Ross, who knew Mary Adelaide from their adolescence, recounted in her memoirs an occasion at a ball at Orleans House in Twickenham when the princess was dancing with the Comte de Paris: she 'collided with me in the lancers and knocked me flat down on my back'.[4] The American ambassador in London, Benjamin Moran, described her in 1857 (when she was 24) as being 'very thick-set', declaring her to weigh at least 250lb.[5] Regardless of this, Mary Adelaide was known for her genial and ebullient nature. In 1883, Janet Ross and Mary Adelaide were reacquainted in Florence when both were living there to ease their financial difficulties. Janet remarked that 'few women possess the charm of the Duchess of Teck; she took interest in everybody and her ringing laugh ... would have made even a misanthrope smile'.[6]

Despite their arranged marriage, Mary Adelaide and Francis seemed to enjoy their life together, socialising and assisting in court events. The birth of their first child and only daughter, May, at Kensington Palace in 1867 appeared to complete their happiness. In journalist Clement Kinloch-Cooke's authorised memoir of Mary Adelaide, we see an ideal picture of domesticity, with May's father, Francis, unusually for a man in his position at this time, relishing the chance to enter the nursery in order to bathe his baby. In a letter to her close friend and royal courtier Lady Elizabeth Adeane (later Biddulph) on 6 March 1868, Mary Adelaide talks at length about her love for her baby: 'She really is as sweet and engaging a child as you can wish to see ... In a word, a model of a baby ... "May" wins all hearts with her bright face and smile and pretty endearing ways.'[7] Mary Adelaide and Francis went on to have three sons: Adolphus (1868), Francis (1870) and Alexander (1874).

Despite their seemingly perfect view of domestic bliss, Mary Adelaide's propensity for partying and her generous charitable benevolence (she gave away a fifth of her income) meant that the £5,000 annual allowance from Queen Victoria was simply not enough for her to maintain her lifestyle. In 1883, the family had to move overseas for two years to escape their creditors. They hoped that by living off the benevolence of relatives they could in some way reduce their debts. They travelled to Italy, Germany and Austria, settling mainly in Florence. At first they went to the private Hotel Paoli on the Lungarno, frequently patronised by the English, and then to the Villa I Cedri at Bagno a Ripoli for the spring, a few miles outside Porta San Nicolo, to the south east of Florence. As one contemporary wrote:

> The various circles of Florentine society vied with each other in their desire to make the Duchess of Teck's stay pleasant and agreeable. It was of course, a great pleasure to the English residents to have Princess Mary (Adelaide) amongst them and her kindness of heart and personal

charm endeared her to all who had the privilege of being presented to her.[8]

It was here that Mary Adelaide's daughter, Princess May, developed an interest in Italian culture, spending much time visiting theatres, galleries, museums and churches. This would later inspire her appreciation of art and collecting, something May passed on to her daughter. There were daily visits to view the Old Masters in Florence such as Raphael, Van Dyck and Titian, along with lessons in singing, Italian and art.

The family returned to England in 1885 and made their home at White Lodge in Richmond. Princess Mary Adelaide was well known for her kindness towards her neighbours and the poor and was eager that her children should learn an empathy with those less fortunate. Kinloch-Cooke recalls in his biography of Mary Adelaide:

> On one occasion, her Royal Highness was taking a stroll … and came across an old woman picking up sticks; the woman seemed tired and the day was cold. Very soon the Duchess was hard at work, pulling down the dead wood from the lower branches of the tree with her umbrella.[9]

This incident was far from unique for Mary Adelaide, who was the first royal to earn the nickname of 'People's Princess' and took pride in assisting the poor. There are accounts of Mary Adelaide supporting neighbouring village fetes and bazaars, helping on stalls to boost sales. This was a trait that she was eager to pass on to her children, who learned the struggles of the lower classes by being taken to visit tenements and hovels. In addition, Mary Adelaide involved Princess May in the work of the Surrey Needlework Guild and the Royal Cambridge Asylum, as well as the Victoria Home for Invalid Children in Margate. Mary Adelaide was an early patron of such charities as Dr Barnardo's, the National Society for the Prevention of Cruelty to Children and the St John Ambulance Association. A publication produced in 1893, *The Gentlewoman's Royal Record of the Wedding of Princess May and The Duke of York*, describes Princess Mary Adelaide as 'one of the most respected and beloved members of our Royal house, whose energy in charitable and philanthropic work deserves the nation's gratitude'.[10]

In 1886, the young Princess May, who was described as 'a remarkably attractive girl, rather silent, but with a look of quiet determination mixed with kindliness',[11] made her debut at court. It was no wonder that she was shy, with such an outspoken and gregarious mother. Yet this slightly aloof and dignified manner soon made her a firm favourite of Queen Victoria and she was singled out as a potential bride for Prince Albert Victor, Duke of Clarence and Avondale, known as Eddy, who was the eldest child and heir of Victoria's heir, Edward, the Prince of Wales. In December 1891 their engagement was announced and as Mary Adelaide remarked in a letter to Lady Salisbury, 'Eddy is radiant and looks it and our darling May is very happy, though at times her heart misgives her lest she may not be able fully to realise all the expectations centred in her.'[12] Queen Victoria herself was pleased with the match and in her diary noted that 'I was quite delighted. God bless them both. He seemed very pleased & satisfied, I am so thankful, as I had much wished for this marriage, thinking her so suitable.'[13]

If May had misgivings about the match, these were well founded. Prince Eddy had, in his grandmother's words, lived something of a 'dissipated life'.[14] The match between his parents Bertie (Prince Edward) and Alix (Princess Alexandra) had come as something of a relief to Queen Victoria. Unlike his father, the saintly, moralistic, Prince Albert, Bertie enjoyed the company of women and living life's pleasures to excess. Alix was a Danish princess and had been chosen as Bertie's wife for her beauty and discretion. The marriage was relatively content, although Bertie continued to have affairs with many society beauties and actresses. In response, Alix gave all of her – at times, suffocating and possessive – love to her five children: two boys, Eddy and George, and three girls, Louise, Victoria and Maud.

Eddy inherited his mother's tall, sinewy frame, yet Queen Victoria viewed Bertie and Alix's children as fairy-like and puny, and this may be why so many later historians took to depicting Eddy as sickly and weak. A contemporary source states that 'the child was not … either weakly or delicate … his general health, indeed, gave no cause for anxiety'.[15]

The life of Bertie and Alix and their Marlborough House set was filled with hunting and shooting parties, balls, race meetings and family gatherings and travel. Wanting to install some discipline into the young princes, in 1871 Queen Victoria appointed Canon John Neale-Dalton to tutor Eddy and George. At times, Dalton despaired at the lack of routine and stability that clearly prevented him from making progress with his charges. Dalton was ahead of his time in some ways, preferring to focus on how to learn rather than what to learn; by teaching his pupils life skills rather than cramming them with facts.[16] By all accounts Dalton established an exacting curriculum for the two boys in his care, believing that they should receive a thorough grounding not just in academia, but also in physical pursuits, as well as the pastimes of country gentlemen such as hunting and shooting. Prince George was considered a good influence on his brother academically and so the princes remained together. Bertie was eager for his sons to escape the harsh regime of the schoolroom that he had been forced to endure under Prince Albert, and he wanted them to see for themselves the constantly expanding British Empire. With Dalton's support, he managed to persuade his mother that the boys would benefit from a cadetship aboard HMS *Britannia* in Dartmouth. This was followed by three years aboard the *Bacchante* and, for Eddy, Trinity College Cambridge and later a stint with the Tenth Royal Hussars, the Prince of Wales's regiment.

Although he was said to possess a benevolent nature, Eddy had scant regard for intellectualism or diligence. Rumours abounded of his predilection for chorus girls and partying. Queen Victoria thought marriage would be the only solution to curb the unstable and immoral prince. She invited Princess May and her brother Adolphus to Balmoral in November 1891, where she could see for herself if May would be a suitable wife for Eddy and found her 'a dear charming girl and so sensible and unfrivolous'.[17]

Thus, on 3 December 1891, at Luton Hoo in Bedfordshire, Eddy proposed to May. 'To my great surprise, Eddy proposed to me during the evening ... Of course I said yes. We are both very happy.'[18] The engagement was announced with preparations in place for a wedding the following February. Queen Victoria was so pleased with the engagement that on 12 December she took the happy couple to Prince Albert's mausoleum for his 'blessing'. For May, brought up to feel that she was somehow less than royal, with her father's morganatic background and her family's recurrent insolvency, this must have seemed tantamount to securing the greatest royal marital prize. She could look forward to becoming the Duchess of Clarence, the future Princess of Wales and ultimately Queen of England.

Sadly, that winter saw a tragic reversal in Princess May's circumstances, caused by a national pandemic of influenza. In early January, Eddy came down with the illness while out shooting at Sandringham and within a few days he had developed pneumonia. He died on 14 January 1892. As Queen Victoria wrote in her diary: 'Poor May, to have her whole bright future to be merely a dream. …This is an awful blow to the Country too! We are all greatly upset. — The feeling of grief immense.'[19] Eddy's younger brother, George, was second in line to the throne. The family were all deeply affected by such a sudden passing. In a letter to his mother, which she recorded in her diaries, Bertie related that:

Poor Boy, he battled so strongly against death … The poison of that horrid influenza had got into the dear boy's brain and lungs, and baffled all science … to rob us of our eldest son, on the eve of his marriage. Gladly would I have given my life for his, as I put no value on mine.[20]

The feeling among the people was of shock and upset at such a premature ending to a life. There was a huge outpouring of grief and immense sympathy for the royal family, not unlike the public demonstrations following the tragic death of Diana, Princess of Wales in 1997. The following day, the *Western Gazette* reported:

The death of the Duke of Clarence plunges millions of all ages, classes, and races in this kingdom into a sorrow of profound acuteness, and into the keenest sympathy with the Prince and Princess of Wales, the Princess May, and every member of the Royal House, who at this hour are so sorely stricken.[21]

Prince George had suffered from typhoid fever just before his brother's untimely death and there were concerns over the succession. The next in line after George was his timid sister, Princess Louise, who had married a mere earl (later Duke and Duchess of Fife) and had thus far only produced a living daughter. In addition, there was a shortage of suitable foreign princesses available to marry the heir to the British throne. George had shown an attraction for his cousin, Princess Marie of Edinburgh, 'Missy', but George's mother, Alix, and Missy's mother, the Duchess of Edinburgh, were both opposed to the match. While serving in the navy, he developed a fondness for a commoner, Julie Stonor, who as a Roman Catholic was equally unsuitable. Princess May's parents were determined that their daughter should not lose out on marriage to the heir and so they deliberately took May to Cannes to recover from her sorrow, where Bertie and his family were staying on his yacht, *Nerine*.

It was natural that May would develop a closeness with Eddy's surviving brother, Prince George, as they were both struggling with grief. Wherever she went in Cannes, Princess May was greeted with compassion for her loss from the locals. Once on a walk to the flower market, when accompanied by Bertie and Prince George, she was overwhelmed by the many bouquets given to her by the people. 'The Prince and George … were completely enchanted by this show of well-bred sentiment towards May on the part of perfect strangers.'[22] As early as 6 September 1892, the *Dundee Courier* reported that 'the rumour is being revived that Prince George and Princess May of Teck will be married, probably in January next'.[23] By February 1893 there was still much speculation that an announcement would be imminent. *Lloyds Weekly Newspaper* reported on Sunday 12 February that 'she has felt greatly pained at the frequent speculations as to her future which have appeared during the past twelve months of her sadness'. [24]

On 3 May 1893 at Sheen Lodge, the home of his sister, Princess Louise, Duchess of Fife, Prince George finally plucked up the courage to ask Princess May to marry him. Both George and May were incredibly reserved and all the gossip and speculation surrounding their possible betrothal must have made the situation awkward for both. As Princess Arthur of Connaught later related:

I don't know whether he was … shy of her … but … he was just about to leave the house without having proposed so [Princess Louise] said to him 'Georgie, don't you think you ought to take May out into the garden and show her the frogs in the pond?' and when they came back, he told them he was engaged.[25]

The marriage ceremony was arranged to be held in the Chapel Royal on 6 July during an 'overpoweringly hot'[26] heatwave. Queen Victoria remarked that 'it was really (on a smaller scale) like the Jubilee, & the crowds, the loyalty & enthusiasm were immense. — Telegrams began pouring in from an early hour … whilst I was still in bed, I heard this distant hum of the people'.[27]

The newly married and named Duke and Duchess of York were given a suite of apartments at St James's Palace, to be known as York House, for their London base, and a small house on the Sandringham estate known as York Cottage, where they honeymooned. York Cottage had once been known as the Bachelors' Cottage and was designed to accommodate any overspill of guests from the main Sandringham house. Designed in an eclectic mix of jarring architectural styles, it was relatively small, especially for a growing family, more akin to a suburban house and yet it would become the favoured home of the couple for the following thirty-three years. Writing to her eldest daughter Vicky, Queen Victoria described it as it 'rather unlucky and sad'.[28]

Yet George disliked entertaining and such a small home ensured that visitors would be few. Furthermore, with his naval background he felt more at home in small, cluttered rooms that reminded him of life on board a ship. His eldest son, Edward, Duke of Windsor, known in the family as David, later said to George's official biographer, Harold Nicolson, 'Until you have seen York Cottage you will never understand my father. It was and remains a glum little villa. It is almost incredible that the heir to so vast a heritage lived in this horrible little house.'[29]

In a misguided gesture of kindness, to save his bride the task of furnishing their marital home, Prince George had already decorated the house with modern reproduction furniture from the popular London retailer and cabinet maker Maple and Co. May, with her love of interior design and art, found this infuriating.[30] In addition, their early marital days at York Cottage were frequently disrupted by the constant and boisterous visits of George's mother, Alexandra, and his sisters, Maud and Victoria, who lived in the neighbouring main house. Alexandra would on occasion rearrange furniture in York Cottage to suit her own tastes rather than respecting May's position as lady of the house.

Despite this challenging start, and with both struggling with their timidity to express themselves to each other, within a few months a gentle fondness had matured into something far deeper, shown in a letter George wrote to May:

> I know I am, at least I am vain enough to think that I am capable of loving anybody (who returns my love) with all my heart and soul, and I am sure I have found that person in my sweet little May … When I asked you to marry me, I was very fond of you, but not very much in love with you, but I saw in *you* the person I was capable of loving most deeply … I have tried to understand you and to know you and with the happy result that I know now that … I adore you sweet May, I can't say more than that.[31]

Their first child, Edward Albert Christian George Andrew Patrick David, known in the family as David, was born almost a year after the wedding on 23 June 1894 at White Lodge in Richmond Park. They would go on to have five more children, who were all born at York Cottage on the Sandringham estate: Albert (known in the family as Bertie), Mary, Henry, George and John.

# 2

# Childhood and Education

Spirit of well-shot woodcock, partridge, snipe
Flutter and bear him up the Norfolk sky:
In that red house in a red mahogany bookcase
The stamp collection waits with mounts long dry.

'Death of King George V'
John Betjeman

York Cottage was already proving to be far too small for the growing family of the Duke and Duchess of York, even with the addition
of a three-storey wing. Two rooms on the first floor were set aside as a
nursery. 'I shall soon have a regiment, not a family,'[1] George remarked
at the rapid arrival of six children. On 7 June 1897 George and May's
only daughter, known as Princess Mary, was baptised by the Archbishop
of York, Dr William Maclagan, at St Mary Magdalen's Church near
Sandringham. Her godparents were Queen Victoria, Princess Mary
Adelaide, Empress Marie of Russia, Princess Victoria, King George of
the Hellenes and the Earl of Athlone (then Prince Alexander of Teck).

In marked contrast to his own upbringing, George preferred to raise
his children with a simpler and quieter life at York Cottage. As his diaries
later revealed, George was a stickler for punctuality with an obsession
over the weather and uniforms. Never one to be considered in any way

intellectual, George was at his happiest when involved in his two hobbies of stamp collecting, to which 'delicious hours have been devoted'[2] and shooting game: he 'had thirty thousand acres over which to pursue pheasants and partridges, woodcock and duck'.[3] George passed on this fixation and pride in wearing the correct uniform to his daughter, who wore the uniform of the VAD while training to be a nurse. During the Second World War she was rarely seen out of her ATS attire.

Princess May kept an album on each child from birth, recording their initial milestones such as cutting a tooth or having their first haircut. However, she disliked the experience of pregnancy and birth, recoiled at any signs of illness and generally took little interest in her children until they were older and had developed their own personalities. Over the years, historians have criticised George and May for being distant and cold as parents. In his ghostwritten autobiography their eldest son, David, who would become Edward VIII and ultimately the Duke of Windsor, described them as 'Olympian figures who would enter the nursery briefly to note, with gravely hopeful interest, the progress of their first-born'.[4] Much has been made of the subsequent difficulties that their children faced as they became adults and their seeming neglect of their youngest son, John, who developed epilepsy and died as a teenager. The way George and May raised their family does seem harsh if we compare it to our age of positive parenting and child-focused learning and if we judge it by how the current generation of royals are raising their children. However, it is important to consider that this was no different to how the offspring of the nobility were raised at this time. Letters and postcards written from George and May, when overseas on tour, reveal their pride and love for their children.

Mabell, Countess of Airlie, a lady-in-waiting to Princess May, related in her memoirs:

I believe that they were more conscientious and more truly devoted to their children than the majority of parents in that era. The tragedy was that neither had any understanding of a child's mind. They themselves had been brought up in loving homes ... but they did not succeed in making their own children happy.[5]

May gave an air of aloofness and rigidity, but as Mabell revealed:

> The Princess received me in her sitting-room at York House, formally
> – almost coldly, I thought – but when we were alone together she
> put her arms round me and kissed me on both cheeks … It was then
> that I began to understand the subtle change in her … only in such
> moments of intimacy could she be herself.[6]

For Mabell, the distance between May, George and their children was
down to their position as members of the royal family in the direct
line of succession, as well as their solemn obligation to the crown.
Furthermore, George and May were both timid and preferred to
express their love through letters to each other rather than in person.
It thus follows that they would struggle to communicate their love
directly with their children. George was fond of his children as babies
but as they matured into childhood, he wanted them to understand
the significance of their role. He was particularly harsh on his sons, and
all the children, including Mary, dreaded being called to their father's
study for some chastisement. George feared that recklessness and dis-
sipation ran in the family because of the behaviour of his father and
his elder brother, Eddy. He had witnessed the impact on his darling
mother, Alix, of the sorrow that came from loose morals and extramarital affairs. George was merely doing what he felt was right to ensure
his children developed a strict moral code of behaviour. As much as
David struggled in his relationship with his father, he did commend
him later for installing this in his children: 'We must never get the idea
that we were different from or better than, other people … He was
determined that whatever else might come of us, we should not be
prigs or snobs.'[7]

Having spent much of his time in the navy, George instilled many
similar values into the children such as discipline, obedience, rigid routine, punctuality and deference to authority, along with an obsessive
adherence to the correct dress code. Photographs and cine film still survive of the children dressed in naval-style outfits carrying out military
drills. This, along with a preoccupation with duty and preparation for

public life, may be why George has often been accused of being a tyrant as a father.

As was befitting for the progeny of the upper classes during that era, the children were kept apart from their parents and were mainly confined within the nursery, which was 'dark and depressing'.[8] The closeness in age between the three eldest children meant that they inevitably spent much of their time together as a trio. With two elder brothers, it was no wonder that Princess Mary became something of a tomboy and had little interest in dolls. The children were cared for by nurses and governesses, often strict and occasionally bordering on sadistic. One nurse was dismissed when it was discovered that she was not only neglecting Bertie but deliberately pinching David when he was taken to tea with his parents, so that he would cry and be forced to return to the nursery.

When she was not on tour or involved in social or public events, Princess May would see her children in her boudoir for an hour each day from 6:30 p.m. Here they would hear her read royal history and learn to crochet and knit, as well as learn songs of the period such as 'The Camptown Races' and 'Oh My Darling, Clementine'. The Duke of Windsor wrote, 'Her soft voice, her cultivated mind, the cosy room overflowing with personal treasures were all inseparable ingredients of the happiness associated with this last hour of a child's day.'[9] This time with their mother was heavenly for the children and in marked contrast to their father's view of children – 'much as he regarded noisy midshipmen when he was captain of a cruiser – as young nuisances in constant need of correction'.[10] George was especially stern with his two eldest sons. Princess Alice, Duchess of Gloucester, notes that 'the Princes were also very much in awe of their father. He was very fond of them and they were devoted to him, but he used to bark now and then … nothing they did ever seemed quite good enough.'[11]

George made an equally terrifying impact on his grandson in the 1930s, showing that the years had failed to mellow him. In his autobiography, his grandson the 7th Earl of Harewood says that 'my grandfather, the King, found it so easy to find fault with anyone … I don't think he really cared much for children and he had a positive mania about punctuality'.[12]

George was far more lenient with Mary and, as his only daughter, she was his favourite child. Unlike his treatment of his sons, he was prepared to overlook a lack of punctuality:

The only person who was allowed to be late for anything, even breakfast, was apparently my mother, [Princess Mary] ... whose instincts must have been similar to those of her two grandmothers, Queen Alexandra and the Duchess of Teck, each of whom was capable of being up to a couple of hours late for meals.[13]

Mary was less inhibited than her brothers but her father's 'frequent jokes at her expense often made her cheeks crimson'.[14] George could be incredibly kind towards women. His subsequent relationships with his daughters-in-law, Elizabeth of York, Marina of Greece and Princess Alice of Gloucester and his granddaughters, Princesses Elizabeth and Margaret, were much more compassionate.

1901 marked the end of the Victorian era and the accession of Edward VII as monarch. George and May became the Duke and Duchess of Cornwall and in November, Prince and Princess of Wales. Life would now be divided between York Cottage, Frogmore at Windsor, Abergeldie in Balmoral and Marlborough House in London. During the year, George and May undertook an ambitious imperial tour. A newspaper article from November 1901 relates a talk given by Bishop Barry at the Royal Albert Institute which claimed that the tour had 'covered more than the circuit of the globe. The Royal couple had gone over thirty-five ... thousand miles, which was far more than the circumference of the world. Wherever the Duke and Duchess went they were received with exuberant loyalty.'[15]

Left to the care of their grandparents, the four eldest children moved into the Big House at Sandringham. May was reluctant to leave her young children but 4-year-old Mary was eager to watch over her brothers. 'Mary, seeing her mother's obvious emotion, threw her arms round her neck and echoed, "Never mind I will take good care of us!"'[16]

Life with Bertie and Alix for the four children was very different to the strict and clockwork regime of York Cottage. The king and queen encouraged their grandchildren to show their 'innate boisterousness'[17] and proved to be indulgent and pandering of their temporary charges, nicknamed 'The Georgie Pets' by Alix. Bertie was very fond of his golden-haired granddaughter and would spend many hours playing with her in the gardens. He would even allow Mary to race pats of butter down his trouser legs as a game. Bertie and Alix believed that 'lessons were less important to children than their happiness'.[18] They 'liked to have us romping around in the dining-room'.[19] They were so eager to ensure that the children were happy, rather than educated, that when they took the children away for a fortnight to Sandringham, their French governess, Mlle Helene Bricka, a rather zealous disciplinarian originating from Alsace, was left behind in London.

May and George kept in touch with their children by letter. On HMS *Ophir*, Princess May wrote to her daughter, who was about to turn 4 years of age:

> We hope these lines will reach you on your birthday and that you will spend a very happy day and have lots of pretty presents given to you. Do you know that Papa and Mama often wish that you and David, Bertie and little Harry were with them on this large ship and seeing all the wonderful things that they are seeing? … Papa and Mama send you all much love and many kisses.[20]

George sent his children postcards and he referred to Mary as his 'Darling Little Butterfly'. 'Has baby [Harry] grown much? Can he talk yet? We have just arrived here from Tasmania. We are all well but longing to see you again.'[21]

The letters George and May sent to their children while they were away on long tours of the empire reveal a natural love between parents and their children; the sharing of pet names, the sending of tokens of affection such as sprigs of heather, postcards of distant lands and ribbons and souvenirs from their expeditions. George and May were making the best out of the difficult situation they found themselves in and they certainly never made any secret of how much they were missing their children. They were terrified that the enforced separation would mean that their children would forget them. These are not the letters of cold and distant parents. It must have been unbearable when they were unable to see their children on their birthdays or at Christmas.

As George and May finally returned from their extensive travels, they set about the task of how best to educate their children. The intention was that Princess Mary would be educated at home rather than attend a private school. May was ahead of her time in establishing an innovative curriculum for Mary that exposed her to an extensive and broad range of subjects. She was taught all aspects of domestic life along with academic and creative subjects; in short 'her education was versatility itself'.[22] This education, coupled with the ubiquitous horseplay involved in having five brothers inevitably ensured that Mary was brought up to be far more resilient and less delicate than previous princesses, such as Princesses Victoria and Louise, the sisters of her father. It proved to be ideal training for her future life spent in public service.

David and Bertie received instruction at home until they were of an age to attend Osborne Naval College as cadets. Mary was considered the brightest of the three eldest children, able to speak French and German by the age of 8. George appointed Henry Hansell, an Oxford-educated schoolmaster, to tutor the three eldest children, although Mlle Bricka continued to teach French. Hansell struggled to control his three energetic charges:

> I must keep Princess Mary apart from the others as much as possible, whenever it is a matter of work. Her disposition is mercurial; one can enforce discipline and order of a sort, but the fact remains that, so long as she is in the room, her brothers cannot concentrate their attention on any serious work.[23]

When Mary was old enough to leave the nursery, a German woman, Else Korsukawitz, was appointed her maid along with a French governess, Mlle José Dussau. Else would become a firm favourite of the children and when she had to return to Germany with the outbreak of the First World War, Mary felt bereft as she had lost her confidante. José Dussau was a brusque disciplinarian who had a strong aversion to boys and would frequently report any of the eldest boys' misdemeanours to their parents. She was eager to divide and conquer the close-knit trio, and thus she encouraged Princess Mary to inform on them: 'Mary … no doubt wishing to please … began to fall in with this prudish attitude; her threat, "I'll tell Mama"… had a powerful subduing effect upon us … Bertie and I discovered … the power that little girls the world over are able to exert over their brothers,' wrote David.[24]

The children were forced to speak French at mealtimes by Mlle Dussau and Mr Hansell. Princess Mary was already proficient in the language but her brothers less so. While Princess Mary was eager to demonstrate her expertise, her brothers would speak in monosyllabic responses. Inevitably the boys developed a dislike of the language that would remain with them into adulthood.

As much as Princess Mary was a conscientious student, who responded well to discipline and complied with rules, she enjoyed playing pranks with her brothers to add amusement to the monotony of their days in the schoolroom. George decided to bring in his former French teacher, an Eton master, Monsieur Gabriel Hua, to act as tutor and librarian. One day, the kind-hearted Hua mentioned that he liked frogs' legs. Princess Mary decided to exploit this and managed to persuade her mother to join in with the joke. The children gathered up their fishing nets and caught some tadpoles, since it was not the season when they would have matured into frogs. They made the cook boil the tadpoles and serve them on toast for dinner that evening. It had been their intention to alert Hua before he ate the unusual delicacy. However, they were unable to stop him, and the demoralised Hua retreated to his room as Princess May jokingly said, 'I am afraid that between *grenouilles* and *têtards*, a French gourmet draws a fine line.'[25] Fortunately, Monsieur Hua accepted the children's apology graciously.

Mary and her brothers inevitably preferred the days when they would be left alone to make their own amusement. Much of this time was spent outdoors, riding their bicycles around Sandringham and the neighbouring villages, climbing trees and jumping onto the 'islands' surrounding the large lake. As well as being more academic than her two elder brothers, Mary was an excellent rider since she had her first pony at the age of 6. She loved horses and swiftly learned to jump fences. 'My sister was a horse until she came out,'[26] Bertie later commented. Despite being the youngest of the three and inherently timid around those she didn't know, 'her yellow curls concealed a fearlessness that commanded our respect. Mary could at times be quite a "tomboy" but at others, supported by her formidable Mademoiselle, she wielded a sweet tyranny over our lives.'[27]

At Sandringham, Mary developed a fascination for plants and gardening that would prove beneficial to her when she became Countess of Harewood. She made a botanic collection of plants and seaweed from the Norfolk region. Mary was an enthusiastic reader of adventure stories, especially those set in exotic locations and considered at the time to be more suitable for boys; such tales as *She* by H. Rider Haggard or *Treasure Island* by Robert Louis Stevenson. She would pore over the poetry of Alfred, Lord Tennyson. The *Idylls of the King*, with its depiction of the story of King Arthur and his knights, was a firm favourite. Along with traditional lessons, Mary was taught deportment, needlework and art; sports such as tennis, fencing and swimming; and music in the form of piano and singing, although her brothers were not appreciative of her musical skills. Outings to historic places including Hampton Court and the Tower of London were organised to bring history lessons to life. Geography was taught using a tray of sand to denote the continents. Mary's natural intelligence led her brother David to later remark that it was a shame that Mary was not heir to the throne as 'she is far cleverer than I am'.[28]

The most important part of the education of a child – that of social interaction with girls of her own age – was, apart from occasional instances, absent from Mary's education. Most of her female relationships were with older women such as her mother, her nurse and her teacher. Even when May arranged for Mary to spend time with other girls such as the children of her ladies-in-waiting, the children would be either much younger or older. This may have been why Mary displayed diffidence and nervousness in the company of strangers: a quality that would remain with her.

Princess Mary later learned essential life skills such as how to drive, as well as shorthand and typing. As she became older, her father would dictate some of his correspondence to her for it to be typed. Undoubtedly this schooling was, as one newspaper declared, 'an education which pre-served the old ideals, while reaching forward to the new'[29] It was an all-round training, designed to prepare Mary not just for a life of royal duty and altruism, but as preparation for whatever her future role in life would be; whether a wife, mother or even a spinster companion to her mother. It taught Mary to be self-sufficient, something that would be evident throughout her adult life. Furthermore, it taught her how to converse on a range of subjects from sport and botany to art, geography and history. Queen Mary may also have been concerned by her own lack of financial resources in her youth, and wanted to ensure that her daughter always had an education to protect her should she lose her royal position.

In April 1903, the magnificent and palatial Marlborough House was finally ready to be used as the new London home of the family. Marlborough House had originally been designed by Sir Christopher Wren and built between 1709 and 1711 as a gift from Queen Anne for her favourite companion, the Duchess of Marlborough. It had been used by the Dukes of Marlborough for over a century until it became a royal residence in 1817. Throughout Marlborough House, murals, tapestries and paintings depicted the history of the building and its previous occupants including the victories of John Churchill, 1st Duke of Marlborough, in the Spanish Wars of Succession and Louis Laguerre's paintings of the 1704 Battle of Blenheim: the ideal sur-roundings for the children to play at being soldiers in its imposing rooms. The house was far grander than the family had ever experi-enced and for once Princess May had been free to decorate it in her own taste. The Duke of Windsor noted that 'it was then and remains one of the finest homes in London, and its spacious drawing-rooms lent themselves to sumptuous entertainment'.[30]

It was in the dining room at Marlborough House that Princess May organised dance lessons for her three eldest children with a class of thirty under the tutorage of the stout but agile Miss Walsh. These classes were an ideal opportunity for the children to connect with their peers and, 'they lifted us out … from our walled-in life in London'.[31] The children would pass some of their time at Frogmore in Windsor and Abergeldie in Scotland. Many of these visits would be spent alone with their mother enjoying picnics while their father was shooting in the Midlands or yachting at Cowes. According to the Duke of Windsor, 'we always had a happy time with my mother … and it was with some regret that we would board the train … to join my father'.[32] There would be the splendour of the Big House at Sandringham for Christmas which was 'Dickens in a Cartier setting'.[33] Even in such opulence the children were encouraged to think of others and watch the distribution of meat to the estate employees.

In 1906, Princess May took her daughter on her first foreign trip, to Trondheim in central Norway for the coronation of King Haakon VII of Norway. The king, the former Prince Carl of Denmark, had married George's sister Princess Maud in 1896, when the Norwegian parliament dissolved its union with Sweden and chose to offer the throne to Prince Carl instead. The occasion was notable as it was the first time Mary met her 3-year-old cousin Olav. Even at such a tender age, Olav was much enamoured of his slightly older relative: 'Little Olav is a dear, he has fallen in love with my Mary, who is rather shy and blushes at his advances.'[34]

As her elder brothers left for naval college – David in 1907 and Bertie in 1909 – Mary felt their absence keenly. She was incredibly close to her eldest brother, David, and when he left for Osborne, Mary became something of a substitute parent to her younger siblings, Henry, George and John. Henry, like his brother Bertie, had knock-knees and a speech disorder and suffered with weak health and fragile nerves. George was the most intelligent and cultured of all of the children. John was eight years younger than Mary and was charming and amusing and so attractive that May and George had difficulty believing he was theirs. John was outspoken, calling his father an 'ugly old man'[35] and tugging at beards to see if they were real. In 1909, John experienced his first epileptic fit at the age of 4 and there were initial signs that he may have had autism. Doctors advised that Johnnie, as he was known, should stay at Wood Farm with his nanny Charlotte (Lala) Bill, presumably for his own safety. In the early twentieth century little was understood about epilepsy and keeping a child in a safe and calm environment would be preferable to expecting him to deal with the many stimuli and inherently hectic life in a royal residence. Furthermore, it was typical in those days for many sufferers to be institutionalised. Yet throughout the period he was brought up away from the family, Mary and Johnnie wrote to each other regularly and developed a close relationship. Mary would call on him almost daily whenever she was at Sandringham.

# 3

# Death of Edward VII and Accession of George V

At 11:45 beloved Papa passed peacefully away, and I have lost my best friend and the best of fathers. I never had a cross word with him in my life. I am heartbroken and overwhelmed with grief.[1]

George V's diary, 6 May 1910

King Edward VII, or Bertie as he was known in the family, had smoked heavily during his lifetime and had been struck down with severe bronchitis in the spring of 1910. However, he refused to give in to his illness and during the last week of his life he undertook many engagements, travelling to and from Sandringham for the weekend before returning to Buckingham Palace on 2 May. His heart was failing and he struggled to breathe. On Friday 6 May at noon he collapsed, but still rebuffed protestations for him to retire to bed. His horse Witch of Air won the 4.15 p.m. race at Kempton Park and he was able to hear the good news before he slipped into unconsciousness. He died just before midnight on 6 May 1910. The following day the new King George V attended his first meeting of the Privy Council.

George was distraught at his father's death and broke down in tears when he informed his two eldest sons of the news. In contrast to his mother, Queen Victoria, who had denied her heir access to any state documents, Edward VII had allowed his son to have a desk next to his at

Windsor Castle, in order to show George cabinet papers, and they had benefited from a close relationship. However, there was much turmoil in the world, with the rising power of imperial Germany and political upheaval at home with a looming constitutional crisis.

In 1909, David Lloyd George's Liberal budget, which had aimed to remedy inequality and introduce social welfare reforms by increasing the taxes on the more affluent, had been rejected by the predominately Conservative House of Lords, despite its popular appeal. New Liberal peers were needed to ensure the government held a majority in the House of Lords. This had forced a general election in January 1910. The election resulted in a hung parliament, with the Liberals under Herbert Henry Asquith winning the most seats and the Conservatives led by Arthur Balfour, allied with the Liberal Unionists (a party made up of a liberal faction), gaining more votes. Asquith formed a government with the Irish Parliamentary Party, a movement campaigning for self-government or Home Rule for Ireland led by John Redmond. In return for their support, Redmond demanded measures to curb the power of the House of Lords, which he believed was the last obstacle to Irish Home Rule. Ulster was violently against Home Rule. Seven days into his reign, George had to decide either to create sufficient Liberal peers if the bill was blocked again or face the prospect of his government resigning. George received conflicting advice from his private secretaries but decided to agree to dissolution of the creation of peers. Politics was further dominated by discontent in the shipyards arising from challenging working conditions and low pay, and the continuing campaign of women's suffrage. For a while these problems were forgotten about as the country prepared to bury its former king and crown his successor.

Edward VII's body lay in the throne room at Buckingham Palace with four Grenadier Guards guarding it, one at each corner. His widow, Alix, was constantly taking people in to see the king or rearrange flowers. The coffin was taken to Westminster Hall where it lay in state for three days and hundreds of thousands of people came to pay their respects.

The state funeral on 20 May was notable since it was the final gathering of many European sovereigns before the First World War. George V rode on horseback leading a procession which included, among many others, George's cousin Kaiser Wilhelm II of Germany. The day prior to the funeral, Mary and David had visited Westminster Hall to see their grandfather's coffin. The hall was in absolute silence and no one noticed the two young members of the royal family standing at the back as thousands slowly processed past the coffin.

Mary and David were both saddened by the death of their grandfather. It was said that one of Mary's happiest childhood memories had been when King Edward had lifted her on to the back of his horse Persimmon and taken her racing around the paddock. During her childhood she would frequently announce her intention to marry a man like her grandfather one day.

For the funeral, the children rode in a glass state coach with their mother and their aunt, Queen Maud of Norway. Edward VII's pet terrier dog, Caesar, led the funeral procession, walking immediately behind the gun carriage carrying the king's coffin. It was a swelteringly hot day and the streets of London from Buckingham Palace to Westminster Hall fell silent, apart from the funeral music played by the band. From Westminster Hall, the procession continued to Paddington Station where the coffin was transferred by train to Windsor and placed on a gun carriage to St George's Chapel at Windsor Castle. As David later said of the event in his memoirs, 'It was all rather overpowering for us grandchildren, even a little eerie; and it was not until all this impressive funeral pomp was over that the full meaning of our grandfather's death registered itself on our young minds.'[2]

As children of the sovereign, the family now had to move home. From Frogmore into Windsor Castle, from Abergeldie to Balmoral in Scotland and from Marlborough House to Buckingham Palace in London. In his will, Edward VII had left Sandringham to his wife, Alix. She could not stand to leave the Big House and so, George and May, now King George and Queen Mary, kept their cramped home at York Cottage until Alix died in 1925. This caused a great deal of disruption and bother for the family, and especially for Queen Mary, since there was not enough room to accommodate the new members of staff who were now needed by the king. As Queen Mary wrote of the matter, 'I confess I am very tired after the strain of the past weeks and now … come all the disagreeables

… if only things could be managed without having rows.'[3] However, George remained insistent that the main house at Sandringham was his mother's home, and as such it would be wrong to make her leave it. Therefore, Alix kept Sandringham exactly as it had been on the day that her husband died. In comparison to the lack of room at York Cottage, Buckingham Palace seemed immense. David, now Duke of Cornwall, found that the palace was 'pervaded by a curious musty smell'.[4]

As the only daughter of the king and queen it was to be expected that there would be much focus on the teenage Princess Mary. This article is typical of the press attention towards Mary at the time, which regularly featured snippets of information concerning her upbringing:

> Our pretty Princess, the only daughter the King and Queen, is thirteen years of age … She is encouraged to take an interest in everything that has gone to the making of the nation's life, and was recently, for instance, taken by her governess to see the relics of John Wesley and Methodism preserved in the City-road, London. Princess Mary always wears a talisman given her by one of her aunts, which is supposed to have been worn by an ancient Queen of Egypt as a charm against misfortune.[5]

As the coronation of the new king and queen approached, there was much trepidation at the magnitude and solemnity of such an occasion. David wrote to Mary in January 1911: 'I do not expect poor Mama and Papa are looking forward to the Opening of Parliament with much pleasure … However, it will in some ways act as a kind of preparation or introduction to the dreadful ordeal: The Coronation.'[6]

Prior to the coronation, on 12 May, David and Mary accompanied their parents to the opening of the Festival of Empire at Crystal Palace. The chief item was a concert featuring an imperial choir of over 4,000 voices with music from the Queen's Hall Orchestra, the London Symphony Orchestra and the Festival of Empire Military Band conducted in part by Sir Hubert Parry. The concert sang Elgar's arrangement of the National Anthem and a 'Patriotic Chorus For Empire and King' written by Percy E. Fletcher.

Inside the Crystal Palace a virtual tour of the British Empire was constructed with three-quarter-sized replicas of each country's government buildings made from wood and plaster. Visitors rode through on an electric railway learning about each country and its products. The history of London and the empire dating from its first dwellers and culminating in 'An Allegory of the Advantages of Empire' was retold in the form of a four-day pageant through the medium of drama, music and song, involving 15,000 volunteers. An Inter-Empire Championship Sporting Event, the precursor to the Commonwealth Games, was organised incorporating swimming, boxing, athletics and wrestling.

On the day of the coronation, 22 June 1911, Mary dressed in magnificent purple velvet robes, trimmed with ermine over a white dress, white satin shoes and stockings. She wore three rows of pearls and had a small coronet on top of her cascading blonde curls. The coronet seemed to cause her a good deal of worry but the Duchess of Teck, the wife of Prince Adolphus, who sat behind her, happily helped to adjust it before the ceremony. Mary had a long train, which was carried by Lady Dorothy Dawkins, a lady-in-waiting to Queen Mary. The king and queen left in the Gold State Coach. Mary was placed in charge of David, Bertie, Henry and George in a third coach, but found it difficult to keep her boisterous brothers in check. As she sat regally in the carriage, they started to poke fun at her dour expression. At one stage Mary's coronet fell into the carriage to the sheer delight of her mischievous brothers. David led his siblings as they processed through the abbey, followed by Bertie, Henry, George and finally Mary, 'a picture of charming girlhood'[7] as she curtsied deeply to her brother. The *Bystander* later reported that:

> One thing that charmed me immensely was … Princess Mary. Duly impressed with the solemnity of the occasion she played her part with a gravity that was positively delicious. To look at her one might have thought that she assisted regularly at Coronations about once a week.

She and the Prince of Wales and the rest of that youthful party got a tremendous ovation.[9]

After the coronation ceremony, the king and queen went on to the balcony at Buckingham Palace to the rapturous applause of the crowds. Colonial troops raised their rifles in the air and officers waved their swords. The coronation celebrations continued the following day when the royal family took part in a royal progress and military parade through London. King George and Queen Mary were driven in an open-top landau through the streets supported by 55,000 troops.

Mary and David both thoroughly enjoyed the coronation festivities and their roles in the pageantry:

> [We] ... had never seen such splendid ceremonies at close range before. We were fascinated by the magnificence of it all – the foreign representatives in their elaborate uniforms, the be-flagged streets lined with red-coated troops, the naval reviews, the full-dress military parades, the gilt coaches, the glittering escorts.[10]

Coronation celebrations continued throughout June, with a Review of the Fleet in Portsmouth, before moving to Ireland in July, where David and Mary accompanied their parents once more. Prior to their visit and with the situation over Home Rule still unresolved, there had been concerns that there might be demonstrations or a hostile reaction to the king and queen, especially since leaflets produced by Nationalist and Socialist elements in Dublin were distributed decrying the visit. Such concerns proved unfounded when the royal party arrived at Kingstown in Ireland on 8 July to receive an unexpectedly enthusiastic welcome of 'the wildest delight'[11] from a crowd of over 40,000.

King George drove through the city of Dublin in an open carriage and thousands came out to see his procession. The visit encompassed a packed schedule of events including race meetings, dinners, garden parties and state banquets but the royal party also called on the sick in hospitals and the poor in slums and opened the Royal College of Science. The king and queen held a court at Dublin Castle, where they met 700 debutantes. Queen Mary was presented with a train of pure Irish point lace from the women of Belfast and in his speech thanking the people of Ireland, the king spoke highly of the Irish cordiality. In an attempt to avoid any criticisms of religious discrimination, they also visited the Catholic Seminary of Maynooth.

Their subsequent trip to Wales culminated in David's investiture as Prince of Wales at Caernarvon Castle on 13 July 1911. The investiture ceremony had been revived by David Lloyd George, who believed that it would do much for Welsh pride, 'a great manifestation of popular enthusiasm ... The occasion will be memorable for its dazzling pageantry, its peculiar historic significance, for the representative character of the great crowds, who flocked from north and south, east and west.'[11] Mary again played a pivotal role and her contribution was acknowledged with the gift of a basket of silver roses.

On 17 July the royal party of king, queen, David and Mary began a five-day tour of Edinburgh, staying at the Palace of Holyroodhouse. Decorations in the streets were described as being on a 'very extensive scale. They are, indeed, the most elaborate the city has witnessed for a generation at least.'[12]

The king and queen left for Bombay in India that November to take part in the Delhi Durbar, an imperial coronation ceremony. Every prince and nobleman in India turned out to show their allegiance to the new king-emperor. George wore the substantial and impressive imperial state crown, which weighed nearly a kilogram. During the ten-day celebrations, George and Mary received some 500,000 people and witnessed a military parade of 50,000 troops. Upon their safe return, a service of thanksgiving was held in St Paul's on 6 February 1912.

While her parents were away on their coronation tour Mary, who remained an inveterate letter writer throughout her life, took it upon herself to correspond regularly with all her brothers, as they were in turn sent off to school or naval college. Mary was now 14 and fast developing similar interests to her mother: a love of interior decoration, fine art and beautiful objects, especially china. When Queen Mary returned to England, mother and daughter would often visit galleries and museums to learn about the Old Masters. Mary was adept at needlework and making garments, a skill which would become useful to her in war work, and she continued her interest in plants and gardening.

The new regal position of her parents forced Mary to overcome her shyness and participate in more official events, something that she always did with solemnity and dignity. When accompanying her parents, Mary would frequently receive an enthusiastic reception, which often caused her some bewilderment. Mary was beginning to understand the importance of her position and her obligations; she knew royal duties would now be an intrinsic part of her life. There was little point in protesting about what she had been born into. The newspapers were fascinated by the relatively young family of the new king and queen and articles often focused on Mary and her upbringing. According to *Tatler* in September 1910, Mary's ambition was to become her mother's private secretary, since her typing and shorthand skills were exceptional, and she spoke French fluently. The *Illustrated Sporting and Dramatic News* related how 'Mary is a real young sportswoman. Her Royal Highness is a fine rider, loves horses and dogs, is a tennis player, and shows a decided taste for golf … is already an angler in aspiration, and loves trout-fishing in reality.'[14]

# 4

# The First World War

Please God, it may soon be over.[1]

George V, Tuesday 4 August 1914

In August 1912, 15-year-old Princess Mary accompanied her mother on an overseas visit to Neustrelitz in Germany, to stay for ten days with Queen Mary's maternal aunt, the Grand Duchess of Mecklenburg-Strelitz, a granddaughter of George III, on the occasion of her ninetieth birthday. They would be accompanied by Colonel and Lady Eva Dugdale, one of Queen Mary's trusted ladies-in-waiting. The visit was meant to be informal: 'I should come quite incognita and want no fuss whatever,'[2] Queen Mary warned her aunt.

Neustrelitz was a small town of about 12,000 inhabitants sandwiched between two lakes, the Zierker See and the Glambecker See, and situated about 60 miles away from Berlin. Mary was driven around Berlin, and she was so enlivened by discovering new places that the party saw 'in seven hours more "sights" than most persons could well manage in three days'.[3] Such sights included the Brandenburg Gate, the Hohenzollern Museum, the Kaiser Friedrich Museum, and the Castle and Museum of Charlottenburg. In the afternoon they visited the pretty town of Potsdam with its magnificent architecture to see the New Palace, the Marble Palace and the Sans-Souci Palace and

Gardens. Mary was impressed most by the New Palace. Using the opportunity to demonstrate her linguistic proficiency in German, she commented that she had never seen anything as mesmerising; moreover, 'she expressed enthusiasm over everything in unmistakable terms of delight'.[4]

They ventured to Hohenwieritz and to the Johanniterkirche (Church of Saint John) at Mirow, to see the family vault of Mecklenburg-Strelitz and reminisced with the grand duchess, looking over family mementoes and photographs. The weather may have been inclement, since there were wintry blasts and persistent showers, but it was a special time for mother and daughter; as Queen Mary recalled in her letter of thanks to the Grand Duchess, 'How quickly the time flew at Strelitz. I never knew a week pass more quickly … I felt quite at home.'[5]

As Mary entered her teenage years, her father, although proud of his only daughter, struggled to engage with her. This is certainly no different to most fathers of adolescent girls. Once at York Cottage on the Sandringham estate he found himself on his own with Mary for a few days and seemed unsure what he should do. Queen Mary advised George to allow Mary into his study and keep him company while he worked on his red boxes. In a letter to his wife, George proudly explained, 'I have invited her to come and sit in my room while I write, she … seems pleased at the idea, although she did not talk much, at least to me, but that will come I hope.'[6] Eventually the two became closer and by 1914 they were seen riding together regularly.

Queen Mary had been brought up by her mother to take an interest in those less fortunate, not simply by donating money but by embracing an active rather than nominal role in her philanthropy. Since 1897, she had inherited from her mother the patronage of the London Needlework Guild, founded in 1882 as a means of supplying socks and jumpers for orphans. Over time, the guild grew to provide items for hospitals, nursing institutions, missions, refugees, the poor, as well as for the armed services during the wars. Besides making knitted and crocheted items, Queen Mary supervised the arrival, checking and unpacking of parcels at the Imperial Institute, dressed in apron and gloves and armed with a large pair of scissors. The charity had been Queen Mary's first and favourite patronage and she had personally made clothing items for the guild since she was a young girl. Many of these guilds were set up throughout the country and therefore in 1911, Princess Mary established her own, amassing over 700 items. Even David was persuaded to make comforters for Mary's collection.

In an attempt to find a final settlement to the issue of Home Rule in Ireland, George called a meeting at Buckingham Palace in 1914. Yet by the summer, events in Europe overtook any political debate at home and so the Irish Home Rule issue was abandoned. George recorded in his diary:

Tuesday August 4th. I held a council at 10.45 to declare war with Germany. It is a terrible catastrophe, but it is not our fault. An enormous crowd collected outside the Palace: When they heard that war had been declared, the excitement increased and May and I with David went on to the balcony: the cheering was terrific.[7]

Mary's diary for the same day records her parents' reception on the balcony:

I got up and looked out of the window; there were about 6000 people …They were singing the National Anthem and Rule Britannia and were shouting for Papa. At about 10, Papa and Mama came out on the balcony and were loudly cheered … the people were rather noisy during the night.[8]

Crowds continued to gather outside Buckingham Palace over the next few days, to show their support for the king and queen.

The announcement of war shocked many who did not grasp the full implications. Some erroneously believed that it would all be over by Christmas, but the war between the Central Powers led by the German Empire and the Allied forces continued for the next four years until November 1918. For both George and the royal family there were further uncertainties and concerns. The German Kaiser and George were first cousins and grandsons of Queen Victoria and Prince Albert of Saxe-Coburg Gotha, with George and his family sharing their Germanic name. Queen Mary was the daughter of the Duke of Teck, a descendant of the House of Württemberg. In fact, most of George's family were German with German titles.

Queen Mary was horrified by the war but resolved to help immediately by organising volunteer workers. As early as 5 August she recorded in her diary that she was preparing 'to help the existing organisations with offers of clothing and money etc … Very busy seeing people about the various relief schemes.'[9] There was an urgent need to provide aid to the families of men called up to fight.

George did not possess any clearly defined blueprint for the role of a constitutional monarch in times of war. However, he understood more than any of his predecessors the need for him and the royal family to be constantly visible, as well as the need to do something tangible, so that he would become a symbolic leader of the British Empire and a symbol of stability and security. Right from the outset of war, George was often seen accompanied by Queen Mary and Princess Mary inspecting the hundreds of recruits before they were sent overseas. His and Queen Mary's own devotion to duty meant that they expected the same from their children. A map was kept in Buckingham Palace showing the public service of all members of the royal family. It used lines and coloured flags to illustrate where each member appeared in public. Every Christmas a chart was prepared for George so that he could 'review the year as a company director might review his balance sheet'.[10]

The British government brought in a system known as 'business as usual' in the early days of the war; a phrase attributed to Winston Churchill at the time. In order to keep Britain stable, it was necessary to carry on day-to-day life. Furthermore, Britain faced the prospect of shortages of food since most came from imports, and fear of shortages led to panic buying and increased prices, particularly of meat and bread. When voluntary rationing was introduced in February 1917, George was among the first to agree to have ration books. Vegetables were grown at Sandringham, Windsor and Buckingham Palace and George agreed to abstain from alcohol throughout the war – although he continued to drink cider, which he did not consider alcoholic. The royal horses were sent to serve at ambulance stations and royal carriages were to be used to convey convalescents. George suggested that Buckingham Palace should be used as a hospital, but it was deemed far too old-fashioned to house the sick and it would have needed considerable structural work to make it suitable.

Bertie was already on HMS *Collingwood* in 1913. Although everyone knew he was a prince, he was known by the more common, anglicised name of Johnson as a means to ensure that he was not treated any differently to his fellow shipmen. The position of David as the Prince of Wales was not so easy. As the heir to the throne, he lamented that there was 'not the faintest chance of being able to serve my country'.[11] He was known to complain throughout the four years. 'Oh! That I had a job!'[12] David was eventually permitted to go to the front to see for himself the terrors faced by the British Expeditionary Force.

Mary was 17 when the war broke out, sheltered and still relatively unknown. She dreaded public appearances, though she always attempted to mask her anxiety. Ellis Silas, an artist, met Mary in May 1916 when he exhibited some of his work and was struck by how introverted the young princess was, almost in the shadow of her much more gregarious mother. Though not 'chic', he wrote, she had 'the most striking features: a lovely complexion'.[13] Her debut in society should have taken place in May 1915. However, all state functions and occasions were suspended, and so it was not until 10 June 1920, dressed in a white and silver gown and with a small coronet, that she finally made her official introduction at Buckingham Palace. Mary suffered greatly in the first few months of the war, when her beloved German maid, Else Korsukawitz, had to be repatriated. As David later described, the family 'wept as we said good-bye to this fine woman whom war, with its relentless disregard for human ties, was taking from our midst'.[14]

Mary understood only too well the anxieties and responsibilities of her parents and wanted to play her own role in the war effort. She could not serve as her brothers did in the military, and yet it was not enough for her to be seen merely accompanying her family on inspections of troops. Mary wanted to have a more proactive role. Such was her zeal to involve herself in helping in some way that when there had been a mention in the newspapers that scientists were short of some of the constituents of explosives, of which chestnuts were a perfect substitute, she collected as many chestnuts as she could from Sandringham.[15] She took part in fruit picking and she had her own allotment to grow vegetables to supplement rations.

Mary regularly supported a variety of campaigns during the war. In 1918 Lady Northcliffe, whose husband founded the *Daily Mail*, set up a fund to raise money for the British Red Cross by collecting pearls to make into a necklace which could be raffled. The appeal was a great success with something over 4,000 pearls being donated and over £100,000 raised, the equivalent of £11 million today. Mary contributed a pearl from her own collection.

Mary began a lifetime association with the Red Cross when she became the commandant of a Voluntary Aid Detachment of twenty-five members at Buckingham Palace, made up of her friends and contemporaries. She would spend three mornings a week engaged in voluntary work sorting files and reports at Devonshire House, the London home of the Dukes of Devonshire. Mary regularly volunteered at a munitions factory canteen in the nearby town of Hayes when she was resident at Windsor Castle between 1916 and 1918. She served food behind the counter and did the washing up. There is an amusing story concerning Mary's time at the canteen which illustrates her mischievous sense of fun. One day one of the workers showed Princess Mary her collection of old fabric samples taken from royal garments once worn by Queen Mary. Mary asked if the lady had shown her collection to Queen Mary when she had previously visited. 'No, ma'am, the Queen came by so suddenly that she took me at the "non plus!"' was the reply[16] From that point onwards Mary continued to reiterate the phrase, whenever she was caught off-guard.

Mary gave her name to a collection of short stories and poems from contemporary authors including Rudyard Kipling, J.M. Barrie and Sir Arthur Conan Doyle: *The Princess Mary Gift Book*. The book supported the Queen Mary's Work for Women Fund finding employment for women, based on the innovative idea that it was better for women to work rather than to accept charity. By the end of the war over 1 million more women were working.

Subsequently, Mary proposed an idea which was in equal measure inspired and naive. She wanted to give everyone serving in the armed forces a small Christmas gift. Since there were more smokers than non-smokers at this time, the ideal gift would be an embossed tin containing such items as a lighter, a pipe, tobacco and cigarettes to boost morale and remind servicemen of loved ones back home. Moreover, producing the gift would generate employment with its manufacture. Her initial idea had been to pay for this using her personal allowance, but the logistics and costs involved were far greater than anyone could ever have imagined, and it was judged unviable. Instead it was decided that she should give her name to a fund and a committee would be formed to turn her proposal into a reality. On 15 November 1914 she issued an appeal:

> I wish you all now to help me to send a Christmas present from the whole nation to every sailor afloat and every soldier at the front. On Christmas-eve when, like the shepherds of old, they keep their watch, doubtless their thoughts will turn to home and to the loved ones left behind …
>
> I am sure that we should all be the happier to feel we had helped to send our little token of love and sympathy on Christmas morning, something that would be useful and of permanent value and the making of which may be the means of providing employment in trades adversely affected by the war. Could there be anything more likely to hearten them in their struggle than a present received straight from home on Christmas Day.
>
> Please, will you help me? Mary.[17]

Beneath the pronouncement was a coupon to be returned to Mary at Buckingham Palace with the donation. 'The coppers of the poor and the cheques of the rich'[18] would be equally appreciated. Donations soon came in, many in the form of small contributions from ordinary people. Four days after the launch of the campaign, the *Sunday Times* reported that the response had already been significant, with £12,000 raised by the second meeting of the committee. In time, the response to the appeal was overwhelming with over £162,000 being raised, the equivalent of over £15 million today.

Many were undoubtedly encouraged to contribute by the youthful and personable attraction of Mary and by what seemed superficially such a simplistic appeal. However, much of the success was attributed to Hedley Le Bas, the advertising executive in charge of publicity for the fund, known for his renowned recruitment campaign concentrating on the image of Lord Kitchener, the Secretary of State for War. The intensity of Le Bas's campaign for the gift fund was compared to a 'Blitzkreig',[19] much like many modern high-profile PR campaigns. Over 40,000 appeal flyers were sent to residential addresses, as well as golf clubs, churches, schools, councils, social clubs, businesses and Masonic lodges. There were collections at theatres, in hotels and shops. Troops who were about to leave for overseas and were temporarily stationed in specific counties were also contacted.

The committee consisted of wealthy and influential people of the time including the First Lord of the Admiralty, Winston Churchill, Lord Kitchener and the Prime Minister, along with notable industrialists, bankers and retired navy and army officers. The gift was an immense undertaking and proved to be even more arduous than had originally been thought. Mary met with the committee for the first time at the Ritz Hotel on 14 October with her mother's lady-in-waiting Lady Katherine Coke.

Initially, the idea had been to give the gift to those who were serving in the army under the command of Field Marshal Sir John French, or at sea in the navy under the command of Admiral Sir John Jellicoe at Christmas 1914. However, with funds still available, distribution was soon widened to include all those who were serving, including nurses, prisoners of war, disabled and injured soldiers and the next of kin of casualties; something exceeding 2.5 million people. It took until 1920 to complete delivery of all the tins, something that the committee could never have envisaged when they first set out.

The gift recipients were broken down into various categories according to where they were serving; whether overseas, British or colonial troops. Smoking was frowned upon for women and it was forbidden for men by certain religions; the cigarettes and tobacco, supplied by John Player and Sons or HD or HO Wills, were thus replaced with sweets, spices or chocolate. Some tins contained a pencil resembling a bullet and for the Indian Ghurkas, spices were given to be used in meals. Over 13 million cigarettes were produced, with over 44,000lb of tobacco. Substitutes for some of the gifts had to be found. The flint in the tinder lighter, for example had originally come from Austria, and when supplies were used up, no further replacements could be found. This was substituted with knives, scissors, cigarette cases, combs or tobacco pouches.

The brass tins, made by the architectural firm, Adshead and Ramsey, measured about 13cm in length by 8cm wide with a depth of 3cm and a hinged lid; similar to a modern tin of luncheon meat. On the top was a bust of Princess Mary, surrounded by a laurel wreath, with the words, 'Imperium Britannicum' and a sword and scabbard either side. Below read 'Christmas 1914' with the monogram 'M' on both sides. Around the lid's edges were the names of the Allied powers: Belgium, Japan, Montenegro and Serbia, with Russia and France at either side. Prior to the gift tin being manufactured, very few brass tins had been made in the United Kingdom. This led to a certain reluctance on the part of manufacturers to complete the task, especially when brass became even more scarce with the 1915 sinking by the Germans of the RMS Lusitania, a liner which had been transporting over 45 tonnes of brass from New York for the manufacture of the tins.

By Christmas 1914, over 450,000 parcels and 2.5 million letters were despatched to France. This is even more remarkable an achievement when one considers that these deliveries were in addition to normal despatches and put considerable strain on an already overworked system. A letter from F.T. Clayton, a special duty officer tasked with distribution of the gifts, to his superior on the 13 December 1914 in the Imperial War Museum archives, illustrates how exhausting and complex this was:

> You have given us simply an appalling task in connection with the distribution of Princess Mary's Fund gifts … if we could have had them in sufficient time to have done it by degree it would have been bad enough, but now that everything has to be done in a hurry, I really don't know how we are going to tackle it.[20]

Servicemen from all ranks treasured their tins, and many were sent home to wives and families to be kept. Mary received numerous letters of thanks from troops for her generosity. In a letter dated 26 December 1914, Sir Henry Rawlinson wrote to the private secretary of George V, Clive Wigram, that 'It is just what I want ... how much we all value her kind gift of tobacco and cigarettes.'[21]

At the Western Front over 100,000 troops were involved in a series of unofficial and temporary ceasing of hostilities on Christmas Day 1914. Both sides sang Christmas carols, and some ventured into no-man's-land where small gifts were exchanged. Henry Williamson, the author known for *Tarka the Otter*, was a 19-year-old soldier serving in 1914. From the trenches he sent a letter home to his mother in which he recalled this unique experience:

> In my mouth is a pipe presented by the Princess Mary. In the pipe is tobacco ... In the pipe is German tobacco ... From a German soldier. Yes, a live German soldier from his own trench. Yesterday the British & Germans met and shook hands in the Ground between the trenches, and exchanged souvenirs, and shook hands ... Marvellous, isn't it?[22]

Many soldiers exchanged gifts from their brass tins and when they spoke to the German soldiers, they were shocked to learn that many had the same hopes and fears as them.

Newspapers began to record the stories of soldiers who owed their life to the tin. One, Private James Brown of the Sixth Battalion Cheshire Regiment, was serving at Neuve Eglise about 6 miles from La Bassée:

> I was cleaning up round the quarters of the regiment, when ... before I knew what was happening, I was struck in the left thigh by a fragment from a shrapnel shell. I had Princess Mary's gift box in my jacket pocket, and this deflected the shrapnel which considerably damaged the box ... The box certainly saved my life, for had it not been there the shrapnel would have entered my groin ... I consider I am the luckiest man in Britain today.[23]

A soldier of the Irish Guards, Private Brabston, was fighting in Givenchy and the tin saved him from a bullet shot direct to his heart. In fact, there were quite a few similar stories appearing in the local and national press during 1915, suggesting that some of these reports may have been slightly embellished.

Mary presented specimens of all the gift items, along with the original proofs and dies, to the Imperial War Museum after the war in 1920. When she toured Canada years later, war veterans would bring out their treasured tins to show her. The success of Mary's appeal can be seen in the fact that even now, over a century since the boxes were sent out, they continue to be treasured within families and a great many are still readily available in antiques shops and on online auction sites. Furthermore, if one artefact could characteristically represent and evoke memories of the First World War, it would be the Princess Mary gift tin. It may have seemed an over-ambitious idea initially, yet it was the main reason why so many people continued to regard Mary as such a benevolent and popular member of the royal family.

# 5

# Nursing

Never so happy as when allowed to do the ordinary work of the average commoner.[1]

*Illustrated London News*, Wedding Special, 4 March 1922

Mary's first official engagement as a working member of the royal family was in May 1917 when, with her brothers, she represented her mother at a variety entertainment show on behalf of the Mesopotamia Comforts Fund at Apsley House in Piccadilly. In the same year at a dinner party, George V overheard one of Queen Mary's ladies-in-waiting, Lady Maud Warrender, confiding in her that people believed that the royal family had Germanic sympathies because of their name of Saxe-Coburg-Gotha and Prince Albert's name of Wettin. Letters along these lines had been sent to the Prime Minister and that year, H.G. Wells had publicly written to *The Times* declaring that it was time to eliminate 'the ancient trappings of throne and spectre'[2] and urging the formation of republican clubs instead.

Subsequently, in July 1917, George issued a proclamation changing the name of the royal house to Windsor. Furthermore, all of his British relatives renounced their German titles and styles and changed their names to sound more British. Battenberg became Mountbatten and Queen Mary's relatives went by their Cambridge titles instead. George implemented new measures to reduce the size of the monarchy by restricting who could use the title of Royal Highness:

> We must endeavour to regard the Crown not as a mere figurehead and as an institution … but as a living power for good with receptive faculties welcoming information affecting the interests and social wellbeing of all classes and ready not only to sympathise with those questions but anxious to further their solution.[3]

In short, the royal family needed to be seen to show empathy for the problems faced by ordinary people. Life at Buckingham Palace for the young princess was undoubtedly stifling as the companion to her parents. David tried to convince Queen Mary to permit his sister to socialise with friends of a similar age and to be able to move around the different royal palaces more freely. Yet Mary, ever the peacekeeper, told David, 'You need not feel so sorry for me … The only things I object to are those rather silent dinners you know so well, when Papa will read the paper.'[4]

Throughout the war Mary, despite her inherent shyness and a slight speech impediment of rhotacism, had become increasingly present at royal appearances with her mother visiting factories, hospitals and children's homes. As she became more experienced, she was often called upon to represent the queen at such events as an open day at Roehampton Hospital in 1917, distributing medals and watches and watching demonstrations of disabled soldiers learning to use artificial limbs. Mary took a keen interest in the work of the Land Girls, an organisation of female agricultural workers set up in 1917 to boost Britain's food production and make up for the large number of male farmers who had been called to the front. Mary visited Cambridge in March 1918 to present badges and stripes to highlight the achievements of the women and was presented with a miniature wooden plough.

Since she had been a young girl, Princess Mary had made no secret of her yearning to become a nurse. As the only girl in a family of boys, it was little wonder that she guarded the youngest with nothing short of maternal pride. Unlike her mother, who would recoil at the sight of illness, Mary showed a natural compassion for any patient. When staying at Balmoral as a young child, the gamekeeper's child had become unwell. Mary nursed the child back to health by patiently sitting by its bedside, reading fairy stories.

Between 1915 and 1917 Mary attended gymnastic lessons with Princesses Nina and Xenia of Russia, daughters of Grand Duchess Maria Georgievna, who was a first cousin of Tsar Nicolas II. At the start of the war Maria, a considerable Anglophile, was on a visit to Harrogate Spa with the intention of curing her daughter Xenia's ill health and decided not to return to Russia. Mary would have heard at first hand about the work of the grand duchess, who had served as a nurse at three military hospitals in Harrogate, where she was a generous patron. Mary was equally aware of the nursing career of her cousin Alexandra, known as Princess Arthur of Connaught. Mary had been a bridesmaid at Alexandra's wedding. Alexandra had trained as a nurse and in 1915 started working at St Mary's Hospital in Paddington. Mary had always been encouraged by her mother to read nursing and medical books. She had passed her Red Cross first aid examinations and attended lectures at Buckingham Palace given by Sir James Cattle on first aid, nursing, hygiene and sanitation.

As early as April 1916 there were reports that:

Nursing, in which she has already achieved marked ability and progress, is one of Princess Mary's latest interests in life. Like everything she does, she has … great spirit and keenness and under the directions of one of the most skilled military nurses in this country, she is quite qualified by any sick bedside.[5]

Thus in 1918, at a dinner held at Windsor Castle to mark her twenty-first birthday, Mary asked her father if she could be permitted to train as a nurse. This was not an easy request since daughters of the reigning monarch were not expected to work or learn a profession. There had been royal nurses before, but usually it was the domain of lesser-known members of the royal family. Mary was unique as the daughter of the king; and yet what better way was there for George to show that he identified with his people than for him to permit his only daughter to train as a nurse?

Mary's preferred specialism was paediatric care and thus she began her probationer's training at Great Ormond Street Hospital on the ward named after her grandmother Alexandra. Any concerns that she might catch an infectious disease such as measles or diphtheria were soon disregarded.

Great Ormond Street Hospital was founded in 1852 as the Hospital for Sick Children. Initially it was a single house offering ten beds, but it soon grew and came to be patronised by Queen Victoria, with the celebrated author Charles Dickens becoming one of its more famous fundraisers. Alexandra Ward was a long room with twenty-six beds and a rocking horse and many of the children on the ward came from deprived backgrounds. Prior to the establishment of the National Health Service in 1948, wealthy benefactors would often pay for a cot or bed in a hospital. Mary's association with Great Ormond Street Hospital had started in 1903, when the Princess Mary Victoria Cot was endowed in her name. The cot had been funded by £300 raised by the Children's Salon and J.S. Wood, editor of the weekly illustrated newspaper *The Gentlewoman*. Mary therefore used *The Gentlewoman* in June 1918 to announce her intention to train as a nurse, under the control of matron Gertrude Payne, in the same way that other special probationers trained. According to the *Illustrated London News*, 'The Matron was anxious to know what special steps to take for Princess Mary's safety in the event of an air raid. The reply was that she was to be treated just the same as other nurses.'[6]

Mary impressed everyone with her willingness to behave and be treated as every other nurse. Wearing the red cotton dress of commandant of a Voluntary Aid Detachment, along with a nursing cap and a white apron emblazoned with a large red cross, no job, however tedious, was off-limits, whether it was making beds, changing nappies, feeding babies, assisting in the operating theatre or applying poultices. She was particularly fond of bathing babies. Matron Gertrude Payne and the eminent children's doctor Dr George Robinson Pirie drew up a suitable training schedule for the princess. As a matron later recalled to the *Daily Mirror*:

No menial task was too irksome for her. There was a case which had to be dressed every day and one morning I took Princess Mary with me to show her how it should be done. The next morning when I went to see the same patient, I found that a fresh dressing had been put on again and when I asked who did it, the patient answered, 'Our Princess and she never hurt me once.'[7]

Mary would arrive at the entrance to the hospital by carriage at 9.45 a.m. every morning. The children would look out of the windows to catch a glimpse of her. When she reached the ward, the children would greet her with a curtsey or bow and she would reciprocate with a handshake. In August 1918 Queen Mary visited the Children's Hospital Great Ormond Street and spent over an hour in in one of the wards in which Princess Mary was a VAD nurse:

The Princess takes duty at this hospital on Tuesdays and Fridays … Her majesty had the satisfaction of seeing her daughter neatly gowned like the other nurses and busily engaged in her ward duties …The Princess was busy in applying surgical dressings and her mother watched the process with evident interest and satisfaction. It fell to the Royal VAD nurse to serve the dinners in this particular ward, and in this part of her duties the Queen also took a hand. Her Majesty waited until Princess Mary had finished her duty for the day and then the Royal Nurse, still in her VAD uniform drove back with her mother to Buckingham Palace.[8]

In a letter to her son George, Queen Mary recorded her visit on 10 August 1918:

This morning I went to the Great Ormond St Hospital to see Mary working in her ward. Both the Dr & Matron are much pleased with her work which she does very nicely & thoroughly. She has nice light hands for the work and takes a great deal of trouble over the children's cases. She dressed a wound of one child; removed a needle with saline out of a baby's side, made small incisions on another child's arm, a test to ascertain whether the child is tuberculous or not – of course to me who knows little or nothing of such things it was a great surprise to find my daughter doing all this in the quietest, most composed manner![9]

There were frequent stories in the newspapers of Mary's empathy and kindness towards both the children and the nurses, such as that of a child named Liza Terry, who had developed blood poisoning and needed a very complex leg injury frequently dressed. Mary aided her recovery by her patience and diligence. There were tales of the princess going out of her way to speak to the nurses and patients, giving the children and nurses, as well as the families of patients, gifts at Christmas and Easter. Wherever she worked, people spoke of her incredible patience and sympathy. The sheer quantity of such stories showed that her nursing experience was far more than just a PR exercise. She evidently gained a great deal of satisfaction from nursing and it enabled her to grow in confidence and overcome some of her shyness.

Mary continued her training over the next two years, eventually being able to serve on the surgical ward to help with hypodermic treatment and assist in surgery. She was praised for her competency as well as her unflappable, patient and compassionate nature. Following this, she remained associated as a vice-patron, and subsequently president, of the hospital, resuming as vice-patron when the presidency was abolished after the hospital joined the NHS on its formation in 1948. Her wedding to Viscount Lascelles in 1922 prompted *The Times* to produce a wedding supplement to fundraise for the hospital, and the princess to donate a portrait of her in her VAD uniform, which is still owned by the hospital. She revisited the hospital at intervals to open new buildings, the last being the new Barrie Wing shortly before her death. The Hospital's Nurses' Home on Guilford Street was named in her honour when it opened in 1934.

Mary continually pleaded to be permitted to tour Allied hospitals behind battle lines during the First World War and to be allowed to visit France, but to no avail. After the Armistice on 20 November 1918, Mary was finally allowed to travel to the silent battlefields as far as Bruges to see the work of the VAD and in particular to focus on women, as part of a humanitarian visit. She was the first member of the royal family to cross the channel after the war, visiting northern France and Belgium including the towns of Boulogne, Abbeville, Trouville, Rouen, Etretat, Dieppe and Tréport. This was the first tour in which Mary had been permitted to come out from the shadow of her parents. It shows her determination and strength of character at the age of 21. Mary was able to conquer her timidity and prove that she had an important role to play in the future.

On her tour, dressed in her uniform of the commandant VAD of the British Red Cross Society, Mary wanted to see the work carried out by British women. She heard of their experiences at the front line and where they had suffered bombing by Zeppelins. She was driven by female VAD drivers and had to sleep in a basic, wooden army hut. She visited the Army Economy Department at Le Tréport and saw the desolation at Ypres. On her visit Mary met Rachel (later Dame) Crowdy, the principal commandant of the VAD, a nurse and social reformer who remained a close friend to Mary. This was a pivotal trip for Mary since it enabled her to understand the capabilities and the work of so many women, which would have seemed impossible before the war. On moral grounds women could no longer be denied the vote because they had contributed so much to the war. The work of women would prove a focus for Mary over the next forty years. Secondly, it was the first trip in which we can see the emergence of character traits that would typify Mary's future role and work and make her such a valued and reliable member of the royal family: her humility, her lack of pretention, her diligence and at times her normality. She was the no-nonsense princess, the woman who could be *one of us*. In a thank-you letter to Rachel Crowdy and the VAD on 30 November, Mary explained the significance of the trip:

I was very sad at leaving France yesterday after my delightful visit, which I thoroughly enjoyed. Thank you very much for all you did to make it so interesting and pleasant. I know how many arrangements it entailed and what a great deal of trouble you must have taken. The way the VADs received me everywhere has touched me greatly and after seeing their work in France, I am even more proud than before of being one of them. The identification disc is charming, and I shall always wear it and value it as a remembrance of a very happy ten days. I am most grateful to you for your kindness in giving it to me.

Will you please tell all the members how really grateful I am. I feel sure privately that you yourself had a great deal to do with it. I think it was wonderful how much I was able to see in so short a time.[10]

This trip would have a lasting impression on the princess, and she would reminisce about her visit in January 1937 after she had faced one of the most difficult periods of her life: the abdication crisis.

# 6

# The Royal Scots Guards and Other Charitable Patronages

I want to be a woman, not merely a Princess.[1]

*Throughout Norwood News*, Friday 7 January 1927

With her siblings scattered in various places during and following the war, Mary became the axis of family life and wrote regularly to her brothers to inform them of each other's news. She always remained particularly close to David, sending him gifts to keep his spirits up such as a tin of chocolates, a calendar and a particularly impressive warm waistcoat that she knitted. David even travelled with a teddy that Mary had knitted for him. In return, David would write to his *mignonne* (French for 'sweetheart') and recount tales of watching Charlie Chaplin films in the division cinema, song parodies and nights out.

David was extremely protective of Mary. At times he felt sorry for her, since, unlike the fashionable ladies with whom he associated, he considered her life to be one of drudgery and far too restrictive. He would encourage Mary to try and get out in London as often as she could to lunches, teas and matinees instead of staying indoors in the palace. Mary heeded David's advice and she began to go out for dances on occasion, learning how to fox-trot with Bertie when he was on leave from HMS *Collingwood*. David sent Mary a portable gramophone for her to listen to in the palace and he encouraged her to become friends with Irene

Denison (later Marchioness of Carisbrooke), a woman he adored at the time. He felt she would be able to advise his sister on how to dress better, how to go out more often and generally how to have a better life – according to David. In many ways, David wanted to mould his sister into the similar cast of women that he found attractive; the flighty, elfin, party-loving, elegant and fashionable social butterfly, a 'type' Mary could not have been further removed from.

Mary carried out her first solo public engagement on 5 May 1917, when she invested a new May Queen at Whitelands College in Chelsea. At the time, Mary did not have her own lady-in-waiting and thus she was accompanied by Lady Villiers, who served Queen Mary. It was a very short ceremony; all she was required to do was to place a chain and cross around the May Queen's neck and it was the ideal occasion to begin her solo engagements. By the following year, it was apparent to the press that the substantial increase in Mary's engagements meant that she would soon require her own household. Among many solo engage-ments at the start of the New Year were visits to Victoria Docks to see how rationed food was distributed, a matinee to raise money for sailors at the Palace Theatre, an exhibition of war photography at the Grafton Galleries, and a visit to Hampstead.

The end of the First World War, the well-publicised work of the royal family and the change of name to Windsor did not automatically signify a period of calm for the royal family. There was still much to concern the king about his position including the rise of communism, unem-ployment and poverty, the demobilisation of troops and the shadow of the Russian Revolution. In 1918 a press office was finally created at Buckingham Palace to inform the press and publicise the work of the royal family.

In European courts it was traditional to appoint members of the royal family as honorary colonels-in-chief of regiments. Queen Victoria introduced this tradition in the latter half of her reign. Queen Alexandra, the wife of Edward VII, had been a colonel-in-chief of the 19th Hussars. As Princess of Wales, Queen Mary had been associated with the 18th Hussars. She took much interest in the role and during the First World War she made numerous visits to their Tidworth barracks to visit casualties. Queen Mary's involvement in her regiment exemplified to her daughter the commitment of such a role.

In 1918, not long after Mary's twenty-first birthday, the secretary of the War Office announced that George V had made her the colonel-in-chief of the Royal Scots. The Royal Scots were the British army's oldest and most senior regiment and the Duke of Kent, Queen Victoria's father, had been their colonel. The regiment first came to England in 1625 to attend the coronation of Charles I, returning in 1633 to fight against the Parliamentarians, and it became part of the British army. Over 12,000 men from the regiment had lost their lives during the First World War. The role of colonel-in-chief involved taking an active interest in all activities of the regiment, visiting deployed troops, sending messages of support, attending regimental dinners and taking part in ceremonies. During her trip to France in 1918 Mary, in her VAD uniform, took the salute of the regiment as it marched through Ypres, an enduring precedent.

In December 1918, Mary undertook an engagement at Canon Street Station to meet prisoners of war who were returning from Germany. She had requested to meet men who belonged to her own regiment. Mary was seen to be greatly moved by the distressing stories given of the hardships encountered by the men, who told how 'no torture or insult was too great for us. Hundreds will never return alive to their friends.'[2] This empathy no doubt came from her own anxieties concerning her brothers and their safety during the war.

A year later, Mary finally visited Edinburgh with the Earl of Bradford to inspect her new battalion at the Redford barracks prior to their departure for India. During her first inspection, Mary addressed the men, presented over eighty medals and decorations and expressed her pride in becoming their colonel-in-chief. Right from the start, Mary took an interest not just in the men, but also in their families. She asked to visit the married quarters and spoke to both wives and children. The press recorded that Mary's new role was certainly not an 'empty title'[3] but involved many responsibilities. 'I am proud to be the regiment's Colonel-in-Chief, and to continue that association enjoyed by … Queen Victoria, who always considered herself as "the daughter of the regiment"' ... I shall follow your career in India with the keenest interest.'[4]

When considering how best to honour the 11,000 Royal Scots men who had been killed during the First World War, a Royal Scots' officer, Colonel Lord Henry Scott, younger son of the 6th Duke of Buccleuch, decided that a club for all ranks would be most appropriate. In 1919 he called a meeting of distinguished Scots connected with the regiment and put his plan to them. This led to the formation of the Royal Scots' War Memorial Fund. Trustees were appointed and a public appeal made which yielded £2,000 in the first week, growing substantially to £17,000. In property values today, this is the modern equivalent of about £5 million. In 1921, Nos. 30 and 31 Abercromby Place were acquired, and No. 29 was purchased some years later. The buildings were altered and adapted to become the Royal Scots' Club. The Hepburn suite and the billiards room were built to the rear of the building in 1929. The club was a success from the start with Lord Henry as chairman, an office he held until 1944. Mary opened the Royal Scots' Club in Abercromby Place in Edinburgh on 10 August 1922 and in March 1927 she performed the opening ceremony of the memorial at the Royal Scots' Regimental Depot at Glencorse Barracks, Penicuik, which took the form of wrought-iron gates.

In the early interwar years, Mary's public life increased. Despite her inherent shyness and propensity to tremble before every engagement, she always demonstrated an 'immense power of application', a quality that would be on show in her later public life.[5]

With a background in nursing, which she fully intended to use to her advantage, Mary began to patronise medical charities such as the League of Mercy, a charity to help the sick and suffering in charity hospitals, which were necessary prior to the founding of the NHS. She took a further interest in charities providing rehabilitation for wounded servicemen and women: one such example being the Blinded Soldiers and Sailors Care Committee, which later rebranded as St Dunstan's Home for the Blind and afterwards, the Blind Veterans. This organisation was established by Sir Arthur Pearson, the founder of the *Daily Express* and president of the National Institute for the Blind. Sir Arthur became blind himself from glaucoma and realised that veterans who had been blinded by gas attacks or trauma could still make an important contribution to society and, with the right support, lead independent lives. In 1915, Sir Arthur set up a hostel in Bayswater which eventually moved to Regent's Park. Here men were rehabilitated and taught new skills such as braille and how to use a typewriter or a new occupation such as basket-weaving, carpentry or book-repairing. Sir Arthur thought many men could learn to overcome the restrictions of blindness with sufficient patience and perseverance. Mary visited St Dunstan's Hostel in May 1917 with her brother David. They were shown around the farm at St Dunstan's where the blind veterans were learning how to handle poultry. Mary was struck by the speed at which the blind adapted and learned new skills. She continued to visit the charity several times including a visit in April 1918 and frequently purchased items from their gift shop for Christmas presents in Regent Street.

In 1920, Princess Mary became the first royal patron of the Not Forgotten Association. This had been founded by Marta Cunningham, a singer from America who had regularly entertained troops and visited injured soldiers during the First World War. Marta felt compelled to ensure that the wounded soldiers would not be forgotten simply because they were out of public view. Every year since 1920, a garden party has been held at Buckingham Palace to honour such men and to boost their morale. The first garden party in June 1920 gave the men tea and cigarettes. When Mary died in 1965, the honour passed to the Duchess of Kent and then to Princess Anne, the current Princess Royal. The latest garden parties now support men and women from over 120 military organisations.

The year 1919 began with the sudden death of Mary's youngest brother, Prince John, at the age of 13. Mary and John were incredibly fond of each other; they corresponded throughout John's brief life and John would often send Mary flowers from his garden. Mary was so protective of John and at times rather overbearing, that he was once heard to comment, 'Oh shut up Mary, you fuss as much as Mother!'[6] John loved being outdoors with nature. He was often seen out playing, cycling or fishing and he adored spending time in Broadstairs with his tutor, where the sea air appeared to improve his epilepsy. The widowed Queen Alexandra was a doting grandparent to John. Although 'Pickle', as he was known in the family, was quite mischievous and loved practical jokes, Mary said of her youngest brother that 'he could coax anyone to do anything'.[7]

On 16 January, John had spent a happy time with his cousin Prince Olav. A couple of days later he accompanied Mary on an invigorating walk. Upon his return to the cottage, John suffered a severe epileptic fit. Afterwards he collapsed into a state of unconsciousness and the royal physician, Sir Alan Manby, was called. The king and queen came to see him but thought it unwise to wake him. They returned to York Cottage and a few hours later, John passed away. Upon hearing the news, Mary wept and was inconsolable. Queen Mary wrote to an old friend: 'For him it is a great release as his malady was becoming worse ... and he has thus been spared much suffering.'[8]

John was buried at St Mary Magdalene Church on 21 January, and the court went into full mourning for four weeks. *The Globe* reported, 'The young Prince was, by reason of his years and the seclusion, which is the wholesome rule of the King and Queen's household, but little known to the public, and the news of his early death comes therefore as a shock of surprise to most people.'[9]

In her diary Mary wrote:

> I went with Mama, Henry and George to Sandringham Church to see poor Johnnie's coffin lying in the choir, it looked lovely surrounded by beautiful flowers. We also saw the lining of the grave with poinsettias and Xmas roses ... We arrived at the church at 11:50 for the funeral service, which was at 12. It was a beautiful service and very simple. The church was very full. After the coffin had been lowered into the grave, Papa and Mama threw some flowers on it. Then I walked to Sandringham.[10]

Mary returned to see the grave the following day, 'which looked so lovely covered with wreaths'.[11] Mary and her brothers wrote on their wreath, 'For darling Johnnie from his devoted brothers and sister.'[12]

Prince John's faithful terrier, Spot, was heartbroken. Estate workers carried the coffin into a packed churchyard accompanied by many of John's friends from the estate. Mary was bereft by the loss of John. Over the course of the next few days, she accompanied her mother as they sorted through John's possessions at the farm. Lala, who was almost regarded as a family member because of her loyalty and devotion to John, would return with the king and queen to Buckingham Palace and later became a nanny to both of Mary's children.

As the family slowly recovered from John's untimely passing, Mary was asked to act as bridesmaid at the wedding of Princess Patricia of Connaught to Captain Alexander Ramsay in Westminster Abbey in February 1919. Princess Patricia, a granddaughter of Queen Victoria, was considered one of the most striking and eligible princesses of her era. There was much talk over her possible future husband, but she eventually married for love and George V permitted her to relinquish her royal title and she became Lady Patricia Ramsay. Since Mary had recently lost her brother, many doubted that she would attend the wedding ceremony. However, she insisted on fulfilling her obligation. Patricia's wedding in Westminster Abbey became a popular and much-celebrated public occasion. The crowds roared as the couple drove in an open carriage through the capital. In many ways Patricia was not dissimilar to Mary and may have proved to be something of an inspiration to her in terms of how she carried out her philanthropic work. She was a working member of the royal family, having deputised for her mother, the Duchess of Connaught, on many occasions including travelling throughout Canada during her father's tenure as governor-general from 1911 to 1916. She had her own regiment, the Princess Patricia's Canadian Light Infantry, and one of her ladies-in-waiting was a well-known suffragette.

# 7

# The Girl Guides

In this disordered world of ours, with its vast opportunities, many pos-
sibilities, and many pitfalls, there stands among its fellows a movement
so full of life and energy, that it is fast pushing its way forward, not only
in the British Isles and Dominions, but over the whole world.[1]
*The Common Cause*, Friday 17 February 1922

Princess Mary's association with the Girl Guiding movement is inherently revealing and typifies the course her charitable patronages would
take over the next forty years of her life of public service. It illustrates
her long-term commitment towards girls and their education. It shows
how she believed in equal opportunities for all, regardless of social and
economic background. Furthermore, it underlines her consistency of
support, comprehensive involvement and the earnestness with which
she undertook all her charitable endeavours.

In 1908 Robert Baden-Powell, a lieutenant-general in the Second
Boer War, wrote a book entitled *Scouting for Boys*. The book was meant
to be a manual depicting how to be a good citizen of the British Empire,
as well as containing advice on survival skills such as woodcraft, observa-
tion and tracking. Baden-Powell had tried out some of his ideas at an
experimental camp on Brownsea Island in Dorset. The success of the
book led to many boys and girls forming their own groups of scouts.

Baden-Powell decided that it would be best to form separate groups for boys and girls, since in those days few girls had experienced camping or hiking. His sister Agnes Baden-Powell therefore formed the first Girl Guiding movement in 1910 in Pinkney's Green in Berkshire. With her fondness for outdoor pursuits and having been brought up in a family of boys, it was little wonder that Mary was attracted to an involvement with the Guiding movement.

A major objective for Baden-Powell had been to:

Bring all classes more in touch with each other, to break down existing barriers, which are only artificial after all and to teach them to give and take in the common cause, instead of being at snarls of class against class, which is snobbery all around and a danger to the State.[2]

Yet Baden-Powell was aware that to add gravitas to his movement he needed to enlist the support of the upper classes and if possible, the royal family.

Princess Mary's association with the Guides began during the First World War. There were many girls who joined the movement at this pivotal moment, wanting to help the war effort but restricted from doing so because of their age and their sex. Princess Mary had taken an interest in the movement at this time through the 1st Sandringham Company in the village and became the Girl Guide president of the county of Norfolk in 1917. The Sandringham Guides had an emblem of a rose and a carnation and the group's colour was royal purple.

The Boy Scout movement had donated a recreation hut to the troops serving in France. Robert Baden-Powell's wife, Olave, had worked in the canteen of one such hut and knew that they were beneficial for the troops. She decided to encourage the Girl Guides to raise money to provide another. The cost of these huts was about £500 and by May 1916 not only had the sum been raised, but they had nearly enough to provide five huts. A hut was installed where it was most needed in France and the remaining funds were used to purchase a motor-ambulance. This was presented to the Army Council by Princess Mary on behalf of the Girl Guides in 1917 at Buckingham Palace. At the presentation,

Mary inspected some of the Guides and was presented with a gold badge of thanks.

Many Girl Guide groups were struggling, and it was hoped that having a link with royalty would improve the situation. Mary was asked to become president of the Girl Guiding movement and the previous president, Agnes Baden-Powell, stood down to vice-president. Mary's first appearance in front of the Girl Guides happened at the Victory Rally in the Albert Hall in November 1919 in front of 14,000 Guides coming from all parts of the empire. The rally was held to commemorate the armistice of the First World War. Mary wore the uniform of a commissioner, complete with gold and silver badges to denote her royal rank. On her arrival, all the Guides stood up and saluted. Mary was enrolled and earnestly gave her Guide promise to Olave Baden-Powell. There were speeches by Robert Baden-Powell and the preacher and suffragist Maude Royden, who asked the audience to consider what Queen Victoria would have made of her great-granddaughter dressed in the same uniform as several thousand others. The guides gave a solemn promise to rededicate themselves to their king and country and held a brief moment of silent contemplation to honour the war dead. Mary barely sat down for the entire two-and-a-half-hour ceremony.

It was around this time that Princess Mary started to hold get-togethers for her charitable causes in the guise of supper parties. The very first party was held towards the end of November 1919 and involved over three dozen members of the Land Army. Mary awarded medals and gave a speech. From her initial patronage of the movement, the royal circular would regularly report on her active and hands-on involvement. One day she decided to call unannounced on the offices of the Girl Guides in Victoria Street and see for herself the work that was undertaken there. The doorkeeper had quite a shock with such an unexpected guest. Speaking about the visit of Princess Mary, Lady Baden-Powell touches on something that was so typical of Mary: the unparalleled interest she took in her charities. 'It was so heartening to find that our Guide President ... knows all about what we are at in the Guide World,' she said, 'and quite feels like "one of us" – shaking hands with the left hand and giving the guide sign, as if she had been amongst us for years.'[3]

In January 1920 Mary inspected 2,000 Girl Guides of Norwich and presented several awards including the Nurse Cavell award to Mrs Gillett, who had saved a member of her group from burning. A rally was organised in Hyde Park in June to enable the new president to inspect guides from all over the country. Several thousand guides were present, and they assembled on the Guards' Drill Ground in preparation for the princess's inspection. However, just as Mary started to walk amongst the Guides, the heavens opened to a lashing of torrential rain with lightning and thunder. Instantly the Guides had to flee for cover in nearby bus and train stations. Mary went to the ambulance tent and soon found herself surrounded by girls on stretchers who had fainted in fear. She was only able to find her car with the assistance of a bodyguard of Guides keeping the crowds back. Mary had no choice but to return to Buckingham Palace. One thoroughly soaked Guide was heard to shout, 'Good thing I got me swimming badge last week.'[4]

In a letter to the chief commissioner for London, Mary expressed her distress at seeing so many Guides 'exposed to torrents of rain, thunder and lightning. In spite of the storm everything, in HRH's opinion went without a hitch … The Princess could not fail to be impressed by the discipline and steadiness of all ranks under conditions which were trying and uncomfortable in the extreme.'[5] That night many mothers spent hours scrubbing their children in an attempt to remove the blue dye from the Guide uniform that had stained their daughters' skins. Subsequent rallies were always held with a proximity to shelter.

Not only was Mary an avid supporter of the Girl Guides, but she was eager to involve her family as much as possible. In July 1920, the king and queen, accompanied by Mary, travelled to Denbigh in Wales to open a sanatorium. The Denbighshire Guides undertook the hoisting and breaking of the royal standard, the king's personal flag, and were inspected by the king and Princess Mary. Queen Mary also visited a Brownie pack in Wandsworth. When the first weekly newsletter for the Guides, *The Guide*, was published in 1921, Mary handwrote a message to be printed on the front cover.

On the occasion of Mary's wedding in 1922, the Girl Guiding movement wished to purchase her a suitable gift. All of the guides were asked to contribute a maximum of a penny. There were approximately 215,000 Guides and Brownies and thus the collection amounted to over £900. In the end several small gifts were presented to Mary, including a diamond and ruby Tenderfoot badge in platinum with additional rubies; the Guide symbol of a trefoil represented the three-fold Guide promise. Mary received an antique silver cheese-tray that had been picked by Queen Mary and a silver Guide statuette of a Guide and a Brownie as well as the Guides' standard, a gift from the Norwich County Guides.

In 1922 Anne Saunderson, an American owner of a Georgian manor house named Foxlease in Lyndhurst, Hampshire, offered the estate to the Girl Guiding movement to be used as a training centre. Her marriage had fallen apart, she could no longer maintain the upkeep and wished to return home. While the house was on the market, Anne had permitted Girl Guides to camp in the grounds. The property was set in over 60 acres of gardens, woods and pasture. As generous as the offer was, the Girl Guides did not possess sufficient funds to furnish and repurpose the house. Lady Mary Trefusis was on the committee of a fund that had been established to contribute to a wedding gift for Mary from all girls in the empire with the name of Mary. The sum raised far exceeded initial estimates and thus Princess Mary decided that it should be given to the Girl Guiding movement to enable them to equip the building for their use, as well as carry out any much-needed repairs. Later, Mary donated a further £4,000, half the sum raised by the exhibition of her wedding gifts. Thus, the Guiding movement was able to open the training centre in June 1922 and train Guiders who came from throughout the empire.

Not only did this charitable donation benefit the Guides, but it encouraged other benefactors to come forward who agreed to adopt rooms for personal furnishing and upkeep. In fact, every Brownie or Guide group contributed in some way and there were many gifts from America. Mary visited Foxlease for the first time in July 1923 for an informal visit. Between its opening and Mary's visit, over 1,200 people from over thirty different countries had already been through its doors. Dressed in her Guide uniform, Mary was met by a guard of honour at the front gate. The main house was named after Mary in appreciation of her benevolence. Once refurbished, it had nine bathrooms and accommodation for twenty. Bedrooms were converted to represent different countries of the empire or different schools who had their own Guide group. There was a barn converted into a hall, which was designed as a perfect venue for camp-fire talks and songs. The lease on the property ran out in 1942 and it became the absolute property of the Girl Guides. A record number of over 1,400 trainees went through the doors that year.

By 1929, the London headquarters of the Guides was proving to be far too small to meet their ever-increasing needs. It was decided that it would be best for the Guides to build their own headquarters in London, at a possible cost of £75,000: an astronomical sum in those days. As usual, Princess Mary made a large donation and encouraged others to add to the fund. Guides and Brownies throughout the country were encouraged to think of imaginative ways to raise money for the building. Mary laid the foundation stone in May 1930 and her mother came to open the building the following year in March.

The acquisition of Foxlease meant that by 1924 the first international conference of the World Association of Girl Guides was held with delegates from forty countries. 1932 marked the twenty-first, 'Coming-of-Age' anniversary of the Girl Guides. This happened during a period of financial crisis, when extravagant celebrations were considered unfitting and so plans were kept minimal. However, a service of thanksgiving was held at St Paul's Cathedral on 28 May, attended by over 5,000 London-based guides as well as Princess Mary. This was to be the largest service ever organised. At the same time Lady Olave Baden-Powell was made a Dame Grand Cross of the British Empire as part of the king's birthday honours. Olave saw this as an honour for the movement as a whole.

Mary's two nieces, Princesses Elizabeth and Margaret, the daughters of George VI were eager to join a Guiding group in order to interact with local children. Therefore in 1937, the princesses' governess, Marion Crawford, spoke to the Guide commissioner at that time, Miss Violet Synge. The first Buckingham Palace Brownie Pack and Guide Company was inaugurated with fourteen other Guides coming from the children of palace employees. Mary enjoyed a close relationship with her nieces and in particular would later share a love of equestrianism and horse racing with Elizabeth. Thus it was that Mary, wearing her president's uniform, proudly enrolled the two princesses in the group. Princess Margaret was a Leprechaun and Princess Elizabeth was a Second of the Kingfisher Patrol.

From the outset Mary made it her priority to visit as many different Brownie and Guide groups as she could throughout the country. She would often invite commissioners and guiders to her London town house, Chesterfield House, and kept an active interest in all aspects of the movement. She regularly visited Foxlease, the Guide training centre she had helped to establish, as well as Waddow Hall in Clitheroe in Lancashire, used since 1927 as an activity centre.

Mary was a well-admired president throughout her thirty-five-year tenure. Such was her popularity that when she died in 1965, a memorial service was held for her at St Peter's Church on Eaton Square which was packed out with Girl Guides. It was frequently said that despite her shyness, Mary always appeared relaxed and content when surrounded by her Guiding family. Members recalled such events as a trip to Foxlease in 1930, when she 'perched on a log eating damper with the staff encamped … and later joining with enthusiasm at the camp fire in the barn',[6] or when she attended the twelfth world conference at the Tower of London, just as the Tower was carrying out the 700-year-old locking-up Ceremony of the Keys; a foreign delegate was heard to say, 'Now I understand your tradition – the Monarchy, the Empire, everything.'[7] As the first royal patron of the Girl Guides, and with her generous donation towards Foxlease, Mary would always hold a unique place in the history of the Girl Guide movement, a cherished memorial of a princess proud to wear her purple and gold draped cords, and one that continues even today. Princess Margaret took over from Mary in 1965 and in 2003 the honour passed to the Countess of Wessex. It is significant that in nearly 100 years of Royal patronage, there have only been three royal presidents.

# 8

# Harry

A British Bridegroom for a British Princess.[1]

*Pall Mall Gazette*, 28 February 1922

He is the wealthiest and has been for some time, the most sought-after bachelor in the United Kingdom.[2]

*Dundee Courier*, Wednesday 23 November 1921

The war had made it impossible to find any suitable marriage partners from the former European royal houses for Mary, while the fact that hostilities had arisen between nations led by Queen Victoria's grandchildren proved that dynastic marriages did not ensure peace. Conscious of this and aware of the fervent anti-German feelings of the British public, in 1917 George and Mary had put forward to the Privy Council when they changed their name to establish the House of Windsor that their children should be free to marry into British noble families. George saw this change of policy to be of historical significance, as it would make the British royal family appear more anglicised. Furthermore, after the war, many – including the royal family and the public exchequer – were struggling financially. It was evident that Mary needed to choose a husband who would have substantial funds so that she would not be reliant on the public purse for an annuity on the civil list. George V was acutely aware of the negative effects of payments to the royal family for their expenses. At the time of the Great Depression in 1931, he even gave up his £51,000 allowance and made further cuts to the civil list to show that he was prepared to economise at such a time of national crisis.

Despite this change, for a while it seemed as though Mary was destined to remain a spinster and take on the role of permanent companion to her mother, in the same way that her father's sister, Princess Victoria, had with Queen Alexandra. Mary may have been George's favourite, but nevertheless she was suppressed by her stifling position.

David continued to express his concerns that Mary would never be able to escape 'Buck House Prison', as he termed it. He and Mary maintained their closeness as they entered into adulthood, which is probably why he felt such a duty to ensure her happiness. 'I don't feel that she is happy ... but she never complains. The trouble is that she is far too unselfish and conscientious.'[3] David believed that Mary would live a more fulfilling life if she were to marry. His pleas to his mother to speak to her husband about a possible match fell on deaf ears. He became exasperated with his sister's seeming self-sacrifice to an endless round of duties with her parents and their unwillingness to consider Mary's future happiness.

Although David had no immediate plans to find a bride for himself, he had since 1918 been conducting an affair with the married Freda Dudley Ward, wife of the Liberal politician William Dudley Ward. David shared his innermost thoughts with his mistress in correspondence including his concerns that Mary's life was:

> The greatest tragedy of all ... Though it's not her fault as it's the way she's been brought up and she's quite happy and not to be pitied as far as she is concerned. But I do resent ... the foul way my father treats her in imprisoning her at court and not letting her lead a normal life and ruining her chances of getting married or even of existing as a girl of twenty-three should do.[4]

To David it was a life that was 'sordidly dull and boring'.[5] Yet David's perceptions of his parents' treatment of Mary were not wholly accurate; as the heir to the throne they were bound to be more exacting of him and it is clear that he found their expectations unrealistic and restrictive.

However, while George and Mary were more benevolent towards Mary, as a female, she had much less freedom than her brothers. In addition, she was a naturally unselfish and dutiful daughter who did not wish to displease anyone, let alone her parents, and loathed confrontation. This explains why at times she would bow down to their wishes and needs rather than her own. Such instances of her selfless behaviour include a time when she turned down the chance to play tennis with Bertie, since she did not feel that she would have enough time to change her shoes and her father was a stickler for correct attire at dinner. On another occasion she appeared at dinner in a modern sleeveless dress, and her father immediately sent her to change. Mary had little interaction with people of her own age, her parents preferring to keep her within their social milieu, as if they needed her to remain unmarried for their own selfish needs. This partly explains why she always appeared older than her years. A British writer who lived in America, Marguerite E. Harrison, recalled to the *Baltimore Sun* after meeting a close friend of Princess Mary:

> She is a girl of considerable originality and independence of character, with a keen sense of humour and a natural human love of a good time, but she has always been handicapped by her mother. Like all girls her age, she had a perfectly normal desire to look smart and up to day, but she always had to dress according to the Queen's ideas. A modest round neck and a string of pearls was the Queen's idea of a suitable evening costume for a young girl … she has been dressed like a prim wax doll.[6]

As is the case today with the media, the press loved to speculate concerning possible suitors for the royal family. In May 1919 rumours circulated of an imminent engagement between Mary and the incredibly handsome Earl of Dalkeith, the eldest son of the 7th Duke of Buccleuch. The Earl of Dalkeith had been a lieutenant in the Grenadier

Guards, the Prince of Wales's regiment, and had served on the personal staff of the king. His family were one of the most noble Scottish families. Princess Mary was a friend through the Girl Guide movement of Lady Elizabeth Bowes-Lyon, the future wife of Mary's brother Prince Albert. Lady Elizabeth was the youngest daughter and ninth of ten children of the 14th Earl of Strathmore and his wife, Cecilia Cavendish-Bentick. Mary visited Lady Elizabeth at the Strathmores' Scottish castle, Glamis, along with her mother. Lord Dalkeith was also a guest at the house party. According to Mabel Monty, a former dresser and lady's maid of Lady Elizabeth, Princess Mary and Lord Dalkeith were attached to each other romantically and had an 'illicit attraction'.[7] Monty claimed that the couple were once caught together by Queen Mary when meeting surreptitiously, but this may be mere conjecture. Lord Dalkeith married Vreda Esther Mary Lascelles in April 1921; his sister Alice would later marry Mary's younger brother Henry, Duke of Gloucester.

The press considered this possible match ideal since Dalkeith was a British nobleman rather than a foreign prince. The engagement was even discussed in parliament.[8] However, these reports were refuted within days by the king's private secretary, Lord Stamfordham. The earl may have been the heir to nearly half a million acres, extending over eight counties, yet, compared to many other noblemen, he was not 'rich enough to marry the King's only daughter'.[9] Rumours circulated concerning Viscount Althorp, eventually the 7th Earl Spencer, and William Bingham Compton, the 6th Marquess of Northampton. These rumours incensed Mary, who could not comprehend the level of interest in her future life.

In 1921 Princess Mary visited the Grand National and attended a house party at Chatsworth, where she was the guest of honour. During her time there, Mary visited several neighbouring attractions including the Speedwell Mine, the Speedwell Peak Cavern and the ancient Peakland Church as well as Buxton and Bakewell. On both occasions Viscount Henry Lascelles, known as Harry, was present. Throughout 1921, Harry had been present at many society gatherings involving the royal family through his family's association with the Duke and Duchess of Buccleuch, who were close friends of the king and queen.

Henry George Charles Lascelles was born in September 1882 and was the eldest son of Henry Lascelles, 5th Earl of Harewood and lord lieutenant of the West Riding of Yorkshire, and Lady Florence Katherine Bridgeman, daughter of Orlando Bridgeman, the 3rd Earl of Bradford and a Conservative politician. Known rather unfortunately as a 'dismal bloodhound'[10] because of his downcast expression, Harry was fifteen years Mary's senior and appeared considerably older than his 39 years. Surprisingly, the match was encouraged by George V. Not only was Harry heir to the Harewood estate, with his own private fortune of £3 million and the ownership of vast amounts of land, he also shared a love of horse racing with the king. Most importantly, Mary would not need to move abroad.

Harry soon became a frequent guest at Balmoral in the summer of 1921. He had also visited the royal family at Windsor and Sandringham, and it was while staying at Sandringham that he asked Mary to marry him.

In her autobiography Mabell, Countess of Airlie, one of Queen Mary's ladies-in-waiting, recounts an illuminating story of the proposal at Sandringham and George V's response to it:

> Lord Lascelles had been invited … to York Cottage … After tea on Sunday, Princess Mary took Lord Lascelles to see her little sitting-room and there … he asked her to marry him. Before answering him, she sped downstairs to tell her mother, whom she found … lying down to rest in one of her lovely embroidered kimonos … After congratulations and embraces she said, 'But we must ask Papa,' and began to think of the most favourable time to do it.
>
> 'Now, please, Mama,' Princess Mary said firmly – remembering that all this while Lord Lascelles was still waiting in the sitting-room upstairs.
>
> The queen, glancing at her kimono, demurred, 'I can't go like this.'
>
> 'Yes, you can,' reiterated her daughter.
>
> So, a solemn procession, Queen Mary in kimono and slippers and the Princess palpitating with excitement, wended its way to the King who immediately gave his consent.[11]

Harry came from a long and noble Yorkshire family. His ancestors could be traced back to the time of Edward II in 1315 and when a John De Lascelles lived at Hinderskelfe or Henderskelfe, between York and Scarborough, which now forms part of the Castle Howard estate.

Harry attended Eton, where he was remembered notably for his role of master of the school beagles. After leaving the school he went on to have a distinguished military career. He attended the Royal Military College in Sandhurst and in 1902 became a second lieutenant in the illustrious infantry regiment the Grenadier Guards. He served as honorary attaché in Paris at the British embassy for two years from 1905, subsequently serving as aide-de-camp to the 4th Earl Grey until 1911. He was a member of the Territorial Army from 1913 in the Yorkshire Hussars yeomanry. During the First World War, he returned to the Grenadier Guards for service on the Western Front. He was involved in the Battle of Hamelincourt and in command of a battalion in the capture of Maubeuge in November 1918, two days before the Armistice. Lascelles was wounded three times during the conflict and suffered from gas poisoning.

In his autobiography, *Old Men Forget*, Duff Cooper recalls a meeting with Harry in 1918 in northern France in a deep shelter at the battalion headquarters, where he was impressed by the 36-year-old viscount, who looked 'extraordinarily elegant and beautifully clean'[12] as well as being surrounded by copies of *Country Life* and the *Burlington Magazine* – the common reading material of the English upper classes. Duff Cooper goes on to talk about the pleasure of dining with Lascelles who was a 'far pleasanter companion than anyone else in the mess. He is cultivated. We talked about wine, books, pedigrees and old houses.'[13] Harry had just purchased the magnificent Chesterfield House as a town house in Mayfair, London.

Harry's distinguished military career was not entirely blemish free. He was tried twice by court martial. The first was on 4 April 1918, when he was a major, known to his fellow soldiers as 'Don', and concerned a 'rag'[14] at a West End music hall. This later turned out to be a case of mistaken identity. However, in his unpublished memoir, Geoffrey Hirst, who served in the Grenadier Guards, details his encounter with Harry, when he was called upon as a captain to take charge of his superior prior to the court appearance. Geoffrey describes the encounter with Lascelles: 'Such a situation could have been an embarrassing one for both of us, but he was a very nice person, who was happy to treat the whole unfortunate episode in a friendly and cooperative spirit, for me at any rate the day passed pleasantly.'[15] To show his appreciation, Harry eventually invited Hirst to the ball given by George V at Buckingham Palace to celebrate the engagement. According to Hirst, Harry did not suffer fools and was forthright in his opinions. He was tried a second time when he had made disparaging remarks about the competency of the general staff, but was again acquitted.

More than anything, Harry was known for his intellect, which Mary obviously found attractive. Much later in 1933, the president of Canada, Richard Bedford Bennett, upon meeting him, came 'back full of Harry's praises; apparently he sat next to him after dinner at Buckingham Palace and was much impressed by his knowledge of Canada'.[16] In many ways Harry was something of a Renaissance man: he was interested in art and culture; and as an avid race-goer he found veterinary science fascinating and would later open the International Veterinary Congress in 1930.

In 1913, Harry stood as a Unionist and Conservative candidate for Keighley. He was by all accounts seen as a worthy candidate and very early on in the campaign, the *Yorkshire Post* reported that the opposition were taken aback by his popularity and magnificent reception. The key themes of the by-election were Home Rule, Welsh Disestablishment and the Insurance Act (an act to amend the earlier 1911 act outlining the terms of National Insurance for industrial workers). Despite his ability to be a rousing orator, Harry was beaten by 878 votes by the Liberal candidate, Sir Stanley Buckmaster. There were rumours in 1920 that he would stand for the Barkston Ash seat, but he sought no future role in politics. Harry took an active role in Yorkshire countryside pursuits. He became joint master of the Bramham Hunt with Colonel Lane-Fox. He was a steward of the jockey club and owned several racing horses. Like Mary's brother David, Harry was a Freemason and a devotee of petit-point needlepoint. He would recite his Masonic ritual while embroidering.

During his bachelordom, Harry had been 'notorious for picking out the smartest and most outré women in England as the object of his rather transitory attentions'.[17] In June 1912 at Ascot, *Tatler* and the *Sketch* reported that he had been seen in the company of the Hon. Victoria (known as Vita) Sackville-West, only child of the 3rd Baron Sackville. A few days later Harry proposed to Vita. Vita took time to consider his proposal:

> I can't think how he found the courage to say it, for he is very timid. Lunch was difficult, but he behaved very well. He has every virtue, but he is not *simpatico*. He is tall, and not too ugly, but he has a silly laugh. He will be very rich. He always looks terrified.[18]

Harry appeared desperate for Vita to accept his proposal and at a house party in Somerset, where Vita spent much of the time engrossed in lawn tennis to avoid having to speak to him, Harry sought to impress Vita's mother by declaring that his father's income of '£31,000 a year from his land alone, plus plenty of cash'[19] was worth considering. Harry was relentless in his pursuit of Vita, even following her to Italy when she accompanied Harold Nicolson for part of his journey to Constantinople. When it appeared that she was about to choose the penniless Nicolson instead, Harry played his trump card by using Harewood as a bargaining tool, suggesting that Vita, with her eye for interior décor, would make the ideal chatelaine of Harewood.

Vita manipulated and toyed with Harry, who she saw as a forlorn and preposterous, yet generously wealthy, figure of amusement. She betrayed his loyalty by using his affection in a merciless and calculating manner. Undoubtedly, she enjoyed the thrill of the chase, in playing one suitor off against the other. Long after her marriage to Nicolson, Vita continued to ridicule Harry within her circle and eventually Vita's lover, Virginia Woolf, used him as inspiration for the transvestite character of Archduke Henry in her 1928 novel *Orlando*.

Harry was not just the heir to the Harewood estate; he had also inherited a vast sum of money from his great-uncle the Marquess of Clanricarde, along with Portumna Castle in County Galway in Ireland. Clanricarde had a reputation as an eccentric miser who hoarded vast sums of money and dressed in the cast-offs of his valet. However, at the same time as living like a pauper, he was a discerning collector of art treasures and a shrewd investor. Clanricarde had been involved in the Irish Land Debates of the late nineteenth century. He did not live on his estates, preferring to live in London instead. Over the years, he earned a reputation as a ruthless landlord who took satisfaction in other people's misery and would evict any tenant who made the slightest complaint. He would never lower the rent on his land and continued to fight against the government concerning Land Reform. He 'stood for all that was bad in landlordism'[20] and the Evicted Tenants Act was principally directed against him. Once, during the First World War, when he was on leave, Harry Lascelles came across his greatuncle at the St James's Cub and out of politeness sat with him for a brief time prior to lunch. Subsequently, when the Marquess died in April 1916, he chose to reward Harry for this act of kindness by bequeathing most of his fortune to him, to the fury of Harry's father, the 5th Earl. Harry had always been interested in fine art, having completed the Grand Tour of Europe in his youth. The Clanricarde legacy enabled him to become one of the most renowned collectors of fine art in his era.

Included in the items bequeathed to Harry was the famous Canning Jewel, a pendant of a triton holding a sword and shield. Originating in Tuscany in the sixteenth century, it was sent by an Italian grand duke to a Mogul emperor and was found in the King of Oudh's treasury during the capture of Delhi in 1857 and sold to Earl Canning, the first viceroy. In 1931 Harry sold the jewel for £10,000 and it was donated by an anonymous American benefactor to the Victoria and Albert Museum. Harry inherited the Clanricarde diamonds, which had been hidden in a bank vault. Two centuries before the bequest, it had been predicted that the diamonds would eventually become the property of a king's daughter. The diamonds were arranged in such an old-fashioned style that they had to be reset before they could be worn by Princess Mary. According to her son George, the 7th Earl of Harewood, in his autobiography *The Tongs and The Bones*:

> My mother showed me odd bits of Lord Clanricarde's mother's jewellery from which Uncle Hubert (Clanricarde) had broken off a piece to stick on a safety-pin as a tie-pin, sometimes dyeing a diamond with blue ink because he wanted it to look like a sapphire or with red ink to make it look like a ruby. A very odd man.[21]

Harry was generous with his inheritance within his family. He offered to pay for his cousin Alan 'Tommy' Lascelles's son to attend Eton and even suggested that the earldom of Harewood would pass to his cousin if he was not able to provide his own male heir. 'I thought it particularly nice of him to have thought of such a thing ... And I like his frankness in saying, "if I don't succeed, yours is the heir of the house." So many men would feel a false shame in ever alluding to the possibility.'[22]

The king held a special council meeting at 6.30 p.m. on 22 November 1921 to give his official consent to Mary's engagement, and an announcement was issued by Buckingham Palace later that same evening. On the day following the announcement, Mary travelled to Brighton to view St Mary's Hall, an establishment for the education of daughters of clergymen, to inspect Girl Guides at the Royal Pavilion, followed by the opening of a nurses' home at the Royal Sussex County Hospital. Almost precipitating the surprise that some may have had over Mary's decision to marry a man fifteen years her senior, the *Graphic* published a much younger and more dashing photograph of Viscount Lascelles, above the caption 'Special gratification is felt in respect that her Royal Highness is to marry a British subject of good old English stock.'[23] In her diary Queen Mary wrote, 'We were very cheerful and almost uproarious at dinner – We are delighted ... Mary is simply beaming.'[24] Queen Mary was fond of her future son-in-law, as well as being assured that Mary would not have to move abroad.

David, who knew Harry through his Grenadier Guards' nickname of 'Don', was relieved that Mary would finally be able to escape from her life of subjugation and seclusion. However, he was not without concern; in a letter to Freda Dudley Ward, he explained, 'Of course Lascelles is too old for her and not attractive … But anyway he's rich and I'm afraid that is a very important thing for poor Mary. I hope to God he'll make her happy, as she deserves that if anyone does.'[25] Mary's other elder brother Bertie was equally pleased. He heard the news while staying at Belvoir Castle with the Duke and Duchess of Rutland and spontaneously stood up during dinner to propose a toast to the couple.

Mary was surprised by the proposal but there is no doubt that she was delighted with the match. The couple had known each other for a while and Mary wrote to her younger brother George expressing her happiness and her belief that the marriage would work. Mary found Harry intelligent and charming. Informal photographs and British Pathé film taken at the time reveal a radiant smile, the antithesis of her usual dour expression. The newly engaged couple had a great deal in common including similar friends, country pursuits, horses, dogs, agriculture, gardening, racing, antiques and fine art. Both were timid and struggled to demonstrate their emotions; both were traditional. Although Mary was only 24, she was most unlike the fashionable women of her time, the boyish flappers who wore their hair and dresses much shorter and shocked the older generation with their smoking and exuberant party-ing. Mary would always seem older than her years and it is interesting that she never employed younger ladies-in-waiting, suggesting a matu-rity and much more cultured tastes. Harry could provide Mary with the lifestyle that she enjoyed and, more than anything else, Mary would stay in her own country. Former members of the princess's royal household maintained that it was a genuine love match and that she was so attached to Harry that if she had not been able to marry him, it is doubtful that she would ever have married.[26]

Of course, there were mutual benefits from the union; Harry would be provided with an heir and Mary would finally escape from the restric-tive chains of being a companion to her parents. She would be free to dress as she chose, concentrate on her work and pursue her interests. Of course, she would always put duty to the crown before her own personal needs and wishes, but at last she could do so on her own terms. The marriage would prove to be Mary's emancipation, for it enabled her to be mistress of her own milieu. From the outset the marriage appeared to be a partnership. Harry's letters to Mary reveal that he would frequently ask her opinion on things; for example, his new royal connections meant that he suddenly became very much in demand to take on prestigious positions such as mayor of Leeds. He did not wish to accept this since, more than anything, he felt that Goldsborough would be too far from Leeds to carry out his role effectively. However, before deciding on anything he sought Mary's opinion. In plans regarding the wedding and their new marital homes, Harry always consulted Mary.

The stilted formal engagement photographs typical of the period suggest that the union was without romance. Harry, although always impeccably dressed, was not particularly photogenic, and Mary appeared to look so sad. However, letters between Harry and Mary reveal that they were like any couple newly in love, declaring their upset at being kept apart because of their other commitments and awaiting with much eagerness the next time they would see each other. Furthermore, one only needs to visit the incredibly palatial and stunning Goldsborough Hall, Mary's first country marital home, to understand the immensely romantic, as well as privileged aspect, of such a union. Mary expressed her joy in a letter to her former tutor Mr Hansell: 'I cannot tell you how happy I am, and I feel I am very lucky. I feel sure you will like my Harry.'[27]

For their betrothal, Harry presented Mary with a single-stone square-cut emerald. The response from the public to the engagement was one of joy and excitement. Crowds gathered outside Buckingham Palace, desperate to see Princess Mary and her future husband. On Thursday 24 November Queen Mary arranged a drive in a landau carriage with Princess Mary and her lady-in-waiting Lady Joan Verney to have lunch at Chesterfield House with Harry also in attendance. At various points of the route the carriage slowed down for the cheering crowd to gain a glimpse of the couple. The crowds were so enthusiastic that at one point a posy of violets was thrown, narrowly missing Harry's face.

A few weeks later on 16 December Mary, accompanied by her mother, was shown around Goldsborough and Harewood by Harry.

Harry's parents were pleased with the engagement and they eagerly welcomed their future daughter-in-law into their family. Mary arrived by train to be greeted at the station in Leeds by her bridegroom's father and sister, Margaret, Viscountess Boyne. It was no surprise that Queen Mary, with her love of beautiful objects and collecting, should be impressed by viewing the remarkable future homes of her daughter. She recorded the day in her diary:

> Dull first then beautiful day … Went over this wonderful Adams house with all its treasures of furniture pictures and china … At 2 motored to see Goldsborough near Knaresborough where Harry and Mary are to live in. It is 13 miles away. Mrs Lamb, the present tenant showed us over the house which is charming and Jacobean in style. [28]

Queen Mary was so enthralled by the union that for the king and queen's official Christmas card that year, she arranged for the front cover to depict a collage of portraits of her daughter and prospective son-in-law. Mary and her mother stayed in Harewood for two nights, sleeping in the same chintz rooms once occupied by Queen Victoria when she had visited Harewood in 1835, two years before becoming queen.

'Princess Captivates the People',[29] declared the *Leeds Mercury* headline, photographing the exuberant Mary, with her trusty umbrella in hand, as she strode out resolutely to view the Harewood estate and to meet Harry's favourite horse, Tommy. Everywhere were 'country roads thronged with thousands of sightseers. The loyal scenes sprang from hearts filled with satisfaction and pleasure at the Princess's choice of a Yorkshireman for her husband.'[30] The atmosphere was one of 'sociable levity rather than the austere primness which is so often apparent'.[31] While this reportage might seem sycophantic to a modern reader, there is no doubt that the engagement and wedding were hugely significant for the British royal family in boosting their popularity and ensuring the support of their people at a difficult time when there had been a winter of discontent with a heavy trade depression, high unemployment and protests. The excitement of a royal wedding could not fail to quash any anti-monarchy sentiments and lift the spirits of the people. The choice of a British bridegroom for his only daughter would enhance the king's position after such a period of instability and uncertainty. This was to be the first national celebration since the end of the First World War.

Shortly after 2 p.m. the royal procession of cars made its way through the streets of Leeds. The waiting crowds were disappointed that the cars were not open; however, this was a typical rainy winter's day. Princess Mary, dressed in a beaver fur-trimmed grey coat, was seen to look so radiant and happy that the *Yorkshire Evening Post* dubbed her 'Her Royal Happiness'[32] as she made her way to Harewood, cheered on by the rapturous crowds, shouting. 'Come back soon. Don't forget tha's Yorkshire now.'[33]

The king and queen shared their happiness by holding a celebratory ball at Buckingham Palace. One of the invited guests, Geoffrey Hirst, described it as 'a magnificent affair, rendered even more striking by the glittering jewels and colourful confections of the ladies'.[34]

The wedding was arranged for 28 February 1922 at Westminster Abbey. It would be the first wedding of a monarch's daughter to take place there since Richard II had married Anne of Bohemia in 1382. In the week before the wedding, a dinner was held between both families at which Alan 'Tommy' Lascelles was present. He describes the evident happiness of the union:

> Their majesties were in most genial mood, and stayed until 11pm, which, I believe, is unusually late for them. We both took kindly to Cousin Mary, whom we'd never met before – she's very fresh and jolly and wrinkles up her nose when she smiles; and from what I could see of her and Harry at dinner, they seem the best of friends.[35]

There was some confusion in the press concerning how to pronounce Harry's name correctly. In the end the newspapers published a rhyme to aid in this.

> Yorkshire team they are a lot
> To play at bat and ball.

> They cannot lick eleven lads
> That come fra' Lascelles Hall.[36]

Lascelles Hall Cricket Club was one of the oldest clubs in England, having been founded in 1825, and the boys from Lascelles Hall frequently won their matches when playing other Yorkshire teams. Lascelles was to be pronounced with the accent on the first syllable.

# 9

# Wedding

No such popular happening as this has occurred in the whole history of the Royal House of Britain.[1]

*Tatler*, 1 March 1922

It is a great happiness to me that I am to remain in my native land and that my life will be spent among [my] own people.[2]

*Pall Mall Gazette*, 28 February 1922

Excitement continued to grow in the short three months leading to the wedding. Mary's brother Bertie wrote to David:

Mary's wedding is causing a great deal of work to many people and as far as I can make out the 28th is going to be a day of national rejoicing in every conceivable and unconceivable manner … In fact it is now no longer Mary's wedding, but (this from the paper) it is the 'Abbey Wedding' or the 'Royal Wedding' or the 'National Wedding' or even 'The People's Wedding' … of our beloved princess.'[3]

David, with his 'inordinate dislike of weddings'[4] and royal occasions, was relieved not to be present for the occasion as he would still be on tour in India. Mary was kept exceptionally busy by wedding preparations. In a letter a few days after the official engagement Mary confided that 'the pressure of business is so great that little time is left for private letters'.[5]

In a major departure from the secrecy of previous royal weddings, it was decided that two still-image cameras were to be permitted to photograph parts of the ceremony in order to satisfy the public's need to feel a part of this momentous occasion. There were sixty film cameras along the route between Buckingham Palace and the Abbey. Frank O. Salisbury, the English portrait artist, sat in a prime location at the abbey in order to capture the ceremony. It was Salisbury who had asked to change the seating of the royal family at the last minute, in order to give a more aesthetically pleasing backdrop.

The wedding was not without some drama. Three days before the ceremony Queen Mary sprained the tendon of her right ankle, making it painful to walk. The Countess of Airlie, who was in waiting to Queen Mary at the time, recalls in her autobiography the frantic last-minute change of dress:

> The original plan had been for full Court evening dress, with feathers and veil, but the Archbishop of Canterbury pronounced this unsuitable for a religious ceremony. The result was a frenzied rush to have new dresses in time. The principal Court dressmakers worked night and day, and certainly not in vain, for the mass of colour in the Abbey gave the impression of a garden in midsummer. The whole wedding was superb in its pageantry.[6]

Furthermore, as 'Tommy' Lascelles recorded in a letter on 18 February 1922, consideration needed to be given to 'the provision of suitable sanitary accommodation for the many old gentlemen who will feel the strain of a long wait'.[7] In the end a makeshift toilet was installed just inside Poet's Corner.

In the build-up to the wedding, Queen Mary involved herself in unpacking the thousands of gifts that came from all over the empire and from the many charitable organisations that Mary supported. Over 1,300 of the wedding gifts were eventually put on display at St James's Palace and 1s admittance was charged, which would go to benefit Mary's charities. The diverse range of gifts included over 1,000 silver teapots and cruets and forty-one feather, lace and antique fans. The officers and men of the Royal Navy collected a staggering £3,000 for a gift, the equivalent today of nearly £150,000. Mary decided to buy only a small gift for herself and donate the remaining amount to the RN Seaman's and Royal Marines' Orphan Home. She graciously did the same with other cash donations.

The 50,000 members of the Voluntary Aid Detachment sent an emerald and diamond tiara with a detachable corsage ornament, and Mary accepted a diamond pendant from the Brigade of Guards as well. The money given to her by 100,000 residents of Leeds – a sum of nearly £7,000 – was used to establish the Princess Mary Infants' ward at the General Infirmary in Leeds.

Mary did not possess a great deal of her own jewellery and thus, when asked what she would like, she requested her own collection. George V gifted her a sapphire parure with a small coronet tiara that had originally been made for Queen Victoria by Prince Albert at a cost of £400 in 1842. Queen Mary's gift to her daughter was a large sapphire surrounded by fourteen brilliant-cut diamonds. Mary received many significant jewels from her family, as well as jewellery from all over the empire. Her fiancé gifted her a diamond negligée necklace, a diamond and pearl brooch made of cushion-shaped and drop-shaped diamond collets mounted in a kite-shaped panel. He also gave her a long diamond pendant with drops of pearl and a diamond rivière necklace, which she chose to wear on her wedding day. The gold for the wedding ring was donated from the Ilridagoch Mine in north-west Wales.

Eight bridesmaids were chosen from the bride's relatives and friends. They were Princess Maud of Fife, the daughter of Louise, Princess Royal, the eldest sister of George V; two of Queen Mary's nieces, Lady Mary and Lady May Cambridge; Lady Rachel Cavendish, the eldest daughter of the Duke and Duchess of Devonshire; Lady Mary Thynne, the youngest daughter of the Marquess of Bath; Lady Doris Gordon-Lennox, a granddaughter of the Duke of Richmond; Lady Diana Bridgeman, the eldest daughter of the Earl and Countess of Bradford; and Lady Elizabeth Bowes-Lyon, a daughter of the Earl of Strathmore, who would eventually marry Bertie and who became more widely known as Queen Elizabeth the Queen Mother.

Harry chose Major Sir Victor Mackenzie of the Scots Guards as his best man. Mackenzie was a 39-year-old bachelor, who like Harry had been educated at Eton and Sandhurst. He served during the First World War and commanded the special reserve battalion of his regiment. He later became a groom-in-waiting to both George V and David as Edward VIII.

Upon his marriage to the reigning monarch's daughter, Harry was asked by George V if he wished to be made a marquess. He turned down the offer, according to his son the 7th earl, since he believed that 'marquisates died out quicker than any other title and he was keen to provide himself and his ancestors with heirs'.[8] Instead he was honoured by being appointed a Knight of the Garter by George V.

The day prior to the pageant, an immense throng gathered along the route from Buckingham Palace to Westminster Abbey. The streets were elaborately decorated by Westminster City Council in the bride's personal favourite colour scheme of blue, white and silver. Lamp posts and guard posts were equally resplendent. Two arches exceeding 30ft in height secured large banners declaring 'Good wishes. May your path unfold in brightness.' Celebrations would be held throughout the empire. British Pathé recorded a film the day before the wedding showing rehearsals of the dignitaries, organisers and military officials, including the Household Cavalry. The East End was packed with hawkers selling wedding souvenirs including Princess Mary feathers, rings, a wedding mascot of a horseshoe, white heather and imitation orange blossom.

The design for Mary's wedding dress was by William Wallace Terry of Messrs Reville, a London couture house and court dressmaker to the queen. Recognising the importance of making the public feel invested in the wedding, various announcements were made in advance and the public were permitted to examine in detail the materials and style chosen by the princess for her dress and trousseau. This was the first royal wedding to feature in *British Vogue* magazine, which declared that Mary was 'a fairy Princess with youth, beauty and happiness as her attendants'.[9]

The First World War had led to greater freedom in how women dressed. Princess Mary's wedding used the typical streamlined, loose-fitting dresses of the period; it was considered simple and yet chic. This fashion was repeated when Bertie married Elizabeth Bowes-Lyon the following year. Royal brides before Mary had used embroidered motifs on their dresses to honour the United Kingdom; Mary chose to pay homage to the entire empire to recognise the contribution of other dominions throughout the First World War. On her dress train were, among others, the maple from Canada, the Welsh daffodil, the lotus from India, the wattle from Australia and the fern from New Zealand. Mary's dress was an under-dress of silver lamé veiled with marquisette, embroidered in English roses and thousands of seed pearls and diamonds over a lattice work. The girdle was studded with rows of pearls with a trail of orange blossom with silver stems. Mary's train was a specially woven blend of white and silver Duchesse satin which was draped with Honiton lace from her mother and maternal grandmother. She wore a simple veil edged with pearls and worn under a tiara of orange blossoms, signifying good luck. Her shoes were made of silver brocade with diamond buckles and a gift from Norwich ex-service workers at the Haldinstein and Sons factory. They were presented to Mary in a golden casket a week earlier at Buckingham Palace. For her going-away outfit, Mary chose a powder-blue charmeuse drop-waist dress embroidered with coral with a moleskin coat and a mole panne travelling hat. Even the contents of her trousseau were released to the public a week before the ceremony, describing the blue, pink and pastel outfits including evening gowns, day dresses and frock coats.

This white and silver theme was continued with the bridesmaids. They wore a similar glistening cloth of silver, with a wide panel back and front over a dress of satin anglaise adorned with flowers. Tulle head-dresses were held in place by wreaths of silver-leaf and they carried bouquets of sweet peas. The white and silver wedding procession made for a medieval-style, ethereal sense of purity in keeping with the dawn of a new post-war era. Harry chose to wear the full dress uniform of the Grenadier Guards, along with the riband and star of the newly conferred Order of the Garter.

There was some apprehension with regard to the weather, since the night before there had been a strong wind blowing. However, on the morning of the ceremony the sun finally came through and it remained fine all day. Queen Mary woke her daughter on the morning of the ceremony, observing a wedding-day custom of the mother being the first to speak to the bride. Mary travelled to the abbey with her father in the same carriage she had ridden in for the coronation in 1911. With the inclement weather of a February morning, Mary wore a Russian ermine wrap, lined with silver and white brocade. She carried a gift from Queen Mary, an illuminated copy of the marriage service. They were escorted by a field officer's escort of Life Guards. Sir Hubert Parry's bridal march was playing as the guests arrived with Mary making her entrance at the west door at exactly 11.30 a.m., her train held by Lady Rachel Cavendish and Princess Maud.

Queen Mary had ridden to the abbey with her three sons and later in her diary recalled that she was 'very proud'[10] of all of her children, especially Mary who had 'great dignity'[11] throughout the day. On arriving at the abbey, Queen Mary and her sons were received by the Dean of Westminster and processed with Queen Alexandra to the sacrarium.

The service began with an address by the Dean of Westminster, Dr Ryle. The later part of the ceremony was led by Randall Davidson, Archbishop of Canterbury. During the service, the choir sang Psalm LXVII, 'Praise My Soul the King of Heaven' and the anthem 'Beloved Let Us Love One Another' was played on the organ by Sydney H. Nicholson during the signing of the register. The register recorded every bride and bridegroom since George II, with many signatures being indecipherable. As they made their way out of the abbey the bridal march from Gounod's 'Romeo and Juliet' played, followed by Mendelssohn's 'Wedding March'. The abbey bells rang out for over three hours.

After the ceremony, Mary and Viscount Lascelles drove from Westminster Abbey to Buckingham Palace for the wedding breakfast. The bridal carriage stopped at the Cenotaph, Viscount Lascelles saluted, and the bride handed a bouquet of pink sweet peas to Regimental Sergeant-Major Barwick, who placed the bouquet at the base of the memorial to the war dead. The roaring crowds went silent. Thus,

Mary initiated a tradition that Elizabeth Bowes-Lyon continued upon her marriage to Bertie by placing her bouquet on the Tomb of the Unknown Soldier. This tradition is still honoured today by royal brides. 'This unexpected and touching incident was impressive as it was simple,' opined the *Illustrated London News*.[12] Even on one of the most significant and personally rewarding days of her life, Mary never forgot her duty and compassion for those who had lost their lives in the First World War.

A great crowd of thousands had assembled near the gates of Buckingham Palace and surrounding the Victoria Memorial in order that when they were greeted by the sight of the newlywed couple on the balcony, there was 'a great ovation'.[13] After a few minutes they were joined by the king and queen with Queen Alexandra, as the crowd sang out the National Anthem.

The main wedding cake (seven were on display) was gargantuan in size, over 6ft high and weighing over 500lb; it had been prepared by McVitie and Price. On Mary's tier were the crests and badges of the Girl Guides and the Royal Scots Regiment. Harry's tier was in the colours of the Grenadier Guards and the Yorkshire Hussars. Mary's brothers Bertie, George and Henry waved off the newly married couple with scatterings of confetti, rice and lucky horseshoes, as the bride and groom made their way to Shifnal before travelling to Weston Park, the seat of the Earl of Bradford.

For the thousands who witnessed the events of the day, it was no exaggeration when *Tatler* declared that the occasion, 'roused a greater enthusiasm throughout the wide dominions of the Crown by reason of the fact that the husband whom H.R.H. chose is a British soldier. No such popular happening as this has occurred in the whole history of the Royal House of Britain.'[14] A wedding supplement produced by *The Times* on the morning, which had doubled its initial print run, sold out within hours and was exchanging hands for an inflated price.

In summing up the true impact of the occasion, celebrated writer G.K. Chesterton declared, 'These are the things that will move any imaginative person, when the pageant of our national monarchy can still pass amid a sympathetic people, in these strange and doubtful days, when the nation has recently passed through so noble a tragedy and when so many crowns have fallen down.'[15]

After the spectacular occasion, Mary wrote to thank her mother for allowing her to marry Harry with a tinge of sadness for the life left behind: 'I cannot tell you how much I hated saying goodbye to you, Papa and the brothers yesterday.'[16]

Queen Mary felt the bittersweet taste of losing her only daughter and watching her leave to start a new life. She tried to remain stoical to prevent Mary from breaking down, yet there was no denying that family life would not be the same without her. 'Mary and Harry left at 3.45. Dreadful saying goodbye. They had a great send off.'[17] Queen Mary later recalled in her diary that 'everybody felt very low'.[18] Queen Mary was facing a secluded future alone with her husband. It led to her telling David in April, 'I miss Mary dreadfully here and her passage seems so empty and silent. It is all rather sad and depressing and this added to the most odious cold dull rainy weather, makes life almost intolerable.'[19]

Even Mary's father felt her loss: 'I went up to Mary's room and took leave of her and quite broke down. Felt very down and depressed now that darling Mary has gone.'[20]

The nation felt otherwise after the ceremony for, as the *Bystander* recorded the following day, 'Princess Mary's wedding has provided more genuine sentiment to the square inch than the challenge of Kaiser Wilhelm and all his Uhlans produced on any one acre of soil.'[21]

# 10

# Honeymoon and
# Early Married Life

Wherever Princess Mary appeared, peasant women curtseyed to her
and children threw kisses and flowers.[1]

*Belfast News-Letter*, Monday 13 March 1922

A special royal train of five carriages, each embellished with pink carnations, arrived at 4 p.m. to take the newly married couple from Paddington
to their first honeymoon location, a small market town in Shropshire
called Shifnal. The couple posed for photographers outside the train and
waved to the crowds who continued to line the route holding flags and
handkerchiefs, desperate to catch a glimpse of the princess. By the time
of their arrival it was already dark, yet this did not deter the waiting
guard of honour made up of Girl Guides and a choir of school children,
along with yet more sightseers and photographers.

Cheered on by the masses who had gathered along the length of
the route, Mary and Harry motored to Weston Park, the home of the
5th Earl of Bradford. Harry's mother, born Lady Florence Bridgeman,
was the daughter of the 3rd Earl of Bradford, who had held many
court positions during the reign of Queen Victoria, including Vice
Chamberlain of the Household, Lord Chamberlain and Master of the
Horse. The Earls of Bradford and their wives had numerous connections
with the royal family. Lady Ida Lumley, the wife of the 4th Earl, had

been a lady-in-waiting to Queen Mary. Lady Diana Bridgeman, known for her resemblance to Greta Garbo, had been Mary's youngest bridesmaid and would go on to feature in Cecil Beaton's *Book of Beauty* in 1930. Weston Park was further renowned for its association with Prime Minister Benjamin Disraeli, who had given Selina, Countess of Bradford a yellow parrot as a token of his affection. Queen Mary's brother, the Marquess of Cambridge, lived nearby at Shotton Hall in Harmer Hill.

It was hoped that the relatively secluded and informal environment of Weston Park, with its 1,000 acres enclosed within high walls, would allow the couple to begin their first week of married life with a degree of privacy. With this in mind, they chose not to accept an offer to install a temporary telephone wire. Yet press attention continued relentlessly during their first week of married life and showed little signs of waning. The couple gave the press staged photo opportunities in the hope that in return they would be free to enjoy some private moments together in the elegant and tranquil grounds. The couple were seldom alone for the start of their honeymoon, since several members of the groom's family had gathered at the house to welcome the princess. A few opportunities to venture out arose, such as a visit to Harry's aunt, Lady Mabel Kenyon-Slaney, at nearby Hatton Grange in Shifnal. Lady Mabel's daughter Sybil became a lady-in-waiting to Mary. The couple attended a church service packed with fascinated onlookers and visited nearby Boscobel House, where Charles II was said to have hidden in the royal oak tree after the Battle of Worcester in 1651. Mary spent the first few days of her marriage writing to her mother and sending thank-you letters to those who had attended the wedding or sent gifts. This must have been quite an undertaking and not something one would expect from a honeymooner; however, it is more an indication of Mary's impeccable manners and daily habit of letter writing. One such thank-you was received by Prime Minister David Lloyd George as soon as 3 March, for a present given by the Cabinet.

As they left for the Continent, Mary and Harry gave a public walkabout in the village of Weston, where they were waved off by enthusiastic children singing the National Anthem and waving flags. This would be only the third time that Mary had ventured overseas.

After travelling to France, they made a fleeting stopover in Paris, where Mary was met by her close second cousin, Lady Patricia Ramsay, whose husband, Captain Alexander Ramsay, was at the time a naval attaché in Paris. Their host for this brief sojourn was Lord Hardinge of Penshurst, the ambassador to Paris, who accommodated them at the British embassy, known as the magnificently grand Hotel de Charost, on the rue du Faubourg Saint-Honoré; it was a former home of Pauline Borghese, the scandalous sister of Napoleon. This imposing and grand *hôtel particulier*, or townhouse, had gardens stretching as far as the Champs Elysées.

The couple's next destination was the fifteenth-century Villa Medici, set among the hills of Fiesole, near Florence, and at the time the home of Lady Sybil Scott, a cousin of Harry. Built in 1458 for the rich and powerful Cosimo de Medici, and a favourite haunt of his grandson, Lorenzo the Magnificent, the house was characteristic of the patrician villas of the Renaissance. Architecturally it was considered simple with white walls and windows lined with *pietra serena* – sandstone. Its *pièce de résistance* were its gardens built on several levels, designed to harmonise with the landscape. There were two terraces, wells and fountains and an avenue of cypress, cherry and almond trees: perfect for seclusion. It was here that many key artists, philosophers and men of letters had met during the Renaissance to debate. Queen Mary had been overwhelmed by its beauty when she had visited with her parents, and she had even drawn up a list of neighbouring locations for her daughter to visit including art galleries and beauty spots.

In preparation for the princess's arrival, Fiesole was bedecked with hundreds of British and Italian flags and the entrance of the Villa Medici adorned with plants and flowering branches of almond and peach. In every room were baskets of roses, carnations, white lilac and cyclamen: a gift from the British residents of the town. The local police took precautions to ensure that the couple would not be disturbed by the curiosity of local people. Police officers and a small group of troops were stationed at the gates to the villa and in neighbouring peasant homes. A police commissioner named Dr Genovest was appointed to accompany Mary and Harry and to ensure their safety. However, this had little effect and did not stop the many crowds who stood waiting at the railway station for their arrival and proceeded to pelt them with flowers, or the frequent visitors to the gates of the villa who would question the Carabinieri. As the *Western Mail* reported on 11 March,

> It is worthy to mention that the municipality of Fiesole … is in the hands of Socialists, who have done everything in their power to render the sojourn of the distinguished couple as pleasant as possible … and have expressed themselves as willing to go to any length, compatible with their principles, to show courtesy to the English visitors.[2]

The Italians were even more enamoured of the princess when they overheard her speaking in fluent Italian.

Early in the morning, Mary and Harry motored into Florence to peruse bric-a-brac, jewellery and antique shops or to visit nearby places of interest. It may seem incredulous for the time, but interest in the couple was so illimitable and support so fervent that they frequently had to cut short their visits to tourist sights after being surrounded by enthusiastic locals. Occasionally they succeeded in outwitting the hordes to go to some of Queen Mary's recommendations. They managed some time at the Santa Maria Novella Church, known for its elegant Tuscan gothic architecture, and funerary monuments, as well as its art treasures including medieval stained-glass windows. Mary was deeply moved by the celebrated mosaic Madonna by Cimabue and the wooden crucifix by Brunelleschi with its perfect anatomical depiction. A further place of interest was the Royal Villa at Paggio a Cajano. Built in the late fifteenth century by Guiliano da Sangallo, tourists came to view its frescoes and impressive panorama of the Tuscan landscape. Other outings included the Boboli gardens; the Palazzo Pitti; the Ponte Vecchio with its shops; and the Porta Romana, a gate leading out of the town, noted for its antiquity.

In light of their desire to immerse themselves thoroughly in Italian culture, the conclusion of their stay was a packed performance at the Teatro della Pergola on 28 March of the popular Opéra-tragédie *Francesa da Rimini* by Riccardo Zandonai. To honour their guests, both the Italian and British National Anthems were played, and the audience gave the couple a rapturous reception roaring, 'Viva la Principessa!' – Long live the Princess!

The highlight of the return journey was a fleeting, private tour of Paris hosted by the Earl and Countess of Granard at 73, rue de Varenne, in the elegant residential area of the 7th arrondissement. Their sightseeing tour comprised the principal sights of the Musée du Louvre and the Cathédrale Notre Dame de Paris. Lord Hardinge, the ambassador to France, gave a banquet in their honour at the British embassy. Paris in 1922 was at the epicentre of fashion. Marriage for Mary meant that she could finally break free from the constraints of having to please her mother in how she dressed, and she thus had no hesitation in patronising one of its prestigious salons. Edward, Captain Molyneux's design house in the rue Royale, was known for its illustrious clients and Molyneux's creations epitomised an effortless yet refined simplicity. It was here that Mary purchased several ankle-length dresses of her own choosing, in shades of blue, to add to her trousseau.

Fresh from such an enlightening and inspirational honeymoon, the couple returned to British soil in early April to begin their married life in their London home, Chesterfield House. Any hopes for a diminishment of public interest and fervour were immediately crushed, when yet another considerable crowd of well-wishers gathered at Victoria Station with a further crowd congregating at the gates of Chesterfield House. More than anyone, the king and queen were relieved by their daughter's return. They had missed her greatly during her honeymoon and to such an extent that the parson at Buckingham Palace had been advised not to mention Mary's wedding during his services. The newlyweds would live in Chesterfield House when in London and Goldsborough Hall, the dower house of Harewood, when in the country. They initially remained at Chesterfield House for a few months since the tenancy on Goldsborough did not end until April 1922 and changes needed to be made to modernise the home.

A short stay at Lynton Springs in Wetherby in May was organised as an opportunity to introduce the princess to her new home and so that she could supervise the renovations at Goldsborough. Not wishing to cause a fuss, their arrival in Yorkshire was kept fairly quiet until the last minute. They arrived almost unnoticed at Harrogate before travelling in a closed car to Lynton Springs. The following day, Harry was seen alone at York racecourse, to much consternation from the public who had ventured to the races hoping to see the princess, while Mary, since the hall was now empty, took full advantage of finally being able to view her new home and make further plans with an architect. Desperate to meet the princess, an uninvited charabanc of ladies arrived at the entrance gates to Goldsborough but were swiftly despatched by a policeman. Those who had been fortunate to meet Mary stated that 'she was quite charming to every one of the servants she met … the dear Princess seemed just an ordinary happy housewife, diligent in arranging a comfortable home and delighted to be herself responsible for it'.[3] Over the next few months of 1922, an army of builders and tradesmen worked on the hall to ensure that the home was prepared for the end of the year.

Chesterfield House was situated in the exclusive area of Mayfair, at the junction of South Audley Street and Curzon Street. The trees of Hyde Park could be seen from its windows. It had been built in the Palladian style popular in the mid-eighteenth century by English architect Isaac Ware for Philip Stanhope, the 4th Earl of Chesterfield, a British statesman who was much admired for his sharpness of wit. The writer Samuel Johnson had visited the house on several occasions, and it had many historical and literary connections. When he opened the house in 1752, Stanhope erected two statues and labelled them 'Adam de Stanhope' and 'Eve de Stanhope' for his guests' amusement.

In 1869, the house was scheduled for demolition but was instead bought by a city merchant, Charles Magniac, who built a row of houses at the rear of the property which became Chesterfield Gardens. During the First World War the house had been used by the American Mission and it was also the headquarters of the League of Nations. In 1921 it was on loan to the government for the state visit of the crown prince of Japan, Hirohito, during his six-month tour of Europe.

The *Illustrated London News* called Chesterfield House 'one of the most famous mansions of Mayfair. Its plain and somewhat sombre exterior … serves to enhance the magnificence within.'[4] The entrance

hall had an impressive marble hall and staircase and bronze balus-
trade which was 'big enough for a military band to play in'.[5] Harry
bought the property in 1921, where it housed many of his art treasures,
along with those bequeathed to him by Lord Clanricarde, as well as
a collection of French furniture. Some of the art on display included
Titian's *Death of Actaeon*, El Greco's *A Night Scene* and works by Bellini.
Harry was eager to restore the house to its former glory and he sought
to purchase family portraits that had been sold by previous Earls of
Chesterfield. The house was renowned for its remarkable white and
gold ballroom and the way in which all the ground floor rooms led
from one into another. In making her London home at Chesterfield
House, Mary would be among many aristocratic families who chose to
live in Mayfair, including the families of the Earl of Reading, Viscount
Curzon and the Marquess of Crewe.

Mary and Harry's country residence would be at Goldsborough Hall,
located 17 miles from York and 7 miles from Harrogate, in the heart
of what was termed as York and Ainsty Country. They would come to
spend the majority of their time there until they moved to Harewood
in 1930. Viscount Lascelles had grown up at the hall during the 1880s
and 1890s and it was subsequently let to a family by the name of Lamb.
The tenants agreed to vacate it and as a welcoming gift gave the princess
a brace of peacocks. At the time of her wedding, Goldsborough was
considered 'a country mansion of modest aspect'.[6] On first seeing the
hall in December 1921 Queen Mary found it 'charming … It could be
made most comfortable'.[7]

Even in the twenty-first century there remains an aura intrinsically
English and antiquated about the village of Goldsborough, with its
abundance of rape seed fields and trees, its cricket green, its local Church
of England school and church and its cottages. It offered enough seclusion for Mary to live a private life as the wife of a country squire, yet it
was still within convenient distance of Leeds and other towns and cities
to enable Mary to continue her public life and build up her patronage of
northern charities.

Goldsborough Hall was an early Jacobean red-brick house, originally
set in over 100 acres. It had initially been the home of the Goldsborough

family: Richard de Goldsburgh had taken his family name from the village in the eleventh century. The family were ruined by litigation and family feuds in the sixteenth century, leading to the original house being destroyed by fire. A three-storey red-brick and limestone hall was built in its place and completed by 1625 for a lawyer named Sir Richard Hutton, who served under Elizabeth I as a serjeant-at-law and under James I as an acting chief justice.

During the English Civil War Goldsborough was occupied by the Parliamentarian army while they destroyed Knaresborough Castle. In 1766 the brother of the first Lord Harewood, Daniel Lascelles, bought the estate and engaged the celebrated Adams brothers, who were working at Harewood at the time, to repair and remodel the hall and to make it more imposing. Bays extending to the roof were added, along with windows on every floor and balustrades. A new entrance hall was built, along with cornices, columns and fireplaces and intricately carved mantlepieces. One of the most spectacular rooms was the library, with its oak-panelled walls. Twelve acres of formal landscaped gardens were laid by Richard Woods in the style of Capability Brown. The garden, with its gently undulating pasture, boosted some incredible trees including a *Robinia pseudoacacia* dating back to 1706, a copper beech dating from the late eighteenth century and a giant Redwood Wellingtonia introduced in 1863.

Mary made many changes to the hall, under the guidance of Leeds architect Sidney Kitson, to make it more suitable for her and a young family. Most of the changes were internal, including adding corridors and extra rooms for servants, as well as ten new baths. There were many new additions to the hall including a telephone and the stained-glass windows showing the union of the Lascelles and royal family on the staircase, along with stained-glass windows given as a wedding present by the Grand Mufti of Jerusalem. The ceilings were restored to their former glory with electric lights replacing the outdated gas lamps.

Mary, with her childhood love of botany, was evidently a keen gardener. She had designed a garden for the *Daily Mail* Ideal Home Exhibition to be shown in March 1922. The main feature of the garden was a waterfall and rockery surrounded by evergreens and shrubs. Mary

loved gardening so much that she had a wheelbarrow made in the shape
of a seat, so that it could be easily transported to wherever the light was
best. The seat was engraved with the short poem, 'The kiss of the sun for
pardon. The song of the birds for mirth. We are nearer God's heart in a
garden, than anywhere else on earth.'[8] In May 1922, she was seen making
many purchases from the Chelsea Flower Show to add to the grounds.
She created a vista to the south of the hall, with the planting of a dwarf
walled terrace and a beech hedged avenue with herbaceous borders
centred around a sundial. The emperor of Japan had given Mary some
Japanese cherry trees – *Prunus 'Shirotae' Mount Fuji*, a flat widely spreading low tree with pure white flowers, as a wedding gift. The famous lime
tree walk was planted by royal visitors during the 1920s including the
king and queen and Mary's brothers David, Bertie, and Henry. The first
tree was planted by Mary and Harry on 22 December 1922 to commemorate their arrival; it is still there today.

Mary continued to make several flying visits to inspect the renovations
at Goldsborough and was occasionally seen perusing the shop windows
of Harrogate. Tenants from the Harewood estate presented a portrait of
Princess Mary by Oswald Birley to Viscount Lascelles as a wedding gift.
The painting, which Princess Mary was never fond of, eventually hung
at the bottom of the staircase at Goldsborough Hall. At the presentation
ceremony, Mary's father-in-law, the 5th earl, stated that he hoped that
one day Princess Mary would be mistress of the Harewood Estate and
'would diffuse the lives of the tenants with a ray of sunshine as she had
already diffused the lives of the family of which she was now an honoured member'.[9]

Unfortunately, and in keeping with most construction projects, there
was a delay forcing an extension of the November deadline. Thus, after a
few visits to London for Christmas shopping, Mary and Harry returned
to Harewood to celebrate their first Christmas as a married couple.
Finally, on Thursday 28 December the house was complete. Exuberant
cheers of welcome from the local farmers, housewives and schoolchildren followed Mary and Harry as the rector formally welcomed them to
their new home. Press attention continued, but Mary was determined to
ignore it in order to blend in like any other inhabitant of Goldsborough.

Within ten days, villagers were becoming increasingly blasé when they saw her striding through the village and queuing in the local shop run by Mrs Falkingham to buy groceries or zipping through the country lanes in her motor car. A few newspapers had already speculated that an interesting announcement concerning the princess would be imminent in the New Year.

# 11

# Royal Family Life

The birth of Princess Mary's baby boy has set all London agog. It is not often that the introduction of a youngster into the World is hailed with such acclamation.[1]

*Sphere,* Saturday 17 February 1923

Princess Mary had been brought up by her mother to take a deep interest in the effective domestic running of a house. Now that she was married and the wife of a wealthy landowner, with homes in both town and country, she concerned herself with all aspects of the households from gardening and interior design to entertaining and meal planning, as well as in the answering of her considerable correspondence. Once a week she would send for her housekeeper to go through the books and to prepare for the week ahead. She would visit the kitchen, the larder and storerooms to see what needed replenishing, and what needed to be bought for meals, along with preparations needed for any guests. She may have been fortunate in having a housekeeper and servants to carry out domestic chores, but Mary enjoyed doing things herself such as dusting, tidying and sewing; she would even clean her own silver.

For Mary there was a certain attraction to be found in living away from London and being able to walk out into the village of Goldsborough and carry out a few errands, without the need for a lady-in-waiting to accompany her. Mary disliked the intrusion of the media, yet it continued unabated in the early years of her marriage. She was frequently followed by 'sketchin' fellows … [making] pictures of her',[2] and no day seemed complete without an article appearing in the newspapers detailing some aspect of her life, from a suggested desire to create a poultry farm at Goldsborough to the contents of her shopping basket and the installation of new blue and gold brocade curtains. Even the villagers in Goldsborough disliked this, declaring 'hasn't she the same right as we have to go where she likes … without people making a song about it?'[3] Harry was equally uncomfortable with this and his new role as a 'celebrity'. In 1923, he objected to a film concerning the Bramham Moor Hunt being released when someone had suggested that he had become a 'movie star'.

Despite the king and queen's reservations that they would lose their only daughter, and Queen Mary's initial feelings of despondency when Mary departed on honeymoon, Mary still saw her parents regularly and accompanied her mother on antiques and shopping expeditions, as well as gallery and museum visits and royal engagements. Inevitably Mary was incredibly happy in her new home, as it offered so many new and less formal experiences. She had been looking forward to participating in the Bramham Hunt but had to postpone her attendance when she realised that she was pregnant.

Mary welcomed in the new year of 1923 by sending out a sprig of white heather to all officers in her regiment of the Scots Guards. She returned to London just as newspapers started to share news of an imminent arrival at Chesterfield House, for which the queen's nurse would be in attendance. This was an age when pregnancy was shrouded in secrecy, especially for royal births, and women were expected to remain unseen at home from the moment that their pregnancy became visible. There had only been the briefest of mentions to Princess Mary's *enceinte* condition, as it was termed. Thus, during the later months of her pregnancy, Mary remained at home knitting and sewing in readiness for the new baby. In 1920 she had designed her ideal nursery for the Ideal Home Exhibition which had been remarkable for its simplicity of design as well as its cleanliness. It featured a lovely idea of a toy cupboard for the teddy bears and nursery rhyme images were stencilled on the walls. There was much speculation that the nurseries in her homes would take on a similar appearance.

Throughout 7 February there had been indications that a birth was imminent. Queen Mary was seen arriving and leaving Chesterfield House several times throughout the day. A large crowd, undeterred by the rain, gathered close by to catch a glimpse of any illustrious visitors and just as is the case today, every detail of the birth was eagerly anticipated by the public. The Honourable George Henry Hubert Lascelles was finally born at 11.15 p.m., weighing a healthy 8lb and delivered by Dr Henry Simson, a Scot and the brother of a famous footballer. The labour had been long, over twenty-seven hours, and Harry was more restless than anyone waiting for the birth. Buckingham Palace announced the new arrival shortly after midnight; with his blue eyes and fair skin, the baby was said to have taken after his mother. This was the first grandchild for the king and queen, who were among some of the first visitors to see their daughter the following day. Lala Bill, who had served as nanny to the family for many years, including being a companion to Prince John, was employed to assist Mary in caring for the baby.

One of the first groups of people to be told of the birth were 4,000 guests attending the Chelsea Arts Ball at the Royal Albert Hall. The announcement was made by means of a giant megaphone from the orchestra and was received with enthusiastic cheers. The following day a veritable avalanche of telegraph boys, postmen, footmen and members of society descended on Chesterfield House. Congratulations and gifts poured in including a layette from the Royal School of Needlework.

There was much speculation about what the baby would be called, with many newspapers guessing that he would be called Henry George after his father. This announcement was delayed until a month later on 8 March and it was explained that his names were in homage to the king, his father and the Marquess of Clanricarde. There was some disappointment in Yorkshire that the baby had not been born at Goldsborough Hall; however, the queen wished to be present when her daughter gave birth and legally the Home Secretary, William Bridgeman, had to be nearby to verify and witness the birth. This custom dated back to the seventeenth century and the 'Warming Pan Scandal', when the wife of James II gave birth to a son and rival families spread word that the child was an imposter. Fortunately, by the time the future Queen Elizabeth II was about to give birth to her first child, Prince Charles, her father George VI decided the practice was outdated and unnecessary.

Nine days after the birth, and with a crowd still gathered outside of Chesterfield House, Mary took George on his first outing by motor car to Buckingham Palace. As the son of a princess and grandson of a king, there was much disappointment that the baby would not have a royal title. During the First World War in 1917, when George V changed the family name from Saxe-Coburg-Gotha and discontinued the use of German titles, he changed the rights to the title of prince and the style of 'Royal Highness', declaring that only grandchildren in the male line would use the title prince or princess. This was something that the future 7th earl would eventually approve of since it gave him a greater degree of freedom throughout his life.[4]

Mary and Harry returned to Goldsborough on 10 March via train, with baby George and his nurse and numerous servants. There was no relief from the crowds waiting to greet them on their return to the hall. The following day many villagers were pleased to see George in his pram being wheeled around the village by his nurse. 'For two minutes they were lost in admiration of the beautifully-robed child.'[5]

Mary's life was one characterised by firsts, especially regarding her position as a member of the royal family at a time of modernisation. In the same way that her wedding had become a public wedding for the people, another family event was momentous, since it too broke the norm of royal christenings being held in private. It had been expected that the baby would be christened in the Chapel Royal at St James's Palace; however, Harry insisted on a Yorkshire christening at Goldsborough. George's christening took place on 25 March 1923, Palm Sunday, at St Mary's Church in Goldsborough. He was baptised by the Archbishop of York, Cosmo Gordon Lang. The king and queen, the Countess of Harewood, and Colonel Lane-Fox, the Minister of Mines, were chosen as godparents. Although the baby cried throughout the ceremony, the event was hailed as being of 'dignified simplicity'[6] since it was so far removed from the usual solemnity and grandeur of royal occasions. Those who came to witness the event were much moved that, although the baby was the grandchild of the king and queen, he was treated 'exactly like the child of the humblest villager'.[7]

The village of Goldsborough was bombarded with hundreds of motorcars and motorbikes, along with horse-drawn carriages. People stood on walls and the roofs of farmhouse buildings to see, and lines of Boy Scouts and Girl Guides attempted to keep the crowds back. The church was packed and the number of people in the village, who came from throughout the county, was declared to be the largest gathering that had ever occurred.

When it became obvious how many people had come to see the royal party and the baby, it was decided to lead a procession back through the village to the hall, at which point the spectators cheered. In the stiff and formal photographs to mark the occasion, it is apparent from her slightly upturned mouth that Queen Mary struggled to contain her joy and pride at holding her first grandchild. On their return to the house, the party lunched in the dining room and Mary cut one of the four christening cakes, one of which had been designed at Leeds School of Art and made in the bakery at the Technical School. In the afternoon, trees were planted to mark the occasion by the king and queen, Lady Harewood and Colonel Lane-Fox. The lack of formality and ceremony and the proximity of the king and queen at what was usually a private and secretive royal family event held in London undoubtedly endeared them to many in the north.

Mary had always loved children. In many ways it was not surprising with her position as the middle child among five brothers. She had chosen to specialise in paediatrics in her nursing and there were frequent stories in the press concerning her kindness towards them. In July 1921 at a children's entertainment gathering held in Victoria Park by the Eccentric Club and the Sunshine Fund, Mary had been unable to leave her car because of all the children who crowded around it. She subsequently entered a lost children enclosure and managed to placate the children who were temporarily separated from their parents. So popular was she that all of a sudden, a crowd of other children appeared claiming to be lost but 'tears soon gave way to smiles'.[8] On that day the public took to calling Mary 'The Heroine of London Children: The Sunshine Princess'.[9]

Mary relished being a mother and took great delight in watching her sons grow. She dressed them in rather twee matching outfits and was frequently seen in the village riding with her sons in her 'governess cart', a small carriage which could be attached to a pony. Such was her popularity that the carts underwent a resurgence in interest after Mary was photographed using one. Mary believed in the importance of family, but she was inhibited by her upbringing and her position. Although she would always be known for her kindness, Mary was embarrassed by displays of emotion and learned to suppress them. Her eldest son later explained that 'though I clung to my mother as a boy and haunted her sitting room and bedroom at Goldsborough, my declarations of affection were regarded I think as slightly embarrassing and something I would grow out of'.[10] As a father, Harry was equally undemonstrative and he did not have any particular affinity with children; certainly he was never the type to get down on his hands and knees and play. Harry preferred to speak to his children as though they were adults and much of their later shared interests came from trips out with their father such as to the football or exhibitions. A mutual respect and admiration developed, and both sons would go on to be in awe of him.

As was the case with the offspring of the aristocracy, George spent much of his time with his nurse. In a letter to her mother in November 1923, Mary explains her son's daily routine: 'Little George is very well and quite happy with Lala. He comes down at breakfast and teatime. He has grown again.'[11]

Another royal wedding occurred in 1923, that of Mary's second-eldest brother, Bertie, and Lady Elizabeth Bowes-Lyon, who had served as a bridesmaid at Mary's wedding. The marriage to a member of the aristocracy rather than to a foreign princess was again as popular as Mary's wedding. Mary and Harry were undoubtedly pleased that the intense press scrutiny of them might be abated slightly by the arrival of a new royal married couple.

Mary consented to become the patron and give her name to the Royal Air Force Temporary Nursing Service in June, which had originally been created in 1918 and thus became Princess Mary's Royal Air Force Nursing Service. Only trained nurses who were widows, spinsters or did not have children were permitted to join. The service had originally asked for George V's consent in 1918 for Mary to be its patron. However, this had been turned down until the service had time to establish itself. Mary visited the service at RAF Finchley in 1924 and the RAF Cranwell station in Lincolnshire in 1925, where she spoke to nearly every single patient and spent much time chatting to the women in the female ward. Mary would pay informal visits to the service where she:

> Thought of herself as one of us ... when seated at a table she would kick off her shoes ... When taking coffee, she filled her cup with sugar crystals and these she ate with a spoon. On one occasion she produced a cigarette case – this was handed round, one noticed, with a rather mischievous smile: smoking at this time was allowed, but not approved.[12]

In November 1923 Mary and Harry and the infant George went to stay with the Duke and Duchess of Northumberland at Alnwick Castle in order that Mary could open a new maternity hospital in Newcastle-upon-Tyne. On 21 August 1924 Mary gave birth to her second son, Gerald David Lascelles, who was born at Goldsborough Hall and christened with David and the newly created Duchess of York as his godparents. He was seventh in the line of succession at his birth. Mary's family was now complete, and photographs taken of her around this time show that she appears more content and possessed, according to the *Sphere*, 'an added charm'.[13] Over the years, Mary and Harry's marriage has led to much speculation and gossip. A recent film depicted Harry as a brutish bully and Mary as a constrained, forlorn wife, but nothing could have been further from the truth, as their eldest son George, later stated in his autobiography:

> My parents got on well together and had a lot of friends and interests in common. Someone years later told my ... wife ... that she had

always felt sorry for my mother 'married to that cold, hard man'…
she had it all wrong. My mother was never so happy to our eyes as
children as when she and my father were embarked on some scheme
together, as they often were, and my father's advice was sought on
every conceivable subject including those on which he could not possibly have been expected to have a view.[14]

The intense press attention on Mary's growing family meant that she was
incredibly popular and thus any cause or campaign to which she gave
her patronage was guaranteed success. During the First World War, the
Five Sisters Window at York Minster, dating from the thirteenth century,
was removed to prevent it from being destroyed during strategic bombing raids carried out by German Zeppelin airships. Mrs Helen Little and
Mrs Edwina Gray set up a public appeal to restore the window in 1923,
as a Yorkshire tribute to the many women who had lost their lives in
the First World War including nurses, members of Queen Mary's Army
Auxiliary Corps of the Saint John Ambulance, the Red Cross, the Wrens
and the Waacs, as well as those killed in air raids. It was a cause close to
Mary, and she immediately gave the fund her full support, donating £50
to the appeal. With Mary's backing, the £3,000 was soon raised within
just over three months. As a contemporary booklet produced to mark
the opening stated, 'Her keen interest thus directly … helped in a very
great degree to bring about the swift response to the Appeal.'[15]

Many of the charities and organisations that Mary patronised benefited from support throughout her lifetime. During the First World War,
Mary had often visited hospitals for disabled servicemen. She had seen
at close hand the work being carried out with artificial limbs and supported organisations which promoted the importance of rehabilitation
and occupational therapy. One such charity was the Disabled Sailors' and
Soldiers' Mutual Association, which had arisen from the Wharncliffe War
Hospital in Sheffield and the work of an artist, Annie Bindon Carter,
who organised many painting therapy sessions to aid former servicemen
in dealing with the psychological impact of war and the loss of limbs.
Annie discovered that she could produce stencils for the men to use
to paint fabric and attach paintbrushes to their stumps. The men, who

might otherwise have been unemployable because of their disabilities, now had a new skill and were able to work. In July 1925 Mary opened in Sheffield the new workshops and headquarters of 'Painted Fabrics' and became their royal patron. She was presented with her own painted shawl. The fabric items were sold by means of exhibitions, some at town hall sales and others in the homes of the aristocracy. In May 1932 Mary agreed to run a stall for Painted Fabrics at Claridge's ballroom. 'Princess Mary, who looked cool and charming in a summer dress, dealt with orders so expeditiously that she might have been used to selling goods behind the counter all her life.'[16]

Mary's chief charitable interest was still nursing. Although she was now a wife and mother, she maintained this interest through visiting hospitals, especially maternity wings, and throughout 1925 she completed an impressive round of such engagements. She opened a new wing at Hammersmith Hospital, the King Edward VII extension at Pontefract General Infirmary, maternity wings at Halifax and Shipley, and in Wakefield she laid the foundation stone to a nurses' home. However, it was soon apparent that Mary was starting to widen her philanthropic work in the north to take on more industrial and social causes. She opened YMCA clubs in Leeds and Bradford and attended the Harrogate Agricultural Show, the Hackney Society Show in Doncaster and the Chrysanthemum Show in York. Mary had visited a training centre for unemployed women and girls in Hunslet and she had ventured to Grimsby to open the Queen Mary Hostel for Deep Sea Fishermen. It was no surprise that in return, the people in the north began to feel proud of someone who they regarded as their own princess.

On 4 July 1925 Mary commenced a lifetime interest supporting women in higher education when she was conferred with an honorary law degree from the University of Leeds. In awarding her such a prestigious honour, the vice-chancellor stated that Mary had done much in her twenty-eight years, especially within the Girl Guides and nursing, to promote the significance of public service for women and girls.

Equestrianism was a mutual interest for both Mary and Harry. Mary was said to be the most accomplished rider of all the king's children.

During the Bramham Moor Hunt season, hundreds of spectators would turn out to catch a glimpse of her. However, Mary did not hunt often, much preferring to watch horse racing instead. She was frequently seen at most racing events, dressed for comfort in sturdy shoes. Before every race, Mary would enter the paddock to inspect the horses. She would watch every second of each race through her ever-present field glasses. Mary and her father attended the Newmarket Races in 1925. This was George's first appearance in public for some time. George was a heavy smoker and in 1925 he had been seriously ill with bronchial difficulties. He was sent on a cruise of the Mediterranean by his doctors to convalesce, but his hatred of foreign travel meant that he protested greatly about whether this was necessary, declaring that he would sooner die at home than have to venture overseas.

Harry and Mary's mutual interest in the Sport of Kings prompted Harry to purchase Egerton House and stud farm in Newmarket in 1925, with a view to the dual purpose of using it as a base for the celebrated Newmarket season of races and breeding their own thoroughbreds. Originally built for Lord Ellesmere in 1891, the red-brick property and stud farm was leased to the king's horse trainer, Richard Marsh, until it was eventually sold to Harry by Lord Ellesmere's third son, T.H.F. Egerton. Egerton stud farm had a reputation for breeding prize-winning horses and a long royal association including being the erstwhile location of secret assignations between Mary's grandfather Edward VII and one of his mistresses, Lily Langtry, who owned a stable nearby.

One of the more unusual organisations patronised by Mary, and possibly a result of Harry's connections within the Masons, was the international lodge fraternity of Oddfellows, who were founded in the early eighteenth century. Mary became an honorary member of the Loyal Harmony Lodge at Knaresborough and her initiation ceremony took place in front of forty members at Goldsborough over the summer of 1925. The Lascelles family had been members of the lodge since 1842 and even Mary's two young sons were enrolled as junior members. The highlight of 1925 for Goldsborough residents was a summer fete organised by Mary in the grounds of the hall to raise money for the church funds and to pay for a local district nurse for the village. Over

6,000 people came from all over the county to see for themselves the beautiful gardens of Goldsborough and no doubt desperate to purchase one of the items generously donated by Queen Mary or one of Mary's in-laws. They were taken aback by the sight of the princess mucking in with the villagers and serving on various stands. It was no surprise that Mary was followed as she made her way from stall to stall.

Despite Mary now having her own family and living for much of the time in Yorkshire, she continued to visit her mother frequently. In London in 1927 Mary and her mother visited the annual exhibition of the Society of Women Artists at the Royal Institute Galleries in Piccadilly, where both purchased pictures and craft items to support and encourage the artists. Queen Mary made an annual visit to see her daughter at Goldsborough Hall on the way to Balmoral. She would stay for three weeks and clearly delighted in the chance to spend time with her grandsons. Together the queen and Mary would patronise local antique shops. The quaint old street of Stonegate in York was a particular favourite. One day when visiting Messrs W.F. Greenwood and Sons, they arrived to find the shop had closed early for the afternoon. Undeterred, Queen Mary knocked on the side door until a shocked assistant opened the door to her unexpected visitor. Within a short time, the shop was surrounded by a large crowd, eager to see the queen and her daughter. On their departure, the crowd burst into cheers and applause. It was this lack of formality and fondness for normality that Queen Mary enjoyed most about her visits to the north and it was clearly an intrinsic part of Mary's life to be able to travel around freely with limited fuss.

Queen Mary was a doting grandmother. When she was not with her grandchildren, she would send them treats of chocolates and animal figurines or special letters from imaginary farm characters she invented, as any doting grandparent would. Close to Goldsborough Hall's front door, Mary installed a revolving summerhouse complete with basket furniture and its own tea service, so that the queen could experience private moments with her grandsons. Similarly, George and Gerald spent many happy hours with their parental grandmother at Harewood walking through the spectacular grounds and learning how to appreciate the glasshouses and flowerbeds. Gerald and his paternal grandfather frequently shared birthday parties since they were both born in August.

Mary had inherited from Edward VII a love of giving gifts to others. She sent an immense number of Christmas and birthday presents and her Christmas card list was more akin to a book. Every December she would buy and parcel up many toys to despatch to sick children. She would always shock store owners as she would carry the parcels herself to her car. She took pleasure in the rare occasions when she would not be recognised and treated as a member of the public. Many of her presents were bought in Harrogate or were the work of disabled ex-servicemen such as figurines and commemoratives from Ashstead pottery. The Ashstead factory in Surrey had been established by Sir Lawrence Weaver, who had received support from Bertrand Clough William-Ellis – the creator of the village of Portmeirion – in establishing his factory for ex-servicemen.

The National Garden Scheme had been established to raise money for district nursing by opening up gardens of character, quality and interest. By the summer of 1928, Mary decided that the grounds at Goldsborough were of sufficient maturity to be part of the scheme. With interest in the Yorkshire princess and her family still at its height, the response was overwhelming, with Mary raising nearly £200 – worth £12,000 today – and receiving 4,000 visitors. Much mention was made of the flower borders and Mary's favourite roses on display. It is a testament to Mary's skill as a gardener that now, nearly 100 years since she first lived at Goldsborough, the gardens remain a reflection of her vision.

1928 was a busy year for travel for Mary and Harry. Their sons were no longer babies and Mary was less apprehensive about leaving them behind in the care of their nurse, with occasional visits from family members. Mary found the history of Egypt and the Holy Land fascinating; therefore in March, Mary and Harry embarked upon a tour of Cairo and Jerusalem, taking only a small entourage with them. Furthermore, although much of the trip was a private holiday for rest and recuperation after a busy round of engagements, it would afford Mary the opportunity to meet the families of serving members of the Royals Scots Guards regiment, stationed in Egypt at this time. This trip would be relatively

low key compared to official royal trips overseas, and they fully intended
to do as much sightseeing as possible.

Prior to departure, Mary purchased special clothing to prepare for
the climate, and she took her typewriter with her, a gift from David,
to create a travel journal. As was her usual custom prior to travelling,
Mary spent a couple of days with her parents dining and having lunch at
Buckingham Palace. At Marseilles they joined the P&O luxurious liner
*Ranchi* for Port Said and were shown their green and gold deluxe cabins
by Miss Elsie Mackay, the daughter of P&O chairman Lord Inchcape.
Miss Mackay later told the press that there had been much merriment
when Mary, who like her father disliked travel, asked if the ship was
steady, since she positively hated ships that rolled.

Upon arrival in Cairo they were welcomed by a guard of honour of
Girl Guides. The following day they intended to journey to Khartoum
via Luxor; however, the extreme heat meant their proposed visit of
Khartoum would need to be cancelled and they ventured to Sudan
instead to buy souvenir trinkets from the local shops. In Egypt, King
Fuad gave Mary the Grand Cordon of the Order of Kamel and the
Grand Cordon of the Order of Mohamed Ali to Harry. King Fuad
believed greatly in documenting Egypt's past and was instrumental in
appointing archivists to translate and catalogue the archives of his paternal ancestors. Mary attended a tea party given to honour her by Princess
Toussoun. Despite the trip being a private holiday, Mary agreed to
inspect her regiment of the Royal Scots and award medals.

There was some disturbance in Cairo just before Mary's trip with a
student demonstration against King Fuad, owning to his dictatorial stance
on some matters; he was a great admirer of Machiavelli and had wide
powers that he used frequently to dissolve parliamentary cabinets at will.
Fortunately for Mary, this did not impact her visit and her agreement to
attend a state banquet given by the king was not criticised. The royal couple
travelled to Palestine as guests of Lord and Lady Plumer and witnessed the
Ceremony of the Holy Fire in the Church of the Holy Sepulchre, said to
be the site of the Crucifixion, Jesus' burial and the Resurrection.

In October 1928, Mary and Harry travelled to Portumna in Ireland
via motorcar and the steamer *Lady Limerick*. Mary had visited Ireland

in 1911 with her parents and received an enthusiastic welcome but this was her first visit to the country as an adult. Two days prior to their visit a deliberate fire had been started at the castle in two coach-houses, causing considerable damage. Three men, who had no doubt caused the arson attack, were seen fleeing from the stables. They were eventually arrested but Harry magnanimously requested that no further action was taken against them. Presumably he may have believed that the attack was politically motivated, and he did not wish to appear to be stirring up any trouble or inciting revenge. Prior to their visit, there had been some concerns regarding the safety of such a trip and the possibility of an attack or kidnap attempt. However, Mary with her 'unflinching courage'[17] and 'pluck'[18] was adamant that the trip would go ahead since cancelling the trip would no doubt jeopardise any future royal trips to Ireland. Special Garda police were appointed and Colonel David Neligan, director of intelligence, liaised with Special Branch. A bulletproof car provided by the Irish Free State army was used for additional safety in transporting the couple. There were fortunately no public demonstrations against Mary's visit or any other major disturbances. The only minor incidents were the distribution of a pamphlet by IRA sympathisers and a small number of women expressing their disapproval by jeering. However, their boos were swiftly drowned out by all the cheering.

As the couple arrived in Dublin, they received a rapturous welcome of several hundred people, mostly women and children waving Union Jacks and anxious to see a real princess, who as the wife of an Irish landowner was considered to be making her homecoming. Mary and Harry were met by Captain O'Sullivan, the aide-de-camp to the governor-general. According to the newspapers 'Princess Mary looked a picture of happiness'[19] and 'Lord Lascelles ... was in excellent spirits ... although he has a proverbial dislike of photographers he submitted cheerfully, "You must have taken about a thousand pictures between you," he remarked when they had finished.'[20]

They made their way to the Viceregal Lodge; as they did so some of the crowd managed to break through the police cordon and surround the car. Mary was greatly touched by the warm welcome accorded by the

Irish people. After breakfast, they drove to Portumna where they won over the local people by visiting schools and institutions, dining with the local parish priest and attending a harvest service at the Protestant church. Harry showed his wife around the family estate, where Mary was presented with a pedigree Irish wolfhound named Patrick of Ouborough as a gift from the Association of Irish Wolfhound Breeders and Mrs H.K. Purcell. It was given to Mary as a way to popularise the breed, not unlike the modern effect on fashion of the Duchess of Cambridge, who merely has to wear a high-street dress at an engagement for it to sell out within hours. Within a few weeks, the breed had suddenly become popular, with the *Yorkshire Post* reporting that:

> It is gratifying, though slightly amusing, to note how invariably the purchase or acquisition of any special dog by a member of the Royal Family leads to an immediate 'boom' in that particular breed. This has never been more marked than in the case of the Irish wolfhound presented to Her Royal Highness, Princess Mary, during her visit to Ireland. I understand that the Secretary of The Irish Wolfhound Club has been nearly snowed under by applications for membership, from people of all sorts and kinds. Certainly, no large breed of dog deserves more popularity than the Irish wolfhound, for no more excellent companion and friend could be found.[21]

Special arrangements were made to transport the dog back to Goldsborough Hall including a basket and return journey via steamer and train. Mary accepted the invitation to become patroness of the Association of Irish Wolfhound Breeders and held this honour until her death. Mary bred a litter of puppies from Patrick and registered them with the Kennel Club. Patrick was put on display at the Ladies' Kennel Association at Olympia in May 1930. The dogs became a feature of life at Goldsborough Hall. As Mary's son George later recorded in his memoirs, the dogs were 'slightly ludicrous … [and] once succeeded to my father's indignation in catching the goat which kept the horses company; the wolfhound puppies … knocked me down when I was six and threatened to lick me to death'.[22]

After Portumna the couple travelled to Ulster and were received at Hillsborough by the governor of Northern Ireland while Orangemen drummed and processed through the castle. The following day they arrived in Belfast. The 10-mile route from Ulster to Belfast was lined with thousands of supporters. At Belfast City Hall, Mary admired the war memorial window and left roses from her bouquet there to honour the war dead. The Belfast visit was a veritable whirlwind of events. They paid a visit to some industrial organisations, the shipyard and proceeded on the Saturday to a meeting of Girl Guides and Boy Scouts and a performance at the Hippodrome. Mary, dressed in her Guiding uniform, went on stage to accept a gift of Irish linen. British Pathé newsreel from the occasion shows the police struggling to hold back the crowds as Mary carries out official ceremony duties.

Mary's Irish visit was significant since she was the first royal to visit the Irish Free State privately. On her return, she gave an informal dinner party at Chesterfield House to show off the beautiful linen that she had received from her Irish visit. Mary had already spoken of her intention to revisit Ireland the following year.

During the 1920s, Mary developed an interest in girls' education. She understood its importance for girls, especially within single-sex schools. Her interest in this field possibly came from the broad, progressive curriculum she had experienced. In recognition of her support she was made patron of the Yorkshire Ladies' Council of Education in 1931, an organisation that financially supported girls and women in education and helped to support such illustrious establishments as St Paul's, Leeds, Wakefield and Bradford Girls' High Schools, as well as the Yorkshire College of Science, which eventually became the University of Leeds. To highlight this, Mary regularly visited girls' schools. One such example of Mary's ongoing commitment to this cause is to be seen in her association with Wakefield Girls' High School. In 1925, Mary distributed prizes at speech day. During the ceremony, the headmistress spoke of her desire for a school hall to commemorate the school's jubilee in 1927. Mary encouraged people to support this cause and the money was raised remarkably quickly. In 1927, Mary returned to lay the foundation stone for the hall and returned to open it in 1930, during which, 'Miss Martin assured her ... that we felt that our dream of a School Hall had materialised largely owing to her interest in the School and her kindness in coming to lay the foundation stone'.[23]

For Mary it was not enough merely to support a charitable enterprise: she derived more fulfilment in seeing the fruition of active involvement. For her, royal patronage had to involve longevity of commitment, dependability and permanence throughout her lifetime – a standard still adhered to by royal patrons today.

# 12

# Harewood

I would not exceed the limits of expense that I have always set myself.
Let us do everything properly and well, *mais pas trop.*[1]

Edwin Lascelles to Robert Adam

On 6 October 1929 the 5th Earl of Harewood died aged 83 from a lung disease, surrounded by his family at Harewood House. His death caused great sadness in Yorkshire. Harry had been at Newmarket at the time and Mary was at Selly Oak in Birmingham, where she had opened the College of the Ascension for missionaries. Mary was upset by the news as she had a close relationship with her father-in-law but still insisted on fulfilling a commitment to the Girl Guides for an inspection at Cannon Hill Park.

The earl's funeral took place a few days later at Harewood and a memorial service was held at St Peter's Eaton Square in London as well as at Leeds parish church. The 5th earl had been quite a private man despite his connection to the royal family. He had a reputation for being a generous and benevolent landlord, who developed the land at Harewood using the principles of agricultural science for land management. Harry would now become the 6th Earl of Harewood; Mary, Countess of Harewood; and their eldest son, George, Viscount Lascelles.

The first owners of Harewood can be traced back to the Domesday Book of 1086 and the presence of three Saxon lords: Tor, Sprot and Grim.

The land was seized and redistributed to Robert de Romelli, a Norman baron. In 1366 Sir William de Aldeburgh, the 1st Baron Aldeburgh, inherited the manor of Harewood through his marriage to Elizabeth de Lisle and built a castle on the site which was 'a mixture of convenience and magnificence'.[2] In 1391, when the 2nd baron died without issue, the castle passed to the Ryther and Redmayne families. The castle was sold to Sir William Wentworth of Gawthorpe in 1600 and ceased to be occupied by the 1630s. Sir John Cutler, a successful grocer and MP, bought Gawthorpe and Harewood, but as he had no male heirs the property was ultimately sold.

The Lascelles family connection with Harewood began in 1738 when Henry Lascelles bought the old manor house of Gawthorpe Hall. Gawthorpe had been the home for sixteen generations of the Gascoigne family and in 1580 it had passed to the Wentworth family, only to be sold when Thomas Wentworth, Earl of Strafford, a leading figure in politics in the period leading up to the Civil War, was executed for treason, leaving the family heavily in debt. Henry Lascelles's son, Edwin, demolished Gawthorpe and erected a new house. Harewood House was located at the top of the hill looking down on the former site of Gawthorpe Hall. Edwin Lascelles had exacting standards; he wanted only the very best in his new home and thus he commissioned John Carr of York to design Harewood House. The foundations were built in 1759 using stone from a local quarry. A few months later, the very fashionable Scottish architect Robert Adam travelled to Harewood to make sketches in order to restore the church. Edwin consulted Adam about the house design and, as well as designing the interiors, he contributed to the exterior architecture, making it impossible even today to ascertain which man designed which part. According to Adam's brother, he 'tickled it up so as to dazzle the eyes of the Squire'.[3] The building work was finished in 1771 and it was very much a faithful collaboration between all designers to create a building that is still one of the greatest treasure houses in the country.

Plaster work was completed by the famous stuccoists, Joseph Rose and William Collins, the decorative paintings by the neo-classical painters Angelica Kaufmann, Antonio Zucchi and Biagio Rebecca and furniture by Thomas Chippendale, who received the greatest commission of his career worth over £10,000 and lasting for nine years, along with an incredible Lancelot 'Capability' Brown-designed landscape of a 32-acre serpentine lake, cascade and carriage drives. Capability Brown was called by this nickname since he would frequently say when speaking to a client that a landscape had great *capability* for improvement. He began his career as a mere kitchen gardener but rose to great success as a landscape gardener and architect. His arrangement of the landscape at Harewood is considered one of his best accomplishments: his key strength lay in making a landscape look as if it had been created by nature alone.

When Edwin died with no heir in 1795, his cousin Edward Lascelles inherited the family fortune and became the 1st Earl of Harewood. Edward's son Edward, Viscount Lascelles, who was known as Beau, commissioned watercolours from J.M.W. Turner and was one of the artist's earliest patrons. Turner, only 22 when he arrived at Harewood in 1797, and other artists – Thomas Girtin, John Varley and John Sell Cotman – were commissioned to paint different aspects of the house. In the mid-nineteenth century, the 4th earl disposed of many of the Turner paintings, erroneously believing that their colours would fade. Later generations sought to return these paintings to their original home. Mary and Harry, with their shared interest in the visual arts, were successful in reacquiring many of the lost Turners and they received *Harewood House from the South-East* as a wedding present from the Countess of Wharncliffe. Typical of Turner's style as a landscape artist, this was painted from the high vantage point of Almscliffe Cragg, with Harewood House depicted far away in order to show the magnificence of the undulating land.

Beau Lascelles was an avid collector of French Sèvres, a highly prized porcelain of the eighteenth century that was patronised by Louis XV of France. It was considered to be some of the most beautiful ever made because of its exquisiteness and finesse. Among the cups and vases, Sèvres manufactured a range of items known as *objets utiles*, or useful items for personal care, such as bidets or false teeth. After the French Revolution of 1789, the porcelain was sold off from Parisian auction houses and it was in these that Beau made his purchases. Beau died before he could succeed his father, though he had already amassed one of the finest collections. It was an interest he shared with Mary, who already had her own substantial collection of pale green Sèvres, which she used on the oak table in her green and gold dining room at Chesterfield House. When Queen Mary saw the Harewood collection of china she was said to be envious of several of the rarer pieces.

The 3rd Earl of Harewood, Henry, and his wife, born Louisa Thynne, the daughter of the Marquis of Bath, had thirteen children and set about extending the house to be more befitting of a Victorian family home. Louisa commissioned Sir Charles Barry, famed for his work on the Houses of Parliament, to carry out major alterations. Rooms were transformed and an additional floor was added to provide servants' quarters and more bedrooms. Barry supervised the addition of Corinthian balustrades, along with terraces with fountains to give the air of an Italian palazzo. The terrace at Harewood, incorporating a formal Victorian garden, was designed to highlight the sublime beauty of the Yorkshire landscape with spectacular views spreading as far as the eye could see.

The 4th Earl, Henry Thynne Lascelles, although a great benefactor to the Leeds General Infirmary, did little to the estate. Later generations considered his greatest accomplishment to be his marriage to Elizabeth de Burgh, daughter of the politician Ulick de Burgh, 1st Marquess of Clanricarde, and sister of Hubert de Burgh-Canning, 2nd Marquess of Clanricarde, who would later bequeath the majority of his estate to Harry Lascelles, the 6th Earl.

The 5th Earl had difficulties maintaining the estate and living within his means. He had to sell several properties including Harewood House in Hanover Square, London, and he subsequently invested the money in worldwide railway companies. Some money came from the Lascelles business in the West Indies but there were many annuities charged on the estate. These financial difficulties meant that he carried out very little work to the house in the thirty-seven years of his tenure, apart from having electricity installed in 1900 at a mammoth cost of £5,000. Harewood House was used as a convalescent hospital during the First World War, which impacted quite badly on the condition of the house.

In 1929, Harewood House still had many Victorian features created by Sir Charles Barry that were no longer impressive and urgently
needed attention after being left for so long. Mary and Harry, with their
mutual love of the country and art treasures, and a much more substantial budget than the previous occupants, were eager to give their home
a new look. Thus began a series of modernisation schemes. One major
undertaking was a partial rewiring since there were not enough table
lamps. This was regretted much later when it was apparent that a complete overhaul and renewal would have been more befitting with the
advent of increased use of electrical appliances. The new heating system
had to be installed with great care to ensure that it would not damage
the Chippendale furniture. Electric cooking equipment needed installing to feed all fifty people who were normally resident at Harewood
along with more bathrooms. Private apartments were modernised, and a
nursery was added to the top floor of the east wing.

The elderly Sir Herbert Baker had originally worked with Edwin
Lutyens and he was called in to alter the interiors to create additional
rooms for Mary, along with the York architects, Messrs Brierley and
Rutherford, who had taken over John Carr's business. Nine bathrooms and two lifts were installed along with an exquisite boudoir on
the ground floor between the east bedroom and the former study, as a
homage to the original style of Robert Adam. A bathroom and separate toilet were added to the suite for the princess with a recessed bath
and silver taps. Mary's dressing room was Baker's largest undertaking and featured plasterwork by Sir Charles Wheeler, a deep apse and
two cupboards either side of the Adam revival mantlepiece to display
Mary's collections of amber, rose quartz and jade, and many Chinese
objects. Two impressive items were a nineteenth-century white jade
'Jue', an ancient Chinese vessel for wine, and a Mughal-style, white,
thickly carved jade chrysanthemum bowl. Most of the rooms were
redecorated, shades of blue dominated, and Mary worked with Baker
on the designs, adding such touches as coats of arms, her monogram,
emblems of the Commonwealth on ceilings and the inclusion of the
motifs of the Girl Guides and the Royal Scots in her bathroom.

Harry was keen to refurbish the old library, as it had deteriorated considerably and needed extensive refurbishment to restore it to its former glory. The room was noted for its Corinthian pilasters and elaborate Adam ceiling. The billiard room once again became the rose drawing room; a perfect example of Adam's meticulous conception of rooms, which included everything from the elaborate ceilings through to the fire iron and door-handles. The 7th earl, Harry and Mary's son, later described Adam as 'like a stage decorator, with an eye to the total effect'.[4] Eventually most of Adam's rooms on the main floor were restored. Undoubtedly the most magnificent room in Harewood was and still remains the gallery, on the west side of the house. It extends for some 23 metres and displays much of Harewood's most spectacular art treasures. It was described in an early Harewood guide book most accurately as 'a room of extraordinary richness and charm … a tour-de-force of controlled embellishment and magnificent content'.[5]

Building work took time and the renovations required considerable planning. The removal from Goldsborough Hall to Harewood took place in many stages. Items needed to be transported from Chesterfield House in London, which was vacated by the family in 1932 and demolished a few years later to make way for a block of flats. It was ten years before Harewood was completely finished. Goldsborough Hall remained in the Lascelles family until 1939 and was repurposed as an independent school.

Like her mother, Mary enjoyed collecting miniature objets d'art. Records of memoranda concerning the removal show that she possessed a curious and unique collection of miniatures of assorted animals including cats, birds, elephants and owls, along with tea sets, artificial plants, perfume bottles, boxes and even a 'laughing God standing on a frog'.[6] Following strict instructions, these were only permitted to be packed by the head of the removal firm. Mary was eager to impress this fascination with miniatures on to her sons and provided them with their own collection in the nursery. She had an extensive collection of fans, from ostrich feather ones adorned with Cartier diamond monograms to eighteenth-century chic fans bedecked with cherubic creatures cavorting among pastoral and heavenly landscapes. One highly prized item was a Fabergé fan jewelled and with gold-mounted mother-of-pearl. Mary collected many other Fabergé luxury objects, and these were normally received as gifts from her grandmother or her mother. She cherished a cigar cutter and a jewelled gold and silver cigarette case, both once the property of her paternal grandfather, Edward VII. Linen was at this time greatly valued and Mary had amassed an extensive collection, with some dating from the Victorian period in 1846, along with different cloths for just about every domestic chore from glass-cleaning to carpet druggets and well over 100 dusters. Mary may have been a princess, but she was incredibly prudent with everyday items. She was a great believer in the wartime adage 'make do and mend' and recycled envelopes, paper and string, storing many such items in the most ornate examples of Chippendale furniture. Her hats were kept in a large cupboard and they would be worn even when they were frayed and faded and pretty much until they fell apart.

The total cost of building work and refurbishment came to over £44,000: something exceeding £2.5 million today. In keeping with Robert Adam's original interior design, much of the Chippendale furniture was extensively reupholstered or restored. Some was even covered with petit-point tapestry embroidered by Harry. Many of the rooms on the main floor had been restored to their former eighteenth-century glory.

When he opened an art gallery in Harrogate in 1930, Harry made a point of stating that it was imperative that art works were not just concentrated in London but could be viewed in the north as well. To this end, he used the money he had inherited from his uncle Clanricarde to purchase exceptional works of art, many from the Renaissance period. These eventually hung throughout Harewood, including works by Titian, Bellini, El Greco, Veronese and Tintoretto. Much of Harry's collection was purchased between 1917 and 1927 and he had consulted the well-known art specialist and historian Tancred Borenius, who worked at Sotheby's auction house and lectured as a professor at University College, London. Borenius was 'an old-fashioned *savant,* who seemed informed and informative about everything, a cultivated man and excellent company'.[7] Borenius became part of the family and he would spend a month every summer between 1929 and 1939 at Harewood. In 1925 he wrote an article about the new Lord Harewood's collection of Old Master drawings and followed this in 1936 with a catalogue concerning Harewood artworks. Furthermore, he became something of an unofficial antiquity expert to Queen Mary, accompanying her on trips to antique dealers in Yorkshire.

Paintings such as Frank Salisbury's *The Marriage of Princess Mary* and its companion *Princess Mary Signing the Register*, commissioned by George V to record his only daughter's wedding ceremony, as well as Sir Oswald Birley's portrait of Mary, were hung among the other family portraits by Joshua Reynolds and Thomas Gainsborough. In 1931, Mary and Harry commissioned Sir Alfred Munnings, one of the finest painters of horses, to paint them both riding. In total Harewood displayed some eighty-four Italian paintings, sixty-two Dutch, eighteen French and ninety English. Mary was particularly fond of watercolours and hung the Turner paintings in her sitting room. The sitting room housed her books until she had so many that they had to be kept in the 'little library'. Of an evening she would go in there to read, knit or complete tapestries.

One hundred new acres of trees were planted, and Mary and Harry continued the tradition they had started at Goldsborough Hall of inviting their many royal guests to plant a tree. New glasshouses were built in the walled garden. In these were grown all manner of plants, such as begonias, orchids and poinsettias and exotic fruits of peaches, figs and berries. In the kitchen garden were beds of kale, asparagus, artichokes and chicory. The gardeners were always particularly proud of the Muscat of Alexandria variety grapes that were grown, which came from an original plant grown in 1793. Mary was pedantic about how grapes were cut: always removed from the stem using special grape scissors, rather than being pulled. Mary's particular favourite plant, roses, were positioned on the terrace. Harry was fond of rhododendrons and the leading botanic garden expert on these plants, Sir William Wright Smith, advised on how best to grow the more peculiar varieties with their unpronounceable Latin names. Mary and Harry took much enjoyment in questioning gardeners when they were planting the varieties, just to hear their amusing mispronunciations. Flowering shrubs and trees were added, and a rock garden was made at the head of the lake. Much of the pastureland was converted into paddocks for racehorses, although Harry rarely saw a return on his investment in the years to come. Mary took an active interest in all aspects of the house including the farm. At Goldsborough, she and Harry had a herd of Guernsey cattle. At Harewood, she raised a prize herd of Red Poll cattle shown throughout England by one of the agricultural world's best showmen, Tom Scaife. Mary was a keen bee-keeper and even brought her hives from Goldsborough, complete with queen bee. Harry and Mary first opened the gardens of Harewood for the British Legion in July 1931 and subsequently the following Saturday in aid of district nursing. The house and gardens were also on display on Wednesdays and Thursdays in June and July for a few hours.

In the winter the 40-acre lake would freeze and the residents from the estate along with Mary's children would skate. Harry would even arrange ice-hockey matches and his wife would play in goal position. To ensure that the lake would be able to support the weight of the many skaters, a member of staff carried out a thorough test in which he:

> Would muster about six gardeners of different weights and acquire a ladder with a hundred-foot rope attached, the lightest gardener would step on the ice and take the ladder aeroplane fashion and push it forward. Each gardener would ... follow ... until the last man, the heaviest, would be well on the ice; then ... everyone ... would have to jump up and down.[8]

It was not until 25 October 1930 that the couple could move into their new marital home. Unfortunately, on their way, they were involved in a car accident in which they collided with a two-seater car. Both cars were badly damaged, though no one was injured. In September 1930, a lunch was given for all the tenants on the estate to introduce the new earl. As a Unionist (later known as Conservative), Harry believed that the legislation introducing greater tax on a large agricultural estate such as Harewood was wrong:

> The whole trend of modern taxation is more and more to put the burden upon capital, and if your capital is sunk in land in the form of

buildings, fencing, drainage, etc., you cannot realise that capital in order to pay taxes, except by selling the land. I am sufficiently old-fashioned to think that this is wrong. The disturbance created by selling agricultural estates is greater than any good which can come from it.[9]

His words were considered controversial at the time, since members of the royal family, even with distant associations, were not supposed to express any opinion on contentious subjects. Yet these words were to prove more than prophetic when he died in 1947 and the family were faced with immense inheritance tax to pay.

Harewood House bloomed in the 1930s and was 'buzzing with activity'.[10] Many of the villagers were employed on the estate as domestic servants, chauffeurs, gamekeepers, labourers and grooms and remained for several generations. The butler, Alfred Blades, served throughout Mary's tenure at Harewood and was known to be incredibly trustworthy, discreet and unflappable. He was an expert concerning Harewood silver and the house's traditions. Blades used to ride a moped on the estate but since he did not possess a licence, he would ride to the archway, dismount and push the bike back to his home. He was quite an eccentric, always wearing his glasses askew in a similar vein to the comedian Eric Morecambe. Yet Blades's knowledge of the house was so extensive that George's second wife, Patricia, credited him for teaching her everything about her role in the house when she arrived in the late 1960s.

In the 1930s, there were regular house parties and a stream of visitors for the race events at Wetherby and York, shooting parties, the Bramham Hunt and Christmas. Mary kept a very detailed visitors' book recording all of Harewood's illustrious guests, including Mary's brother Bertie and his wife Elizabeth, who visited in December 1931, and David in 1933. There was Princess Alice, Countess of Athlone; Lady Patricia Ramsay; Cosmo Gordon Lang, the Archbishop of Canterbury; Hugh Lowther, the 5th Lord Lonsdale, known as The Yellow Earl and the founder of the Automobile Association. The royal guests would mingle with the leading figures of horse racing. Queen Mary came every year for ten days on her way to Balmoral and insisted that her visits would be quiet family gatherings even though she delighted in speaking to the crowds of villagers and estate workers who came to greet her upon her arrival. Just as at Goldsborough, she enjoyed visiting local antiques centres and shops in Yorkshire. Mary would regularly accompany her mother to visit Henry Widdall, a dealer in antiques at Beverley, or Henry Blairman, a dealer in Harrogate, to purchase items which would be sent on to Harewood for Mary or Buckingham Palace for the queen.

According to his son Henry, later Duke of Gloucester, George V hated Harewood.[11] However, when one considers how George preferred the cramped quarters of York Cottage, it is easy to see why he disliked the huge estate. He did, however, enjoy hunting at Harewood where he was 'a legendary performer at the butts'.[12] When the king and queen visited together, security had to be increased with a need for police and security men to patrol the estate as well as various equerries and aides-de-camp. In 1933, King George and Queen Mary stayed at Harewood when visiting Leeds to open the town hall. They travelled in procession from Oakwood to the town hall, and the king inspected the guard of honour in Victoria Square. A record number of people turned out for the event from all over Yorkshire. Prior to Mary's arrival as a resident, it had been incredibly unusual for a monarch to visit the north. Mary's grandparents, Edward VII and Queen Alexandra, visited the north in 1908 and even stayed at Harewood with the 5th earl and planted a tree on the estate to commemorate this momentous occasion. The local newspapers reported that 'some 250 years, it is said, have passed since a crowned king of this country was seen in Leeds'.[13] One cannot underestimate the gratification it would have given to the people of Yorkshire that a king would come to visit the north regularly, as well as it being an astute exercise in public relations for the monarchy, albeit unintentional.

House parties were planned with painstaking care; sometimes an increased serving staff was required to cater for thirty or forty guests. Prior to each event or dinner party, Mary and Harry would inspect the table in the state dining room to ensure that everything was perfect. Extravagant floral displays in silver or gold ware that had been approved by Mary would be placed throughout the house, each one different and reflecting the changing seasons. Music would play from a gramophone given by King Amanullah of Afghanistan in the music room. At

Christmas, holly and greenery would be dipped in flour and Epson salts for a glittery effect. As Mary's son George later wrote, 'Christmas meant a full house of relations, walks with different people to talk to, elaborate games, special food and staying up late.'[14] For their first Christmas in the house, Mary and Harry attended church twice on Christmas morning with a number of their house guests. Mary's favourite Cairn terrier, Peggy, waited for her mistress at the door of the church, and Harry read the lesson. Mary held a children's party with a magician for her sons and a dozen of their friends where she joined in many of the games herself.

In a year the house would get through 600 bunches of grapes, an equal number of figs, 1,000 peaches and nectarines, 100 pears and many strawberries as well as gages, plums and Morello cherries. According to the 7th earl, there was a knack to eating Harewood pears, which involved 'cutting them in half round the middle, removing the core from the centre and then scooping them out with a spoon'.[15] Harewood figs were so good that they were said to have their own 'special flavour'.[16] Between April and August the family would move to London for the season accompanied by many staff members. When not entertaining, the family lived quite modestly and so rationing during the Second World War was not such a shock to them. With the Second World War, entertaining was put on hold.

Mary was known for her timidity and nervousness and was therefore keen on the idea of privacy when off duty. She hated any intrusion from the media. Although Harry owned two Rolls-Royce cars, horses were still used a great deal for transportation and roads were relatively quiet. Mary enjoyed driving her sons around in a pony and cart. Harewood was an ideal estate on which to raise children and Mary's two sons would wander freely throughout the estate, frequently visiting the various hives of activity to seek out their own entertainment. There was the joiner's headquarters in the estate yard, with its scent of wood shavings, all the farmyard buildings with their pigsties and cowsheds as well as the stables. The lake, which had its own herd of Canadian geese and Whooper swans, was ideal for all kinds of activities such as rowing and trout fishing. The children learned to ride from an early age and would venture out on their ponies most days, seeking out the reassuring anecdotes of the groom, who happily regaled them with tales of his former role as a huntsman. Riding was a natural way of life at Harewood and occasionally it gave way to cycling. Sometimes the children would venture to watch Leeds United play at football or to the cinema and the nearby shops or they would visit a zoo with their mother. They joined the village cricket team and played against other villages. There were picnics in the Yorkshire Dales, as well as visits to Bolton Abbey and the local towns.

During her tenure at Harewood, Mary immersed herself fully in all aspects of running a stately home. Mary and Harry gained a special pleasure from regularly going out into the grounds together and attempting to hack away at the overgrown rhododendrons. They took an interest in village life, helping out with the Women's Institute flower show and presenting prizes or participating in Brownie or Girl Guide meets. Harewood House became 'something of an establishment fit for meeting all the requirements necessary for royal occasions and regal living'.[17] In short, a royal palace.

Mary and her brothers in 1910. Left to right, back row: Prince Albert ('Bertie'), Princess Mary, Prince Edward ('David'). Front row: Prince John, Prince Henry, Prince George. (Arthur James Hope Downey)

The Princess Mary gift tin belonging to Henry Williamson. (Anne Williamson)

·1914·

With

Best Wishes

· for a ·

Happy Christmas

· and a ·

Victorious New Year.

From

The Princess Mary

and Friends at

· Home ·

· · · ·

A Christmas card to the troops that accompanied the gift tin. (Anne Williamson)

Queen Mary with Princess Mary as a nurse at Great Ormond Street Hospital. (George Grantham Bain Collection, Library of Congress)

Nurses at Great Ormond Street Hospital admiring the painting in tribute to Princess Mary. (Great Ormond Street NHS Foundation Trust)

Henry, Viscount Lascelles, known as Harry. A somewhat dashing photograph given that he was said to be unphotogenic. (Tuck DB Postcards)

The wedding of Princess Mary and Viscount Lascelles on 28 February 1922. Back row, left to right: Lady Doris Gordon-Lennox, Lady Elizabeth Bowes-Lyon, Viscount Lascelles, Princess Mary, Major Sir Victor Mackenzie, Lady Diana Bridgeman and Lady May Cambridge. Seated, left to right: Lady Mary Cambridge, Princess Maud, Lady Rachel Cavendish and Lady Mary Thynne. (Weston Park)

Honeymoon at Weston Park in 1922. Mary is seated third from the right. Harry is standing second from the right. (Weston Park)

Four generations of the royal family in 1923: George V; his mother, Queen Alexandra; his daughter, Princess Mary; and her first-born son, George. (TuckDB Postcards)

The British Industries Fair, February 1933. Princess Mary with her brother Prince George, her mother, Queen Mary, and the Duke and Duchess of York. (Tuck DB Postcard)

A bronze bust of Princess Mary by F.E. McWilliam, on display at the Parkinson Building at the University of Leeds as a tribute to her chancellorship of the university. (Author's Own)

10 May 1954: Princess Mary receives an honorary degree of LLD from the University of St Andrews, one of eleven honorary degrees she received from various institutions during her lifetime. (D.C. Thomson & Co. Ltd)

August 1960: Princess Mary inspects the First Battalion of the Royal Scots in Dundonald.
(D.C. Thomson & Co. Ltd)

May 1964: Princess Mary presents colours to the Perth County and City branch of the Red Cross. (D.C. Thomson & Co. Ltd)

September 1964: Official visit to Newfoundland. (Royal Newfoundland Regiment Museum)

September 1964: Princess Mary meets veterans in Newfoundland. (Royal Newfoundland Regiment Museum)

Harewood House today. (Victoria Fletcher)

Bedales postcard image of Princess Mary, 1926.

Tuck postcard image of Princess Mary, 1915. (Ernest Brooks, Tuck DB Postcard).

Tuck postcard image of Princess Mary, 1930. (Speight, Tuck DB Postcard)

Bedales postcard of Princess Mary and Viscount Lascelles by Carl Vandyk, 1922. (Carl Vandyk)

# 13

# The Death of George V

He was the servant as well as the King of his people. His life was surrendered to Duty.[1]

Scotsman, Tuesday 21 January 1936

The 1930s would prove to be a significant period in Mary's royal life. As the older generation of monarchy began to decline and wrestled with increasing ill health, the next generation emerged and the prelude to a new royal era could begin. It would soon fall upon Mary to support her favourite brother, David, as he inherited the throne. In the New Year's Honours of 1932, George V bestowed the title of Princess Royal on Mary, the previous incumbent, the king's sister Princess Louise, Duchess of Fife, having died the year before. The title had first been used in 1631, when Charles I awarded it to his daughter Mary, thereby establishing the tradition of the title being awarded to the monarch's eldest daughter. Mary was the sixth princess to receive the title, and although it had little significance apart from distinguishing the holder from other princesses, the occasion was widely celebrated, especially in the north, where the *Yorkshire Post* reported that:

During the last ten years many cities and towns in the North of England have been honoured by a visit from Princess Mary, whose radiancy of disposition, unaffected manner and capacity for genuine sympathy and understanding, have intensified the loyal reception always accorded her.[2]

Queen Mary was now 65 years old and she needed her daughter to spend more time in central London in order that the new Princess Royal could begin to deputise for her mother and take on some of her patronages. With this in mind, in January 1932 Mary and Harry moved out of Chesterfield House and into 32 Green Street, Mayfair, purchased by Queen Mary as a present. The new residence was much smaller than Chesterfield House, being a four-storey red-brick town mansion forming part of the exclusive Grosvenor estate. It was built on the corner with Dunraven Street in 1897 as part of the early Georgian revival by the same architect, Sidney J.R. Smith, who had constructed the original Tate Gallery building in Millbank.

Although she spent a considerable amount of time in London, Mary still maintained her patronage of northern charities and organisations. Just a few examples of these include the opening of the Ministry of Pensions Hospital in Leeds, and two new wings of the nurses' home at the Leeds General Infirmary. In recognition of her contribution to Yorkshire, in July 1932 Mary became the first woman, as well as the first royal, to receive the freedom of the city of Leeds. The mayor stated that the award was 'symbolic of the charm and capacity a woman can carry into public life'.[3] In her acceptance speech, Mary expressed her pride at being the first woman to receive this honour. Harry spoke in his role as county lord lieutenant and added that by presenting this award to Mary, the city had shown:

> Two social principles …the first principle that the activity of a woman is real power in the World and that their beneficent influence is of real importance to a city like Leeds. The second is that it is not necessary to take an active part in … political life to play one's part in the World effectively.[4]

This seems an ambitious speech for him to make and it is evident that he was not merely offering his support to his wife's work, but acknowledging the increasing role that women were starting to play and the social reforms that were taking place. This was a time when many feminist groups including the Women's Freedom League and the London and National Society for Women's Services were active in such campaigns as adapting the social insurance system making it fairer for women, defending married women's right to work, increasing the number of female MPs and demanding equal pay, as well as the need for improvements in maternal health and wider availability of birth control.

In May 1932, Mary's life as a mother entered a new phase when her eldest son, George, went away to an all-boys' preparatory boarding school – Ludgrove at Cockfosters – at the tender age of 9. The school had a sporting tradition and it was customary for the children of the aristocracy to be sent to board at such a young age in preparation for their Common Entrance examination to enter public school. Harry had attended Eton College and therefore wanted his sons to maintain the tradition. Since local schools did not prepare pupils for entrance to Eton, Mary had to accept the inevitability of her sons leaving home at this young age. As someone who could repress her emotions, Mary had to demonstrate resilience and accept the inevitability of George's and ultimately Gerald's departure. Being the youngest member of the family, Gerald suffered most from his brother's absence and missed his companionship until he too left for Ludgrove. By all accounts, though, the active curriculum with a strong emphasis on outdoor pursuits meant that George found his experience at boarding school generally happy, apart from the loneliness, which was particularly keen at night, when he struggled to fall asleep. To compensate for her children's absence in term time, Mary would organise a hectic schedule for the school holidays. A stay with Harry's sister and brother-in-law Lord and Lady Boyne at Burwarton in Shropshire always proved popular for the boys, due to their affection for their Aunt Madge. Additionally, the holidays were spent attending royal events and house parties in London, staying at Windsor Castle and Buckingham Palace or going riding with their mother, watching football matches at Leeds and attending the York Races.

Mary was one of the hardest working members of the royal family. In addition, in the 1930s, it had become the expectation that a royal visitor would give a prepared speech at each engagement. This was quite demanding for Mary, not only because of her natural timidity, but since she frequently did several engagements in one day. Mary struggled to speak in public and found it challenging to compose speeches. In many of her letters it is apparent how onerous a task this was for her and a subsequent cause of continued anxiety, since Mary would often tie herself in knots and overthink her concerns prior to an event. Furthermore, the total of her engagements almost equalled the number that her brother David, the heir to the throne, undertook. However, for a period of about two years, Mary was unwell, and it was referred to in the family as her 'infirm state'.[5] Mary was frequently fixated with her health and she could be something of a hypochondriac; however, for once, this illness seemed serious.

In August 1933, at a luncheon in Rotherham, where he was deputising for his wife, Harry stated that the princess had become extremely unwell as a result of all the public engagements she had undertaken during the blistering summer heat. The official diagnosis at this stage was overstrain but there were reports of a nervous breakdown. It was quite a common diagnosis at this time, when, as Rev. Neville Davidson preached at Glasgow Cathedral, there was a prevalent 'atmosphere of restlessness and instability that many men and women in our times were overstrained, highly strung, easily upset'.[6] The seriousness of the illness was downplayed in the press, but Mary was unable to carry out any engagements for quite some time. She had lost over 2st in less than four months. Harry added further, 'I do think the public ... does ask a great deal of the Royal Family. I do not think the Public realise how few of them there are to do the very large number of functions.'[7]

There is no doubt that Princess Mary was suffering from overwork. During May and June alone, she had travelled to engagements in Manchester, Lancaster, Brentwood, Oswestry, Shrewsbury, Liverpool, Derby, Edinburgh and London. This was something that frequently concerned Queen Mary. Many years later she complained to Mary's eldest son, George, in the same way that she had complained to Harry before the Second World War: 'You must persuade her to do less.'[8]

At first, Mary's doctors had discovered a toxaemia, which they believed was caused by an infection in her appendix. She underwent an operation to remove her appendix in November 1933 for which an entire surgical unit was set up in her Mayfair home. The operation was performed by Sir Thomas Crisp English, illustrious as one of the first surgeons to carry out appendix operations, once considered incredibly difficult. The residents of the estate were equally concerned about Mary's illness and operation, with one explaining to the press that 'the Princess is very much our own and has mixed with us a great deal'.[9] Sir Thomas continued to check up on Mary's health for two weeks after the operation and, in recognition of his care and skill, she sent him a monogrammed piece of furniture. She continued to send him a Christmas card every subsequent year.

Mary was never particularly enthusiastic about travel overseas but for the purposes of her convalescence, in February 1934, she and Harry took a private cruise ship tour of the Mediterranean, stopping at Morocco, Gibraltar, Tangier, Egypt, Jerusalem and Palestine. While they were away, their eldest son George had to have a minor operation to remove an abscess on his neck. Messages were sent to Mary and Harry from the king and queen to keep them informed but it must have been a worrying period.

Upon their return to Harewood for Easter, it seemed that the warmer climate had a positive effect on Mary's health, and she appeared to improve, managing to attend the race meetings at Newmarket where, for once, Harry's horse Hempseed won. However, over the next few months, Mary began to struggle again and it was not until June 1935 that she was diagnosed and operated on for the condition of exoph-thalmic goitre, known as Graves' disease: an endocrine disorder often associated with stress and typified by an enlarged thyroid, bulging eyes and an increased heart rate or tremors. Two serious operations within just over eighteen months of each other and no sign of full recovery suggests that there was uncertainty among her doctors concerning her illness. Fortunately, this operation was successful and by the beginning of July, Mary seemed to be on the road to recovery, managing a brief trip to the races at Newmarket before returning home to Harewood to convalesce for the rest of the summer.

1935 marked the Silver Jubilee of George V and it should have been a time for great festivity but as Mabell, Countess of Airlie depicted in her memoirs, the king had been unwell for some time and the mood of the period was somewhat subdued:

> The King seemed tired and discouraged in the last two years before his death ... sometimes he felt bewildered in an epoch which was so alien to his whole mentality. Communism to him was still identified with the horrors of the Russian Revolution; he had a profound distrust of Fascism ... and considered Hitler's regime – rightly – a menace to the peace of the World. Most of all he was distressed by the industrial gloom in Britain ... he was surprised and wounded by the attacks levelled against the monarchy by some of the socialists.[10]

A national holiday on 6 May would see the culmination of public celebrations with a glorious procession from Buckingham Palace and a service of thanksgiving at St Paul's Cathedral. Street parties and celebratory events were organised throughout the country, and the commemorative day climaxed in an appearance on the balcony of the entire royal family including Mary and her sons. The king and queen were seen throughout the week taking carriage rides through London, accompanied by their granddaughters Princesses Elizabeth and Margaret. The many thousands who celebrated the event displayed, according to British Pathé, 'the most impassioned demonstration of loyalty within memory'.[11] The king recorded in his diary his disbelief at such devotion: 'I'd no idea they felt like that about me. I am beginning to think they must really like me for myself.'[12]

By the end of 1935, Mary's two younger brothers had married: George to Princess Marina of Greece in 1934 and Henry to Lady Alice Montagu Douglas Scott in November 1935. Of the king and queen's children only David, the direct heir to the throne, remained unmarried. David's unmarried status and his propensity for relationships with married women exasperated George. He had already told Prime Minister Stanley Baldwin that 'after I am dead, the boy will ruin himself in twelve months'.[13] As Prince of Wales, David had relationships with several women, including a sixteen-year affair with Freda Dudley Ward and one of five years with Thelma, Lady Furness. Like any infatuation, they usually petered out. However, by 1934 David was becoming increasingly dependent on the twice-married American Wallis Simpson, and she appeared to exercise an excessive influence over him. Wallis and her husband Ernest had been presented to the king and queen at a reception given at Buckingham Palace on 27 November 1934, just before the wedding of George and Marina. The king was incensed by what he regarded as the sheer effrontery of David parading his mistress before the court. The king's concern over the relationship was affecting his health considerably. Fortunately, by way of a gentleman's agreement with Lord Beaverbrook and Lord Rothermere of the British press and out of respect for the crown, nothing regarding David's private life had as yet been written in British newspapers.

After the Jubilee celebrations, the king confronted David about his personal life. David insisted that his relationship with Wallis was purely platonic and that he was not involved in an affair with her. The king appeared to accept David's explanation and he agreed to invite Wallis and her husband to the state ball and to Ascot.

As the Jubilee year drew to an end, George's health problems worsened and were compounded further by the death of his favourite sister, Victoria, known as Toria in the family, on 3 December 1935. Unsurprisingly, George was overwhelmed with grief for the sister he had been devoted to throughout his life and to whom he spoke daily on the telephone each morning. The state opening of parliament had to be cancelled and George never appeared in public again, although he did attend his sister's private funeral. A few weeks later on the 18 January 1936, it was finally announced in the press that the king was suffering from 'signs of cardiac weakness which must be regarded with some disquiet'.[14] The family assembled at Sandringham with Mary summoned from Yorkshire. They stood around the dying king's bed while he passed in and out of consciousness, and as David later recalled:

> While we were whispering together in the room, my father suddenly roused himself. He asked Mary whether she had been skating … My

father's mind must have been travelling back into the past and to the wonderful skating parties that he and the rest of us had there.[15]

The following day the king became progressively worse. Queen Mary took a walk with Mary, David and Bertie in the grounds and finally admitted that the family should prepare for George's imminent death. David travelled to London to inform the Prime Minister, Stanley Baldwin, of the king's condition. While he was away, a council of state had been appointed of the queen, David, Bertie, Henry and George in order to deal with state documents. As David later recalled in his auto-biography, 'when a King starts to die the whole world crowds in for the death-watch, to follow with morbid curiosity every detail in the pathetic process of mortality'.[16] Despite the assembled family members and officials, the house was eerily silent. As the end approached, the Archbishop of Canterbury travelled to Norfolk to pray with the king. George was given oxygen and a cardiac specialist, Sir Maurice Cassidy, was called for, but it was too late. The archbishop later recalled in his diary:

> The Queen was still amazingly calm and strong, the Prince of Wales full of vitality and talk, and touchingly attentive to the Queen ... Dawson consulted us about the famous bulletin – 'The King's life is moving peacefully to its close.' I put on my cassock and went with him to the King's room. The Queen and Princess Mary were there, with the doctors and nurses ... As it was plain that the King's life could only last for a few minutes, I felt that I must leave the Queen and her family alone ... I was told afterwards that the sons ... were painfully upset ... it was the Queen, still marvellously self-controlled, who supported and strengthened them.[17]

George was given a lethal injection of morphine and cocaine by his physician, Lord Bertrand Dawson, to ease his suffering and so that the King's death could be reported in the morning edition of the Times rather than in the evening papers. That afternoon, the Privy Council met at St James's Palace for the declaration of the accession of Edward VIII.

'Am brokenhearted',[18] Queen Mary recorded at the top of her diary entry for 20 January in bold letters. 'At five to twelve, my darling husband passed peacefully away. My children were angelic. He looked so peaceful … David very brave and helpful for he has a difficult task before.'[19]

The king's body was taken to the church at Sandringham and on Thursday 23 January moved to lie in state at Westminster Hall. On 27 January George's four sons stood guard over their father's coffin for twenty minutes; Queen Mary saw this as 'a very touching thought'.[20]

The funeral was 'a terrible day of sadness'[21] for the family. In her diary, Mary wrote: 'Dense crowds everywhere and silent. Only noise beside rumble of carriages and horses' hooves was orders to troops lining streets. Many people fainted in crowds. Most impressive service and mercifully I did not break down.'[22] Once again, as she did throughout her life, Mary suppressed her emotions. It was to prove a troubling omen for the year that lay ahead.

# 14

# The Abdication Crisis

How very kind of you to write to me. I appreciate it more than I can say … Last year has indeed been a very sad one for us all. I feel sure that things will be happier under our new King and Queen and that they will do their utmost to follow in my dear parents' footsteps. At the moment, I am recovering from a cold and have been voiceless since December 23rd … I have completely got over my operation and was very well until this cold came upon me … It seems a long time since we met. What an interesting visit to France I had in 1918.[1]

Letter from Princess Mary to Dr Rachel Crowdy, 2 January 1937

Ever your devoted sister, Mary[2]

Letter from Mary to her brother David, 7 October 1937

Thus began the year of 1937 for Princess Mary. 1936 had indeed been unbelievably sad for the family – although 'sad' is an understatement. The year had rocked the family in a cataclysmic, shocking manner that would take decades to overcome. They had all been affected on a personal as well as a public level. It would later be known as the Year of the Three Kings: George V, Edward VIII and George VI. It is clear from this letter that Mary was experiencing a physical manifestation of her angst. At the end of the letter she appears slightly whimsical in looking back to an earlier time in 1918, when as a family, they had dealt successfully with the challenges of the war and the uncertainty of their future as a royal family. It was duty that had taken them through the dark days of the Great War. Yet at a time when they should have been looking forward to a new monarch who was seen to have great 'charisma'[3] by both his family and his people, they were once again facing uncertainty regarding the future of the monarchy. It was no wonder that Mary felt despondent.

The sentiments shared by the whole country were the same as those later expressed by Mary's son in his autobiography, when he declared 'I know I found it as shattering as everyone else.'[4] David was condemned for putting private life above duty. 'But it was hard for the younger amongst us not to stand in amazement at the moral contradiction of a code of duty on the one hand and on the other the denial of central Christian virtues – forgiveness, understanding, family, tenderness.'[5]

Much has been written about the abdication over the subsequent decades. The attitude of the public was of shock and loss that a divorced American had stolen their king. There are those who believe that the country had a narrow escape from a king who wished to intrude into politics and failed to grasp the role of a constitutional monarch. Others might consider that his abdication over wishing to marry Wallis Simpson was merely a ruse to avoid the duty with which he had always struggled. Some may feel that his subsequent exile was a life wasted. Yet the abdication has never been considered from the angle of a sister to her brother or, more importantly, from a close sibling relationship. David and Mary were devoted to each other growing up and this remained the case throughout their lives. Mary frequently acted as peacemaker between her brothers and her parents. She was always self-less and diplomatic. She hated upsetting anyone, least of all her family. In a letter to David written on 7 October 1936, a few months before the abdication, we see Mary's need to tiptoe gently around members of her family for fear of upsetting them, even over something so innocu-ous as the correct attire and the appropriate time to move out of full mourning over the death of George V to half-mourning. We see how Mary reminds David of his devotion to his mother:

My Darling David,

While I was staying with Mama the question of mourning came up and Mama said she thought it would be nice if I wore half mourning till January. I said I would do so if she would like it. I felt however, I had better write and tell you this as it would not do for you and the brothers and sisters in law to go out of mourning if I was still wearing it … I feel I must tell you that you gave Mama great pleasure by accompanying her to Marlborough House when she moved there last Thursday. I know she was much touched …

Best love darling David, ever your devoted sister.[6]

Once the funeral of George V had passed, the new Edwardian age could begin and at first the signs were favourable since David had 'expressed determination to follow in his father's footsteps in upholding constitution government and asked for the Nation's support in his heavy task of sovereignty'.[7]

Throughout the dull early months of 1936, Mary stayed in London to look after Queen Mary, to aid in sorting through the king's letters and possessions and to help her mother with the move from Buckingham Palace to Marlborough House. Queen Mary relied on Mary more and more after the death of the king and Mary rose to the role of companion and comforter, scarcely seeing her children. They spent a great deal of time rearranging furniture and organising the division of spoils between family members. David had generously allowed Queen Mary to take any items that she needed. They often dined with David and with the Kents, George and Marina, as they discussed the redecoration of rooms at Marlborough and the packaging of Queen Mary's many objets d'art. In April, Mary returned to Harewood, where both she and her 11-year-old son Gerald had to deal with the measles.

During 1936 a family disagreement arose from David and Harry's mutual dislike; Mary's loyalties were tested to the utmost. Throughout the 1930s, David pursued a belief in the importance of upholding good relations with Germany as a means to avoid another war. David had been seen to associate with fascist sympathisers such as Oswald Mosley. In 1935, David made a speech to the British Legion urging them to 'stretch forth the hand of friendship'[8] to the Germans. The following day, David was summoned by his father, who was disturbed by what appeared to be David contravening the royal code of impartiality. However, when George V died, David maintained this belief of appeasement. There were such serious concerns about David in his political meddling that Stanley Baldwin asked MI5 to start surveillance on him, including phone tapping.

In April 1936 Harry, in his position as president of the West Riding Territorial Association, gave a speech, when opening the new drill hall, about the international situation:

> I recommend you read not so much the story of the last twenty years, but the story of the first twenty-five years of the last century. There you will find the story which is repeating itself today. That enormous upheaval produced Napoleon. Today both Mussolini and Hitler have been produced. We do not want to interfere with the internal political affairs of foreign countries. It is only when they come to use their methods outside their own country that we are obliged to become interested. If you examine the methods of Herr Hitler in his own country, you will find that it is very difficult to draw any parallel with them in any other walk of life except that of the gangster. This was where the Territorial Army must protect us … When you are talking with a highwayman or a gangster, you will do so much more comfortably if you are armed with a bullet proof shirt.[9]

Furthermore Harry congratulated the Territorial Army at a time when 'political leaders of every party were telling us that armed forces were unnecessary in order to secure the safety of our country and that our best way of keeping out of war was to have no means of defending ourselves'.[10] This political foresight angered David, who wrote immediately to Mary and told her that she had to stop Harry from speaking out in this manner. This admonishment came not from the fact that a member of the royal family had shown political bias, but that the opinion was not in keeping with David's belief concerning appeasement. Harry was, however, very much his own man and he certainly had no intention of listening to David even if he wished to placate his wife.

As 1936 progressed, David's reliance on Wallis augmented and her name appeared regularly on the court circulars as the king's official guest at functions. The family were certainly aware of David's fascination with Wallis Simpson, but they had never openly discussed it with him, hoping that he might lose interest in her given sufficient time and that he would grasp the absurdity and impossibility of marriage to a divorced woman who still had both former husbands living. Yet he would not, and this affair seemed far more serious than any previous friendships the prince had experienced. Queen Mary voiced her concerns to her lady-in-waiting Mabell, Countess of Airlie, when she asked if her children had ever given her cause for disappointment. 'I answered that I thought all sons … disappointed their parents at some time,' said Mabell. 'Yes, one can apply that to individuals, but not to a Sovereign.'[11]

During the summer of 1936 David and Wallis cruised aboard the yacht *Nahlin* in the Mediterranean and rumours circulated that Wallis was about to divorce her second husband with the inference that the king intended to marry her, although the British press still maintained their silence over the king's private life.

David made his intentions clear to Prime Minister Stanley Baldwin on 16 November 1936. The king was the head of the Church of England and the Church did not allow divorcees to remarry. Baldwin believed that the British people would consider the marriage to be morally wrong and would not support Wallis as queen. That night David dined with his mother and Mary at Marlborough House and afterwards, in his mother's boudoir, he expressed his desire to marry Mrs Simpson despite the opposition from Baldwin. Furthermore, he added that if necessary, he would abdicate. Both Mary and his mother listened with sympathy until they heard his threat to abdicate, which they met with utter shock and disbelief. They failed to comprehend how he could even consider giving up the throne. For, as David later recalled: 'My mother had been schooled to put duty, in the stoic Victorian sense before everything else in life. From her invincible virtue and correctness, she looked out as from a fortress upon the rest of humanity, with all its tremulous uncertainties and distractions.'[12]

David had once said of his sister, who resembled her mother greatly, with her innate sense of duty, that she would be far more suited to the role of monarch. As her own son later said of her in his memoirs, 'We did not talk of love and affection and what we meant to each other, but rather and even that not easily, of duty and behaviour and what we ought to do.'[13] David knew their perception of duty and yet he still implored both women to put this aside in favour of their familial loyalty to him and meet Wallis. He was convinced that this would enable them to understand his reasoning, yet 'the iron grip of Royal convention would not release them'.[14]

Cosmo Gordon Lang, the Archbishop of Canterbury, had severe concerns about the coronation ceremony and in administering the sacrament of Holy Communion, since at that time the Church was reaffirming its marriage laws and he considered such a marriage degrading to the monarchy. David suggested the idea of a morganatic marriage, a marriage between people of unequal social position with any children of the union having no claim on succession rights, titles or property. This was not unknown in Queen Mary's father's family, since her paternal grandfather, Duke Alexander of Württemberg, had married Countess Claudine Rhédey von Kis-Rhéde in 1835. The countess was considered non-royal by the German laws of succession. As far as it concerned David, a morganatic union would enable him to marry Wallis, but she would not become queen consort and any children of the marriage would not inherit the throne. David's idea was supported by Winston Churchill, a mere MP at the time, who wanted David to remain king, having known him since he was invested as the Prince of Wales. However, the morganatic plan was rejected by both the cabinet and the Dominion governments. David gave Baldwin an ultimatum: if he could not marry Wallis, he would abdicate.

Over the next few days, David informed his brothers of his situation. They needed to know because with increased reports in the American media, it was proving difficult to keep the British press quiet. Finally, the first comment concerning the relationship appeared in the *Yorkshire Post* on 2 December. The king's matter was being discussed by all people from the common man in the street to the aristocracy and members of parliament. Everyone had an opinion and on 4 December 1936 the *Daily Herald* reported: 'Within 48 hours it was general knowledge that a grave constitutional issue had arisen between the King and his ministers and the possibility of his immediate abdication had become the one topic of conversation from one end of the Empire to the other.'[15]

Mary and her mother attended church on 29 November, but David saw little of the two of them until he had made his decision. On 9 December Queen Mary wrote in her diary: 'Mr Walter Monckton [David's legal advisor] brought him and me the paper drawn up for David's abdication of the Throne of the Empire because he wishes to marry Mrs Simpson!!!!'[16] Never one to deviate from correct punctuation, the use of four exclamation marks by Queen Mary records her utter shock. She continues: 'The whole affair has lasted since Nov 16th and has been very painful. It is ... terrible ... to us all and particularly to poor Bertie.'[17] The Prime Minister informed the House of Commons of David's decision on 10 December. 'The more one thinks of their affair, the more regrettable it becomes.'[18]

After the abdication, David had to go into exile in Europe while his next brother, Bertie, became king. It was important in those days to maintain propriety and so David and Wallis needed to remain apart until Wallis's divorce was finalised. Wallis remained in Cannes in France with Katherine and Herman Rogers, close friends she had known since the 1920s. At 7 p.m. on 11 December, Mary and Queen Mary together journeyed to Royal Lodge to dine for the last time with David before he left for the Continent. They listened to the broadcast given by David from Windsor Castle, which, in spite of its contents, they considered dignified. David returned to Royal Lodge at 10.30 p.m. and the tension between him and his family appeared to have abated despite this being such an anguished and desperate occasion. Mary left to take Queen Mary back home and the brothers remained behind for a short while longer. The family said what they hoped would be a temporary goodbye to David, before he left for Austria where he would be the guest of Baron Eugen and Baroness Kitty de Rothschild (Kitty was a friend of Wallis) at Schloss Enzesfeld, situated south of Vienna. Mary, ever mindful of propriety, sent a letter to Prime Minister Stanley Baldwin, thanking him for helping the family through such a difficult time. In her diary, Mary expressed her shock and sadness at David's decision.

Bertie adopted the regal name of George VI, to signal that the crown would be returning to the traditional ways of George V. He was clearly terrified that he was ascending a throne that was about to crumble. The family needed to show unity. Queen Mary perhaps typified the family's reaction to David's abdication in believing that he had let both his family and his country down. Lady Airlie later recalled 'her unspoken condemnation of a Sovereign who had allowed his personal feelings to take precedence of his kingdom. I had realised then that her own nature, so gentle in her private life, had a side which was as steel.'[19]

In a letter to David in July 1938, Queen Mary expressed her feelings at the abdication:

> You will remember how miserable I was when you informed me of your intended marriage and abdication and how I implored you not to do so for our sake and for the sake of the country. You did not seem able to take in any point of view but your own ... I do not think you have ever realised the shock, which the attitude you took up caused your family and the whole Nation. It seemed inconceivable to those who had made such sacrifices during the war that you as their King refused a lesser sacrifice. My feelings for you as your Mother remain the same, and our being parted and the cause of it, grieve me beyond words.[20]

Queen Mary spoke of her feelings towards David as a sovereign and as a son as being two separate emotions. The same duality of feelings were exhibited by Mary, who was shocked by the abdication in the same way that the rest of the family were, yet she still maintained that she had a duty to David as his beloved sister. Mary felt that David's main fault lay in his inability to comprehend the gravitas of the situation. The full extent of her mixed feelings can be seen in her first letter to David sent a fortnight after the crisis on 21 December 1936. She may not have understood his actions, but her love and depth of feeling for her brother are clear. The reference to the prayer book is particularly touching.

> My Darling David,
> I have been thinking of you so much especially these last weeks and now you are away from all of us abroad. I hope you like the house where you are staying and are benefitting by the rest and change. The strain during those troubled days must have been very great for you as I know how much I have felt it. I am amazed at your leaving everything, but it is difficult often to understand someone else's feelings particularly one's own relations. I am hoping you do not feel very lonely and cut off. It is difficult to know what to wish you for xmas as it is not as if you were married yet. Still I send you my best wishes together with a prayer book. George told me that the night you left you wanted one. I am also sending you a small framed photograph of myself taken recently. I expect you have forgotten that in 1910 on your birthday you gave me a prayer book with Prince of Wales' feathers on it. This book has been everywhere with me ever since. Curiously enough the book I am giving you is green though a different shade to mine, it was the only good one …
> Best love darling David, your devoted sister Mary.[21]

Mary's duality of emotion was reflected in the divided mood of the nation. A muddle of overpowering sorrow and shock, along with feelings of disappointment and, of course, fierce antipathy towards Wallis, who would forever be considered by many to be the villain of the event. David was clearly in Mary's thoughts throughout the Christmas season. Her position of intermediary between her brothers and her parents had always meant that she acted as go-between, and this was no exception. Mary spent Christmas at Harewood trying to recover from her cold which prevented her from attending church on Christmas Day. She attempted to carry on as normal, sending her annual sprigs of white heather to her regiment of the Royal Scots in Edinburgh and donating to the fund to help repair the roof at York Minster. She journeyed to Sandringham on

16 January, where she lost no opportunity in speaking to Bertie immediately, to ask if it would be feasible for her to visit David in Austria. Bertie agreed, perhaps surprisingly as he had already refused the Duke of Kent a visit, and so Mary wrote to David with some possible dates.

The family left in England maintained a united front during this time, visiting Newmarket and Egerton House to inspect horses and attended church together, where a crowd of 3,000 loyally greeted the new king and queen. Queen Mary was surrounded by all her children and their families, apart from David. It was now exactly a year since George V had died and this was the first time in a long while that the family had been together. Understandably their thoughts continued to focus on the recent crisis.

Mary returned to Harewood where she carried out a few engagements. She deputised for Harry, who had been struck down with flu, and opened a boys' club in Shipley and the area conference of the women's section of the British Legion. Mary and Harry arrived in London from Leeds on 5 February. Before travelling to Vienna on the Orient Express and almost as if to seek approval for her imminent visit, Mary dined with her mother. She and Harry left London on 6 February and arrived in Vienna the following day to find David waiting for them on the platform looking lonely and forlorn.

He was living in a Louis XV-style castle. They were to stay for a week, acting as tourists as a means to avoid talking about the real reason for Mary's stay. The newspapers reported Mary's visit and observed that the Duke of Windsor embraced and kissed his sister. They arrived to a crowd of photographers and to cheers from well-wishers. To the newspapers it was considered 'a visit of sympathy and affection'[22] since it was well known that Mary had a vehement dislike of travel overseas. There were some untruthful reports circulating that Mary had been sent out to try and dissuade David from his marriage to Wallis. Herman Rogers, who was at the time with Wallis in Cannes, gave a statement to the *London Evening News* denying the rumours and stating that the marriage would go ahead as soon as possible.

David was hopeful that they would be able to discuss arrangements for his wedding: 'I'll be able to give them a lot to say and arrange for our wedding when they return.'[23] He naively believed the wedding would be a significant royal family event. The newspapers maliciously reported that David was still trying desperately to negotiate an acceptable financial settlement with his family. This incensed Wallis, who was overheard by Harry shouting down the phone to David.[24] Before their departure, David took Mary around the sights including Schönbrunn Palace and the little Palace Theatre, and they paid a private courtesy visit to the Austrian President Miklas.

On the return journey to Harewood, Mary and Harry stopped off at Marlborough House to inform Queen Mary of their visit. Once home, Mary wrote to thank David for his hospitality:

> My darling David
>
> ...
>
> We are most grateful to you for all your kindness and for the excellent arrangements you made for our visit which we much enjoyed ... If only the time had not gone so quickly. I cannot tell you how sad I felt at leaving you as I realise how lonely you must feel ... Mama seems well and I gave her your links and the list, the 'book' ... and she is most grateful for them all. I do want to thank you for the book you kindly gave me and the guide books etc ... I showed these to mama yesterday...
>
> Your devoted sister Mary.[25]

Upon his return, Harry mentioned to the new King George VI that he had been shocked by the Duke of Windsor's belief that his family would accept Wallis. 'I have a feeling that David has told her that she will be received by his family with open arms as soon as they are married and that his whole future will be jeopardised if she thinks this is not so. I am therefore very much afraid of intimate conversation.'[26] In her next letter to David, it is interesting that Mary never mentions Wallis or David's impending wedding. The closest she gets to showing how she feels is when she states, 'I do hope that you are not too lonely. I often think of you and those days we spent together.'[27]

David consulted the king through his close friend and cousin Lord Louis Mountbatten, known as Dickie to his family and friends, concerning the most suitable date for his wedding. Dickie had always presented himself as a faithful supporter of David, although his loyalties were torn since he had since been appointed as Bertie's personal naval aide-de-camp. Dickie visited David in Austria and he later claimed that he had offered to be David's best man. David agreed to delay the wedding until after the coronation on 12 May, unaware that his family would not be attending. On 5 May he received a letter from Mountbatten informing him that not one member of David's family or even the royal household would be present.

The glorious summer gave rise to a spectacular coronation at Westminster Abbey of King George VI and Queen Elizabeth. Events had taken place throughout the month of May and in a move to suggest continuity, the coronation had been very similar to that of George V in 1911 and the spectacle had done much to show a United Kingdom. Mary arrived at the abbey in her ermine robe and crown, flanked by her two young nieces Princess Elizabeth and Princess Margaret, and with her sons as pages.

David married Wallis on 3 June 1937, in front of a mere seventeen guests in the intimate setting of the music room at the Château de Candé in Monts in Touraine. A specially made altar was erected and a Church of England ceremony conducted by Rev. R. Anderson Jardine, who had volunteered to carry out the ceremony despite receiving a warning from the Bishop of Fulham telling him that he had no right to do so. The royal family were conspicuous by their absence, most of them, including Mary, choosing to be at the Coronation Derby at Epsom instead.

In October 1937, Mary maintained the incredibly diplomatic facade. It was almost as if she ignored speaking of David's abdication and marriage for fear of upsetting herself. Her letters begin to take on a more chatty tone, thanking David for sending stamps to her sons, giving details of riding with her boys, Queen Mary's rheumatism in her leg which still permits her to be 'as energetic as ever'.[28] 'Hoping you are flourishing.'[29]

In Mary's letters to David concerning the abdication crisis, we see that she did not cease to put her duty to him as a sister first. She may have appeared outwardly cold and distant – exhibiting the 'grit' of Queen Mary – but her letters reveal another side: that of a close sibling, wanting to understand and help. Mary did on occasion have to consult her mother about visiting or seeing David, not out of fear, but out of kindness and wanting not to upset her mother or Bertie. Mary was the great peacemaker. She had an immense sense of family, that as her son later recalled, 'was inculcated early on ... as with Queen Mary it was very strong indeed'.[30]

Despite Mary's loyalty to David, she clearly felt, as did most people, that David's abdication was, as Sir Alan Lascelles put it so succinctly, 'the most tragic might-have-been in all history'.[31] In November 1937, the *Daily Herald* contained details of action taken by the Duke of Windsor with regard to a book named *Coronation Commentary*, by Geoffrey Dennis. The book contained details of the supposedly more accurate series of events leading up to the abdication, namely that Wallis had been David's mistress prior to their marriage and that the real cause of the abdication was not that David wished to marry Wallis, but that his ministers 'wanted to get rid of him' and that he had been 'giving way to drink'. It refers to David cancelling an engagement in Aberdeen and sending his brother, Bertie, and sister-in-law in his place. It claimed that 'things left undone, duty neglected, papers curiously neo-Kaiserish way annotated ... muddling ... fuddling ... meddling'.[32]

Press attention on the Duke of Windsor continued throughout 1937 and indeed for the rest of his life. Mindful of the importance of supporting the new king, many articles started to appear criticising David for his behaviour when king and suggesting that the country had been fortunate that he had abdicated. In November the Labour MP Herbert Morrison had written an article advising that David needed to 'fade out' of public life: 'His visits to the distressed areas and his indication of impatience with the situation and even with the government were bound to be pleasing to our people but they were constitutionally dangerous.'[33]

The duke was clearly thinking of selling his story. On 2 December 1937 newspapers reported that he had decided no longer to authorise a biography by a well-known author, Mr Compton Mackenzie.

Mary threw herself back into a busy round of engagements supporting her charities, yet she would continue to see David whenever he visited England. Regarding David's abdication and subsequent life in exile, there were two important issues that were never resolved fully, that of the duchess's title not being of a Royal Highness; and the financial settlement. These would impact greatly on David's future behaviour and his relationships with his family.

# 15

# The Outbreak of the Second World War

We, no less than men, have real and vital work to do.[1]
Queen Mary, in the *Scotsman*, Monday 13 November 1939

By 1939, storm clouds were gathering throughout Europe with the expansion of the Third Reich, signifying that the prospect of war was increasingly inevitable. In March 1938 the Nazis, under Adolf Hitler, seized power in Austria by force, known as the Anschluss. Following this, Hitler claimed that his last territorial claim in Europe would be occupation of the Sudetenland, a predominantly German-speaking area in Czechoslovakia which had a natural fortified border with Germany. On 30 September 1938 the Munich Agreement was signed by Britain, France, Italy and Germany, without the agreement of the Czech government. This permitted the Germans to annexe Sudetenland in return for appeasement, which seemed to them a far better alternative to war. An elated Chamberlain returned to Britain on 30 September and was enthusiastically received as he stood on the balcony of Buckingham Palace with the king and queen. It was felt that this was the man who had managed to halt war and secure peace with the Nazis. Unfortunately, appeasement would ultimately fail, when in March 1939 Hitler invaded the rest of Czechoslovakia. The situation reached a general crisis in late August 1939 as German troops continued to mobilise against the Polish border.

For the royal family, it was business as usual. In July 1938 the king and queen made an official visit to France to show solidarity and to strengthen the bond between France and Britain. As a reminder of the circumstances Britain was attempting to avoid, namely war, their tour paid tribute to the First World War, beginning with the inauguration of the Britannia monument at Boulogne-Sur-Mer and ending with the Australian war memorial at Villers-Bretonneux. Likewise, the king and queen travelled to Canada and the United States in May 1939, in an effort to secure friendship and an alliance with American President Franklin D. Roosevelt. Mary and her two younger brothers were appointed counsellors of state following the Regency Act of 1937, to act on behalf of the monarch when he was abroad. This had been passed to account for the heir presumptive, Princess Elizabeth, being under 18.

Although the British were desperate to avoid another war, preparations were made just in case, with the anticipation that there would be high civilian casualties from German bombings. Barrage balloons were installed above cities and key industrial areas. Outside Buckingham Palace, sentries dressed in service khaki and helmets replaced the bearskin guards. Hospitals were evacuated of patients and sent to places of greater safety. Children in their thousands left their parents behind and went to live in the countryside under the care of their teachers. Similarly, at Sandringham the royal family including Mary and Harry had taken part in a mock air raid or an ARP drill and Bertie had recently purchased a fire engine for the estate.

For Mary, her anxiety concerning war must have been heightened since her sons were now well into their teenage years and would soon be of an age to carry out their National Service. George was almost 16. A popular boarder at Eton, he showed an interest in cricket, football and literature. In January 1939 newspapers contained details of the *Harewood News*. Typed by George and Gerald on a typewriter given to them by their father, the newsletter frequently contained reviews and details of films, theatre productions, sporting events, as well as gossip and racing tips supposedly from Harry. Many of these tips later featured in the National press. The newsletter was distributed to 200 readers on the estate as well as Queen Mary, who awaited its arrival with great anticipation. At one stage the newsletter caused some quite serious difficulties for the two boys with the War Office, when they published an article concerning an anti-aircraft gun site near Leeds, and they inadvertently revealed the classified information concerning other site locations around Leeds.

Mary, along with the rest of the family, had anxieties concerning David, who had been trying for several years to return to England. On 8 May 1939, David and Wallis had journeyed to Verdun in France for a tour of the battlefields. There, David was commissioned by American Network NBC to make what he considered a peace broadcast to America, which the BBC refused, for a variety of reasons, to broadcast. David, who had witnessed at first hand the devastation of the First World War, believed that something should be done to prevent another war. It was meant to be 'an appeal to reason in light of World conditions'.[2] David called upon Europe to settle its differences through negotiation rather than by taking arms. The speech was heard by millions and although he had many supporters, it was considered defeatist by the government and an act of unwarranted meddling by the royal family. David was interfering in matters that did not concern him:

> I break my self-imposed silence now only because of the manifest danger that we may all be drawing nearer a repetition of the grim events that happened quarter of a century ago … I speak simply as a soldier of the last war whose most earnest prayer that such cruel and destructive madness shall never again overtake mankind.[3]

The broadcast was heavily criticised and David was forced to issue a statement declaring that he had been 'sincerely convinced … a personal and non-political message might be of some value'.[4]

The family was no doubt exasperated by David at a time when his relationship with his mother was further strained concerning the dedication of his father's tomb. David had given £4,000 when he was the monarch to build George V's tomb for St George's Chapel. In return he had asked to be informed when the tomb would be dedicated. He knew he could not attend but he still insisted on being told. The ceremony took place on 12 March 1939, David received no notice and he held Queen Mary to blame for this slight, which made him furious.

On 23 May, Queen Mary had been returning to Marlborough House in her maroon Daimler limousine with Lord Claud Hamilton, her comptroller, and Constance Milnes-Gaskell, her lady-in-waiting, when her car was hit by a 2-ton lorry containing a load of steel ARP sirens. No one was killed; however, the car was overturned, and Queen Mary found herself thrown out of her seat and across the feet of Lord Claud. The passengers were trapped in the vehicle and men with hammers and stepladders rushed to free the passengers. A lady who lived nearby came to help Queen Mary and took her into her home where she gave her a strong cup of tea and some aspirin. Queen Mary was badly bruised on her back with a damaged left eye which meant that she had to wear a patch. Her stoicism had endeared her greatly to the British press and to the neighbouring lady who had provided her with refreshment that day. Mary wrote telling David of the accident and Queen Mary was very touched by David's apparent concern for her. Although Mary was troubled by her mother's accident, this did not prevent her fulfilling a royal engagement at the Memorial Hospital at Haverford West in Dyfed on 25 May and Mary agreed to deputise for her mother during her convalescence,

By March 1939, and in contravention of the agreement in Munich, Hitler occupied the rest of Czechoslovakia. He strengthened ties with Japan and formed a military alliance with Italy before invading Poland in September. Prime Minister Neville Chamberlain issued an ultimatum to Hitler to withdraw from Poland, but his request was ignored. By 3 September, Britain was once again at war with Germany.

The Duke of Windsor arrived in London in September 1939 to see the king, believing that war might signal the end of his exile. The purpose of his visit had been to discuss two possible roles that had been offered to him: deputy regional commissioner to Sir Wyndham Portal in Wales or liaison officer with No. 1 British Military Mission to French GCHQ under General Howard-Vyse. The latter was more appealing to the duke and he accepted it. None of the other members of the family were aware of his visit and no arrangements were made to accommodate him with the family. The only person who gave David a cordial welcome was Winston Churchill, who had just been appointed First Lord of the Admiralty in the war cabinet, a position he had held during the First World War.

As soon as war was declared, Queen Mary was inundated with offers of help, especially with regard to nursing services. She issued a statement on 19 September expressing her gratitude for the swift call to service by so many women. Furthermore, along with her daughter, she acknowledged the members of Princess Mary's Royal Air Force Nursing Service. In a special feature on 'What well-knowns are doing today', the *Sketch* showed a photograph of Princess Mary in her ATS uniform inspecting troops. During the war, Mary relished the opportunity to journey to wherever she was needed and undertake engagements throughout the UK. Many of these involved the armed forces or organisations such as the Red Cross and Voluntary Aid Detachments. She was rarely seen out of uniform. *Tatler* reported that Mary 'is setting a magnificent example to the country in the matter of pulling one's maximum weight against those unpleasant things we are fighting'.[5] Mary was in better health since the outbreak of the war and appeared far more self-assured and less nervous in public. She only suffered from minor illnesses during the war including a nasal operation in May 1940 to alleviate some of the symptoms of hay fever that she experienced.

It was felt that Queen Mary would be safer if she moved away from London to the country to stay as a guest of her niece, the Duchess of Beaufort at Badminton in Gloucestershire. Queen Mary transplanted her entire household of over sixty people, which must have been quite daunting for the duke and duchess. Mary continued to visit her mother, sometimes spending several days with her. At Badminton, Queen Mary developed an obsession with clearing the estate. She disliked untidiness and she abhorred living amid anything that was not neat. She took it upon herself to rid the grounds of ivy, hedges, brambles and weeds, using a variety of implements and enlisting the additional support of any lady-in-waiting or visitor. This was called 'wooding'. Even Mary was not immune from being called upon to give a hand when she visited her mother.

When the Second World War broke out in September 1939, restoration work on Harewood had only just been finished. During the First World War, Harewood had been used as a hospital for officers. In 1940 Mary and Harry decided that it should once again be used as a convalescent hospital, the west wing and the long gallery becoming a makeshift ward, the paintings protected by hardwood, while the family moved into the east wing. Other paintings and treasures were stored in the sub-hall under the main entrance. Mary regularly invited women from the Princess Royal Hospital supplies depot to sew and prepare items needed for hospitals and convalescent homes and to help knit jumpers for the Navy League. A doctor was put in charge of the hospital and a matron managed two sisters and fifteen young VAD nurses, with Mary assisting at times. There were six orderlies to carry out the cleaning and serving of food. The convalescents were mainly suffering from burns, machine-gun wounds, smashed legs and pneumonia. Many of the patients felt that their experience was palatial compared to the severities of war and there was much to make their experience on an estate enjoyable. The land on the estate had been given over to fruit and vegetables to supplement rationing, and patients benefited from the supplements to rationing of fresh eggs, chickens, pheasants, grouse, rabbits and hares.

Harry was equally determined to do his part in the war effort. He inspected cadets and marshalled every man on the Harewood estate into his own Dad's Army. Equipment was limited, as were uniforms, which were often far too big or small. The hospital continued to care for patients until well after the war in 1947. Ronald Rooke, who wrote a diary of his experience in the British army during the war, recalled that Mary was a frequent sight in the north of England during the war and would often call in to see troops and have dinner with them in camp. Patients would play bridge, listen to music or read or even take walks in the extensive grounds and Mary organised additional entertainment including films once a week and concerts. There would sometimes be dances where the nurses, orderlies, kitchen staff and officers all joined in. On more than one occasion, Mary would even dance with an officer herself.

# 16

# War Work

I am so glad to see ATS girls doing new kinds of work ... that really releases men.[1]

The Princess Royal, in the *Newcastle Evening Chronicle*, Tuesday 28 October 1941

British Pathé newsreels from the Second World War show an abundance of monochrome film in which Mary is inspecting troops, frequently row upon row of women, and always turned out in her immaculate uniform of the Auxiliary Territorial Service (ATS). Throughout the war Mary visited and inspected many units of the ATS as Yorkshire controller, eventually becoming controller commandant in 1941, an honour of which she was immensely proud.

The origins of the ATS are to be found as early as 1916, when the Women's Army Auxiliary Corps was founded as a voluntary service patronised by Queen Mary. The corps had been involved in many vital non-nursing positions such as cooks, cleaners, telephonists and clerks. Since 1920 talks had been held to establish a peacetime corps of women but this took much time owing to lack of funding and the reluctance of male servicemen to accept the important role women could play. The discussions became more formalised from 1934 and eventually on 9 September 1938 a royal warrant was issued establishing the new Women's Auxiliary Territorial Service.

In a letter to Captain Margesson, the Secretary of State for War, Mary wrote of her delight at being associated with the service: 'I am very proud indeed to accept … May I say how interested I am to inspect the ATS in various parts of the country and I have been impressed during recent months to see what a high standard of efficiency has been reached.'[2] A new military law had been passed concerning the conscription of women; at first this was only for childless widows and single women from 20 to 30 years of age, as a woman's priority was still seen to be caring for her family. However, as the war progressed, the age limit was amended to women from 19 to 43. Many more women with families signed up, requiring the introduction of nurseries and more flexible working hours. Women were not required to fight, and the majority signed up for civil defence or the Land Army.

Mary's royal patronage of the ATS did much to show the value and prestige of the service and she was involved in all aspects from dress to personnel, to the decision of a befitting name. As an avid listener of the wireless radio and someone who carried one wherever she went, Mary understood its immense power as a form of communication and as a means to promote a cause. In June 1940, she gave an impassioned broadcast on BBC Radio appealing for women to join up to the ATS, stating that, 'the time has come for every woman in the country to answer the call to service. Do you realise that every girl you can see wearing an ATS uniform is replacing a soldier and thus increasing our fighting strength?'[3]

In 1950 when giving a speech to 5,000 service and ex-service women at the Royal Albert Hall, to celebrate the fourth annual reunion of the Queen Mary Auxiliary Corps, Mary explained how her association with the ATS came about:

It may perhaps interest you to know that my association with the A.T.S. almost came by accident. A commandant had to be found for the West Riding and my husband had some difficulty in finding someone suitable. Partly as a joke, I asked if I should be suitable … and before I knew where I was, I found myself in the Service. That was certainly a very happy chance for me, and I can only say that it has given me the greatest pride.[4]

Over 250,000 women, from a wide cross-section of social backgrounds, worked for the ATS during the Second World War. In many ways it enabled some women to learn new skills and break free from menial careers in domestic service and in factories. Women were able to take on management roles within the ATS, something that few could aspire to in the interwar years. Following from her aunt's example, Princess Elizabeth joined the Service in 1945, learning basic car mechanics and driving an ambulance. It took a great deal of time for the work of the ATS to be accepted by men. Mary herself became exasperated at the way in which men perceived the service, some women even being referred to by soldiers as 'officers' groundsheets'. Eventually the ATS took on many vital roles during the war, leading to the realisation that women had a substantial role to play in the war effort not merely in freeing men to go to the front line, but in serving as mechanics, drivers and telephonists and working alongside aircraft gunners as 'gunner girls'. At the start of the war the women mainly worked in the United Kingdom but by the end they were seen worldwide including in Africa, Europe, the Caribbean and the USA. Furthermore, they partnered with regiments of the Royal Ordnance Corps, the Royal Artillery, the Royal Engineers and the Royal Signals Corp.

As Mary would later say in her preface to Dame Leslie Whateley's story of the ATS, *As Thoughts Survive*, 'the ATS started with many disadvantages of inexperience, but with the great advantage of enthusiasm. From out of this there grew a solid regimental discipline and true military adaptability.'[5] Mary visited the various different regions of the ATS throughout the war, attended nearly all of the monthly conferences and frequently met the ATS directors at Marlborough House, showing an incredible familiarity with the service. Mary's involvement with the ATS would be described later by Leslie Whateley:

> I had already heard of the intense interest she (Mary) had in our Service, and that this did not rest at inspecting units and attending various Headquarter conferences. Those with whom she came into contact had only to mention that someone was ill, or something

urgently needed, and the Princess Royal never spared herself until the need was met. The invitation to stay the night was just another instance of her thought and kindness to us all.[6]

Leslie Whateley gives one example of Mary's intervention and ability to solve problems. The ATS had needed a restroom for the women working for the Royal Corps of Signals in the War Office. It seemed an impossibility. As Mary was leaving the offices one day, a note was thrust into Leslie Whateley's hand from a senior signals officer asking Leslie to consult Mary. Mary asked to see the note and smiled. A short time later, a restroom was provided courtesy of the princess.

In addition to her work with the ATS, Mary was commandant-in-chief of the British Red Cross and controller of the West Riding Territorial Service. Her life of public service during the Second World War became even more demanding with a relentless schedule of engagements. In the first four months of 1942 alone she helped to raise morale by visiting seven different RAF station hospitals run by the Princess Mary Nurses. Mary frequently visited five military commands, Commonwealth regiments stationed in the UK and often toured gun posts. Along with her work with the services and in visiting hospitals, Mary took on several civilian charitable organisations continuing her work with the Girl Guiding movement, the YMCA and the League of Mercy.

Just as George V had recognised the importance of the royal family being on display during the First World War, George VI maintained this tradition and the royal family were permanently on show, frequently visiting towns and cities that had been bombed. Mary went to witness for herself the devastation caused in many bomb-damaged northern towns. She paid numerous trips to Sheffield since it was a heavy industrial city with steelworks and armaments factories. Her involvement with Sheffield formed part of her work for the Air Raid Precautions Committee. Mary supported the Navy League, the Sea Rangers and the NAAFI, along with organisations to provide comforts to servicemen and women stationed overseas. Mary's relentless work during the Second World War resulted in her receiving the award of honorary rank of general in the British Army in 1956.

Mary was still attached to the Royal Scots as colonel-in-chief and inspected her regiment many times during the war, although for reasons of national security this was not often publicised. By 1940, Mary was colonel-in-chief of six further military regiments: the Royal Corps of Signals, the Indian Corps of Signals, the Canadian Scottish, the Australian Signals Corps, the Royal Canadian Signals, and the Royal New Zealand Signals Corps. Mary's association with the Royal Signals Regiment had begun in 1935 when George V had appointed her its colonel-in-chief. The Royal Signals were a mounted regiment and it seemed a fitting association in light of Mary's prowess in horse riding.

In April 1940, while on a visit to inspect the YMCA canteen at Harrogate, soldiers from the regiment were travelling and offered the opportunity to stop and have refreshments in order to see the princess. Mary spoke to the men and discovered that their favourite meal was egg and chips. She inspected her favourite place to visit at a service base – the kitchens – and gave the chip pan a customary shake before stopping to ask a man playing darts how he managed to carry out each shot. This lack of formality and ability to relate to others ensured that many people were often subsequently shocked when they were later told who she was. Mary took an interest in two Commonwealth regiments stationed in the United Kingdom and became their commander-in-chief: the Royal Canadian Signals Corps and the Canadian Scottish Corps. In 1940 Mary visited the Royal Signal Corps and took part in sending a message photographed using a special process which sent it onto a different device in another room. It was in essence a very early fax message.

Perhaps Mary's most significant contribution during the Second World War was her work for the Regional Blood Transfusion Service health campaign in 1941. During the war there was an enormous need for blood transfusions, and donation centres started to form across the country. On 3 February Mary broadcast a speech on the radio promoting the importance of giving blood for both servicemen and women and citizens, who could be injured in air raids, road, industrial and mining accidents or even just for routine operations. A week later, few donors came forward owing to a lack of understanding of the process. Mary realised that something more substantial needed to be done to promote the campaign. She thus agreed to give a donation at the Leeds School of Medicine in front of invited members of the press. While she gave blood, she expressed delight at how painless the procedure was and spoke of the importance in the Leeds and West Riding areas of donating. Mary's campaign was so successful in breaking down concerns the public had over donating blood that over 10,000 people in the local area signed up within a week. The National Blood Transfusion Service was finally established in 1947.

Back at home, Harry was almost 60, an age considered quite elderly at the time. In September 1941 he underwent a minor operation, for which he spent time in a nursing home. Although he had 'some very uncomfortable days'[7] he recovered in time to attend the British Legion County Conference in Hull on 22 November, since he and Mary were both distressed that Hull was 'having such a bad time'[8] with the bombings. Hull became the most seriously damaged city during the war with half of the city eventually destroyed and 95 per cent of houses damaged. From the early months of 1941 it suffered several serious intensive raids from the Luftwaffe right through until July.

As was to be expected during wartime, there were some difficult and sorrowful times ahead for the family. In 1942 the royal family were hit by an incredible tragedy involving Mary's by now youngest brother, George, Duke of Kent. By all accounts George's marriage to Princess Marina was happy and they had three children together: Prince Edward (born in 1935), Princess Alexandra (1936) and Prince Michael (1942). Queen Mary was especially fond of George as he shared her passion for collecting and she thought the marriage was strong, since 'the women of that … family make good wives. They have the art of marriage.'[9] The couple lived in Coppins in Buckinghamshire (inherited from Princess Victoria) and while Queen Mary resided at Badminton, George paid her frequent visits, where they would call on the antique shops of Bath. The duke served with the RAF during the war and on 24 August 1942 he set off by plane from Scotland to fly to Iceland to inspect RAF bases. The aircraft crashed on Eagle's Rock near to Dunbeath in Caithness; all of the passengers and crew were killed apart from one, Flight Sergeant

Andrew Jack, who was a rear gunner in the craft. George was only 39 years old and was the first member of the royal family in nearly 500 years to die in active service. His body was taken first to Dunrobin and afterwards to St George's Chapel, Windsor, for the family service.

George's funeral took place on 29 August. It was thought inappropriate to hold a large funeral during the war when so many people had lost their lives in service, so his was that of a member of the Royal Air Force. The family were devastated by his death, but Queen Mary recognised that she needed to support the duke's young widow for the sake of their children. David was equally sorrowful over his brother's tragic demise but was unable to return to England from the Bahamas, where he had been appointed governor-general. He therefore attended a memorial service at Nassau Cathedral and, according to one of his aides, he 'broke down at the beginning and wept like a child all the way through'.[10] Queen Mary spent a few days at Coppins, and returned to Badminton where Mary, cancelling some of her engagements due to mourning, visited for a few days to console her mother and to continue Queen Mary's battle with the 'wooding'. Queen Mary recorded in her diary: 'I am so glad I can take up my occupations again – Georgie would have wished me to do so.'[11] Following on from the Duke of Kent's death, Mary became the president of Papworth Hospital. It had been founded in 1918 as a hospital to aid discharged soldiers in recovering from tuberculosis. Mary had visited the hospital with her parents after the First World War. The Duke of Kent had been the grand master of English Freemasonry; his death meant that all lodges went into a period of Masonic mourning for six months and his successor was Harry, who was installed in June 1943 by his brother-in-law George VI.

In October, Mary visited Belfast for the first time since 1928. As with her first visit, she received a warm welcome and was distressed to see how greatly the city had been damaged by air raids. The purpose of Mary's trip had been to visit hospitals and witness for herself the Ulster war effort, particularly the work of women. She began with the Samaritan hospital, a place she had previously visited in 1928. The hospital had expanded a great deal since she had last seen it to include a nursery wing and a nurses' home. Mary's next point of call was the Belfast Hospital for Sick Children, where she spoke to many child patients including an 11-year-old boy who had been badly injured by a bomb blast and two children hurt by American army vehicles. Mary expressed her concern for the number of street accidents that were occurring and yet passing virtually unnoticed. Her visit included calling in on the Ulster Gift Fund headquarters to see knitted comforts and hospital supplies that were being sent out to troops. Mary inspected a parade of ATS women the following day and proceeded to a military station of the Royal Corps of Signals and a military hospital, where she was impressed by the first mobile canteen made rather ingeniously from a converted pram.

In October 1942, the First Lady of the United States, Eleanor Roosevelt, paid a visit to England with American troops to inspect British forces and to meet the king and queen. She was greatly impressed by the work women were doing, especially work which had previously been undertaken only by men. Mrs Roosevelt stayed overnight with Queen Mary at Badminton, and Queen Mary presented her with two photographs of herself sawing wood. Mrs Roosevelt met and dined with Mary, who was staying with her mother at the time. Mrs Roosevelt spent an hour in conversation with her two hosts and was impressed that the pair continued to knit comforts throughout their conversation in a kind of unremitting unison. Mrs Roosevelt was immensely impressed by Mary, who seemed a mine of knowledge on all aspects of the war and the work of women, but she later admitted to finding it somewhat problematic trying to navigate all the points of etiquette in a royal household.

# 17

# Prisoner of War

It was all rather pointless and foolish, but they thought we could be useful as hostages, and we had to take this at its face value.[1]

George Lascelles, Lord Harewood,
*The Tongs and the Bones*

A little after his nineteenth birthday, Guardsman 2622986 joined the family regiment of the Grenadier Guards. Known to his family as George, Viscount Lascelles was inevitably concerned by his new role, renaming the date the 'End of Civilisation'[2] in his diary. Initially trained at the Guards' Depot in Caterham in Surrey, George later said of his training experience that 'there was a period of intense physical activity, much square drill, some rifle and other military training and quantities of good plain food'.[3] Following this instruction, he was given a short reprieve of a few hours and permitted to visit his mother at Windsor Castle until the following day. After a mere eight weeks of basic training, George was sent to Sandhurst where he found his new life, 'arduous and ... militarily less than complete'.[4] He was afterwards sent to Windsor for the final stage at Wellington barracks. While awaiting deployment overseas, George spent an enjoyable week with his mother in London visiting theatre shows and sampling restaurants. Eventually he found himself in Algeria.

Unfortunately, by June 1944, George had been wounded and captured by the Germans at Monte Corno on the Italian front. A statement was released from Harewood stating that 'Princess Mary's son ... is reported wounded and missing and believed to be a prisoner of war.'[5] Harry later revealed the full story to an audience at a luncheon in Hull:

> Viscount Lascelles was on a patrol covering a party of Royal Engineers, who were clearing roads ... when he was wounded ... He was apparently too ill to move, so he was put into an Italian house close by and an ambulance was sent for. That was all that was officially known, except that the ambulance was found next morning on the road without any sign of men in it ... There had been a minor German counterattack at that moment which caused the capture of Viscount Lascelles ... One is proud of knowing that his misfortunes are the result of an attempt to execute his duty to the best of his ability.

George was incarcerated at Colditz high-security prisoner-of-war camp. As the nephew of the king, George was one of what was termed *Prominente* prisoners, meaning they were the relatives of VIPs, considered a possible bargaining tool by the Nazis. Other *Prominente* included the nephew of Queen Elizabeth and the nephew of Winston Churchill through his wife, Clementine. Adolf Hitler signed George's death warrant in March 1945 but the SS general, Berger, the commander of the camp, refused to sanction this knowing that the war was coming to an end. George was eventually released to the Swiss. During his time in prison George had been able to listen to between 500 and 700 records from the camp's library, which no doubt explained his later passion for classical music and opera. It was said that few could equal his musical knowledge.[7] George was released in May 1945 but was able to write to his family from late 1944.

During George's time as a prisoner, Mary and Harry were understandably terrified of what might happen. Mary received many messages of support and she was able to report in November 1944 in a letter to Dame Rachel Crowdy that George had recovered fully from his wounds and although it was 'a very guarded letter ... and one can only hope things will not be so hard in this camp'.[8]

Fortunately, Mary's younger son Gerald was not in such a precarious position. At first Gerald worked in a munitions factory under an assumed name and later served in The Rifle Brigade. He was stationed in Holland and would write long descriptive letters to his parents.

In August 1945, Lord Harewood had undergone a serious operation following a period of ill health lasting several weeks, which meant that he had to cancel many engagements. The newspapers reported that 'it seems not unlikely that the strain of waiting for tidings of his son ... may have impaired the Earl's physique and lowered his powers of resistance'.[9] Mary had been anxious about the surgery but in a letter to her Mother on 20 August she wrote: 'I am more than glad to be able to send a good report of Harry and now you will see in the papers that his progress is very satisfactory.'[10] Mary had chosen to inform the newspapers of her husband's illness possibly in a move to prevent misinformation.

As much as Mary had been concerned over her husband's health, she had concerns over her son, who had recently returned from being held as a prisoner of war and was obliged to return to the army until at least late in 1946. In an appendage attached to a letter to her mother and headed, 'PRIVATE', Mary explained that George was 'rather unsettled and I fear rather dreading the thought of going back to the military square'.[11] Mary consulted her mother for advice about George's future position in the army:

Harry and I have been wondering as to the possibility of George going on somebody's staff but till VJ Day arrived, hardly liked to suggest it. We even wondered whether he might go to Uncle Alge. I did just mention the possibility to George who sounded rather pleased about it. Of course, I don't know at all, whether Uncle Alge has a vacancy or would be willing to take George nor do I know what Bertie would think about it. If you think this suggestion might do, may I leave it to you to deal with as you think best ... Am so sorry to bother you about this but feel you will understand.[12]

Uncle Alge was Queen Mary's brother Alexander, 1st Earl of Athlone, who was governor-general of Canada. Mary, with her belief that her position should not afford her certain privileges, was for once requesting something that was most uncharacteristic of her; she was asking her mother as a former queen to intervene and give George a much safer position. However, given that he had just returned from Colditz and little sympathy was given to the emotional wellbeing of soldiers, and nor was there any awareness of post-traumatic stress disorder, it is not surprising that Mary did this. She was clearly trying to ensure that her husband did not have to suffer further worry over his son after his operation and she needed to protect her family. The extent to which Queen Mary intervened is not clear, but George did serve his last year as a soldier as aide-de-camp to his great-uncle.

After VE day in June 1945 Mary accepted an invitation from the National Young Men's Christian Association to visit Northern Ireland as the guest of the governor and Duchess of Abercorn and to receive purses on behalf of the YMCA War and National Service Fund Appeal, which provided amenities for servicemen who were stationed there including eighty canteens, tea cars, a mobile library and seven huts. Her schedule for the four-day visit was packed with visits to inspect the Hillsborough branch of the Red Cross along with inspecting other Red Cross detachments, a gala performance at the Empire Theatre in Belfast, a visit to the Samaritan hospital which she had opened in 1928, a visit to the Hay Park children's hospital, a visit to see Irish linen and a rayon cloth factory. She inspected units of the ATS and detachments of the Women's Legion in Northern Ireland and visited the Ulster Girl Guides at Ravenhill Rugby Grounds. Although peace had been declared in Europe, this was a significant appeal for the YMCA as they still needed to support armies who were fighting in the Far East and give support to servicemen and women who were returning to civilian life.

The war finally came to an end on 2 September 1945 when Japan formally surrendered. It had lasted for just over six years and it would take much longer before a sense of normality was restored. The sense of duty and stoicism shown by Mary and other members of the family against Nazi Germany and their contribution to raising public morale had led to a surge in public esteem for the royal family, who were perceived to have fought the war together with their people. David may have given up his people for Wallis Simpson, but George VI and the rest of the family had done much to restore their people's trust.

# 18

# Death of Harry

Twenty-five years of perfect love and companionship.[1]

Princess Mary's tribute to her husband

The British winter of 1946–47 was particularly harsh, with freezing temperatures and heavy snow leading to further hardship. With disruptions to fuel supplies and power and the deaths of many animal herds, some businesses had to close temporarily, and communications were disrupted. Mary and Harry were fortunate in that both their sons returned alive from the war, and yet the concern over their eldest son had impacted greatly on them both, especially Harry. From 1945 onwards, Harry's health appeared to decline. He had several internal operations with a further one in May 1946.

Furthermore, the task of returning the house to its former condition was onerous since Harewood continued to be used as a hospital and convalescent home until the spring of 1947. The hospital needed to be taken apart, many rooms needed restoring to their previous use and works of art and furniture had to be returned to their original positions. Much had deteriorated during the war, as there had been insufficient time and money to carry out any necessary repairs. With Harry unwell and both sons away (George was a student at Cambridge and Gerald was working in Germany), much of the work had to be put on hold.

In early 1947, Mary and Harry went to stay at the Imperial Hotel in Torquay to celebrate their twenty-fifth wedding anniversary. It was hoped that the weather would be slightly better in the south to aid Harry's health. David sent Mary a commemorative gift of a silver bell and she was touched by this gesture. For the first time, Mary had begun to acknowledge Wallis in her letters to David, enquiring over her health, suggesting that antipathy towards Wallis was diminishing. They returned to Harewood in the midst of the worst blizzard of the century. At the end of April, Harry seemed to be slightly better for a short time, as he presided at a grand festival of English Freemasons in London, where he was re-elected as grand master.

It was announced in the newspapers at the end of May that Lord Harewood was now suffering from cardiac complications and bronchial asthma. Plans to open the house to raise money for the Queen's Institute of District Nurses were put on hold. George was told to come home immediately, only to find his father laughing that the doctors had sought fit to contact Gerald and tell him to return from Germany. Despite his stoicism, Harry died at 1.15 a.m. on 24 May 1947 following a heart attack. Upon hearing of her brother's death, Harry's sister Margaret, Viscountess Boyne, said to Mary, 'You and I know that the world can never be the same again.'[2]

Queen Mary sent a wreath of pink and white carnations 'in loving remembrance from a devoted mother-in-law'.[3] Mary's tribute was a cross of Harry's favourite rhododendrons and, in a rare public show of emotion, she wrote 'In gratitude for twenty-five years of perfect love and companionship.'[4]

George VI flew up to Leeds to attend the earl's funeral. The simple ceremony was held in the All Saints' Church in the grounds of Harewood. To the newspapers, Harry was one of the 'outstanding Yorkshireman of his generation'.[5] Memorial services were held on Thursday 29 May at York Minster, which Mary and her sons attended, and at St Mark's Church, North Audley Street, where Mary and Harry had worshipped when in Mayfair. The London service was attended by members of the royal family, as well as Masonic dignitaries.

For Mary, the shock of Harry's death proved to be overwhelming. In a letter to Lucia, 8th Viscountess of Arundell, dated 28 August, she wrote apologising for not attending Lucia's daughter Mary Monckton-Arundell's wedding:

I said how very sorry I was not to be able to attend [the] wedding on account of being in mourning ... as you will realise my beloved Harry's death is a shattering blow, but I am doing my best to carry on as he would wish. I am fortunate in having my two sons to make a home for.[6]

Harry's death was perhaps something Mary had naively never considered, and her son George later explained this:

During my father's life, she found it uncongenial to make a move without his support and very rarely did so, and for this reason the first years after his death were for her very difficult indeed. Family and close friends were constantly round her, she hated to be left alone even for a meal, much less for a whole day, and there was almost always a lady-in-waiting of roughly her own age with her – someone younger she would not really have cared for.[7]

Over the years there has been much uninformed gossip and conjecture over Mary and Harry's marriage. In 2019, the film *Downtown Abbey* portrayed their marriage as a loveless match. Much has been said that Lord Harewood was pompous and aloof, and much that is far worse. Yet, as George said of his father's death:

That was not how his friends knew him, how his battalion in 1914–1918 remembered him, how those he had helped (including tenant-farmers who could not pay their rent) knew him, how his family felt about him: ... I lost potentially the best friend and mentor I could ever have.[8]

While Harry did act regally at times, this masked an inherent shyness, something that his wife and his eldest son both suffered from. Harry was an intelligent man; in the House of Lords, he gave several speeches that demonstrated his wide knowledge in a range of issues such as veterinary science and the situation in Palestine, as well as the preservation of art treasures and the Museum of London. He passed on his love of football to his eldest son, who became president of Leeds United Football Club. He was cultured, a man of taste and wisdom, and he and Mary had many similar interests such as horse racing, gardening, art and antiques. Harry was kind like Mary and there were many stories of his compassion towards men in his regiment, as well as towards those who lived on the Harewood Estate. As one newspaper said in its obituary, 'to me the outstanding thing about Lord Harewood was the degree of affection and respect with which he had come to be regarded'.[9]

Many believe that Mary never truly recovered from the loss of Harry. She remained at Harewood as the dowager countess, but she hung on tightly to any last reminder of her husband, however small. As her head gardener related, 'it was well known amongst the gardeners that anything Harry had planted was more or less sacred and had on no account to be removed'.[10] In later years Mary would even have her Christmas card photographs taken against a backdrop of a portrait of Harry in a similar vein to Queen Victoria mourning the premature death of Prince Albert. Although she continued to carry out many of her royal engagements, Mary did not seek out social activities and remained for much of the time away from the gaze of publicity. In the first years after Harry's death, Mary surrounded herself with family and close friends, anyone with whom she could reminisce about Harry. Mary became more of a companion to her mother and both appeared to rely on each other in their widowhoods.

This was the first time in her life when Mary did not keep up with her correspondence as religiously. In his diaries, Ronald Storrs, a friend of the royal family and the princess through his work in the Foreign Office as governor of Jerusalem (and later Cyprus), mentions his surprise at the lack of response from someone who was usually so punctilious. After several attempts he finally received 'a little silver owl and card from Princess Mary: relieving me strangely because I'd had no reply to my last three letters of which one was careful condolence on H's (Harry) death.

I had therefore thought that for some unknown reason … I'd offended her or even lost her friendship.'[11]

A further rumour that has escalated and become something of a misconception is that Mary refused to attend the wedding of Princess Elizabeth and Philip Mountbatten on 20 November 1947 because of her annoyance at the Duke of Windsor not receiving an invitation. This belief finds its roots in Ronald Storrs's diary, when he mentions going to visit Sir Henry McMahon, a former diplomat, and his wife. 'They knew all about Princess Mary's absence from the wedding in anger at the Duke of Windsor not having been invited.'[12] However, within the same diary entry, Storrs recalls having to leave the couple after only half an hour, finding them rather tiresome, suggesting a discourse of gossip rather than fact.

In November 1947, just prior to the wedding, Mary explained the real reason for her non-attendance at the wedding to her close friend Dame Mary Tyrwhitt. The letter is marked 'PRIVATE' in large capitals. 'I would like you to know that after all I shall not be coming to London. I felt that the wedding festivities might prove too great a strain. I am very disappointed to miss the wedding. November 17 or 18 the Press must announce I have a chill or something of the sort.'[13] Harry's death undoubtedly had caused her such great anxiety and upset that she feared she was on the brink of a further nervous breakdown similar to that in the 1930s.

Mary was in official mourning for Harry for a period of at least six months. *Tatler* reported as late as 5 November 1947 that Mary was still wearing full mourning dress. Weddings are family celebrations which evoke intense emotion and happiness. It would have been difficult for Mary to attend such an occasion when she was struggling with the grief of her husband's passing, not to mention the fact that Elizabeth's wedding was to be held in the same place that Mary had married Harry over twenty-five years previously.

Mary later attended the wedding of Princess Margaret in 1960, an event to which the Duke of Windsor was not invited. Furthermore, in early December 1947, newspapers contained reports of articles the Duke of Windsor had written for *American Life* magazine in which he had written about his childhood and how Mary 'dominated him and his brother, the present King'.[14] While many of his supposed revelations were innocuous, selling a story to the press was not the behaviour expected of a member of the royal family and as such would have exasperated Mary. As much as Mary loved David, she showed a faithful loyalty to Bertie. David had been working on his articles for over a year and so it is doubtful that his presence at the wedding would have been welcomed by any members of the family.

After the Second World War, Britain was bankrupt. 1945 saw the emergence of a new Labour government under Clement Attlee, who had won the general election with a massive majority and nearly 50 per cent of the vote. The Second World War had led to deep social changes in Britain and this produced a yearning for societal reform. The Labour slogan of the election had been 'Let Us Face the Future' and signified the necessary changes that were needed to rebuild the nation after the war. During Attlee's tenure over 200 Acts of Parliament were passed including controls to limit extreme levels of wealth and poverty.

Death duties were first introduced in Britain in 1894 with a mere 8 per cent being paid on an estate. By 1938 death duties on an estate valued at £100,000 rose to 20 per cent and by 1950 they had increased to 50 per cent on an estate of £1 million. Many landowning families had tried to get around this by gifting property to the next generation, provided that it was done within three years of the owner's death. However, this period was raised to five years in 1946. After the war something in the region of 500 estates were being broken up or sold off, if they had not already been decimated by wartime mistreatment.

The 24-year-old 7th Earl of Harewood, still in shock from his sudden ascendency to the title, faced a monumental task when he inherited Harewood in 1947. There were still huge repairs needing to be done on the house. Crippling death duties meant that he had to pay £800,000 on an estate that had been valued at £1.4 million. George's solicitor laid out a map of the estate and, using a compass and pencil, drew a circle, declaring that everything outside of the circle needed to be sold. It was a third of the estate. As the 6th Earl of Harewood's brother-in-law the Duke of Windsor remarked to Queen Mary:

It is a crime how three decades of Liberal and Socialist legislation destroyed a uniquely English way of life – the great country estates of Britain ... so much of the traditional elegance we used to know ... is vanishing ... until one hardly has the heart to revisit the haunts of one's youth.[15]

Death duties, along with a lack of interest in preserving Britain's architectural heritage, an increased need to rebuild cities and affordable housing after the war and a shortage of serving staff meant that many stately homes had no option but to be pulled down at this time. The priority was to keep Harewood House standing. It may not have appeared so at the time, but Harewood was fortunate in avoiding demolition.

In June 1950 at the Queen's Hotel in Leeds, the new earl employed Hollis and Webb to auction ninety-nine lots over two days including a public house, farms, smallholdings, cottages, sports grounds, allotments and land. Many of the buyers had been tenants for centuries. The following year even more was sold including land in seven villages in Wharfdale, Nidderdale and the Plompton estate. A total of nearly 15,000 acres was sold. Anthony Blunt, keeper of the queen's pictures, came to Harewood and advised about which artworks to keep and which to sell. It must have been a deeply unpleasant experience for Mary and her son having items scrutinised and judged as to their financial rather than sentimental value. Items of furniture were auctioned, and the gardens were made less labour intensive by, among other things, turning the Italiante parterre to grass. The parterre was not restored until as late as 1994.

There were many changes on the estate, as the emphasis was now on commercialisation and making Harewood pay its way. The house and gardens had been open on occasion for charity but in 1950 George had to take the decision to open Harewood to the public on a more formal basis. Advertisements invited paying visitors to see 'Yorkshire's Greatest

Treasure House' with the five state apartments encompassing the rose drawing room, the green drawing room, the gallery, the dining room and the music room. The newspapers claimed that 'there is indeed much of interest and beauty to be enjoyed … Woodland walks are aflame with rhododendron blooms and … drifts of deep red primulas and clusters of narcissi'.[16]

Although she had to support her son, Mary was often seen to hide in the top woods when visitors arrived, and she planted large bushes in strategic positions to prevent visitors seeing her at work in her rose garden. With more visitors coming, who wanted to see impressive gardens, it was still vital to use as much of the garden as possible to grow vegetables to sell. In the past, fruit had been grown and eaten by the family and their guests. Now the best fruit was commandeered and sold to a fruiterer in Harrogate, 'the emphasis being on selling everything whenever possible'.[17] These changes meant that there was a significant increase in the amount of work to be done on the estate but fewer staff to carry it out. Visitors would steal from the greenhouses anything that could be moved, including garden implements and fruit and vegetables, and thus these areas eventually had to be closed off. By the mid 1950s business was booming, Harewood was recognised as a tourist attraction and it was time to expand. Visitors were now permitted to see much of the east wing of the house on the ground floor. The estate started to produce roses and ornamental conifers. The old bus serving tea and minimal lavatories needed updating and so a new cafeteria was opened in the former stable block along with a car park.

George VI gave Mary the use of a six-bedroomed flat at St James's Palace for a London base, where she was able to entertain family and friends. It was where David would visit her when he came back to London and Queen Mary would also call on her daughter. Possibly as a habituated result of George V's obsession with time, Queen Mary's visits were extremely punctual. She would arrive at 5 p.m. on the dot, enjoy a hasty tea with her daughter and leave exactly an hour later.

As the dowager countess, Mary continued to involve herself fully in the estate. She was immensely proud of her herd of dual-purpose Red Poll cattle. When in residence at Harewood, Mary would spend her Sunday afternoons on the farm. Racing had always been an integral part of her life with Harry. She continued to attend race events, even attending the Derby three weeks after Harry's death to support one of his horses, and she continued on a smaller scale the stud farm set up by Harry on Otley Road in 1929. Harry had never been particularly lucky in horse breeding, but Mary eventually came close to a winner with the horse Pretende. After the war, Harewood became the centre for three-day event horse trials, the organisation of which gave Mary much pleasure. The event was so successful that it became known in the equestrian community as the northern equivalent of the Badminton horse trials. Prior to the event, Mary could be seen inspecting the grounds, wearing dark glasses and carrying a stick with which to point out holes that might prove a danger to horses or to spike litter with. Mary was an avid spectator throughout the trials and always presented the awards on the Saturday. Thousands of people came to witness the event until a particularly virulent outbreak of foot and mouth disease in 1960 put an end to it. After Harry's death, Mary still went regularly to Newmarket races, staying at either Palace House or Queensbury House.

The world of horse racing relies greatly on good fortune and given that this was among Mary's greatest interests, she had always been incredibly superstitious. Whenever she saw a single magpie, she would bow three times. In the summer when the birds were out in force, this caused an almost continuous nodding to ridiculous extremes. If Mary saw a piebald horse, with its distinct black and white markings, and superstitiously considered a sign of bad luck, she would remain silent until she had seen a dog. Once a horseshoe was found on a footpath and Mary gave instructions to her gardener that it should not be touched since the lucky horseshoe had appeared on the same day that one of the princess's horses had won at Redcar.

Mary was known on the estate as having a distinct 'lack of hauteur'[18] and acting in a down-to-earth and occasionally eccentric manner. For instance, when a chef was preparing a grand banquet at the house and found there was no fresh mint, the princess thought nothing of getting in her car and driving to buy some in Harrogate. She would find much hilarity in being greeted by shopkeepers as 'missus' or 'luv'. Mary felt at home in the countryside and her love of country pursuits enabled her to converse more easily with people and overcome in part her shyness. Sir David Munro, the director of the Royal Air Force medical service, related in his memoir meeting Mary with his wife: 'At a tea-party I have heard her exchanging with my wife methods for killing wire-worm in potatoes. One might have thought them two women chatting over the garden-fence of their respective vegetable plots.'[19]

# 19

# George and Gerald

The family atmosphere was all important to the Princess Royal.[1]
*Birmingham Daily Post*, Monday 29 March 1965

When speaking of her children growing up, Mary remarked that 'the struggle in our house is for the piano. In my time it used to be for the ponies.'[2] Music figured significantly in both her sons' lives. For George, it was classical and opera, and for Gerald, jazz. While imprisoned during the war, George had used his time wisely to study *Grove's Dictionary of Music and Musicians* as far as the letter 's'. As a student of English at King's College Cambridge, he would spend his evenings entertaining his friends from his extensive record collection. It was thus no surprise that in 1948, while he was at Cambridge, the composer Benjamin Britten, whom he had met several times, asked George to become president of the recently established Aldeburgh Festival, in the small town in East Suffolk where Britten lived. Originally, the festival was designed to be a modest festival of classical music, but it expanded to encompass poetry, literature, drama and art. It was at the 1948 Aldeburgh Festival that Benjamin Britten introduced George to Marion Stein.

Maria Donata Nanetta Paulina Gustava Erwina Wilhelmine Stein was born in Vienna on 18 October 1926. Marion was the daughter of Erwin Stein, a successful Jewish musician and editor, and his wife, Sofie Bachmann.

In 1938 following the annexation of Austria to Nazi Germany, Erwin Stein moved his family to London, where he worked for Benjamin Britten's music publisher. With such a background, it was little wonder that Marion displayed signs of a musical gift. Marion first attended Kensington High School before moving to the Royal College of Music. She received piano training from Frank Osborn and travelled to Brussels for further study. Marion's family were close friends of Benjamin Britten and when a fire destroyed their apartment in 1944, the family temporarily lived at Britten's home in St John's Wood for eighteen months. According to a contemporary of Marion's, Arthur Boyars, the poet and musicologist, when asked at the age of 13 to write an essay on her ambitions, Marion had chosen to write that her ultimate wish was to marry into the aristocracy.

After their introduction at the Aldeburgh Festival in 1948, Marion and George began their courtship, meeting again at Cambridge and subsequently at the Salzburg Festival. By May 1949, Marion became headline news when the car of the 7th earl was seen constantly outside her home in Melbury Road, Kensington.

When George told his mother that he wished to marry Marion, 'her reaction was quite simply to say, "Good God!" and then walk on in silence. In the end she … seemed to find the idea less peculiar … and eventually said she'd like to meet Marion.'[3] Marion was invited to visit Harewood, which George later revealed must have been something of 'an ordeal for her'[4] meeting the king's sister. All that seemed to concern Mary about Marion was whether she was able to cook.

In 1978 the diarist Kenneth Rose recalled a meeting with Marion in which she spoke of her engagement to George. According to the Royal Marriages Act of 1772, George needed to ask the king's permission. George VI agreed with the codicil that George must gain the permission of Queen Mary, who, according to the family, was against the idea. George asked his mother to speak on his behalf to Queen Mary about the engagement. He continued to ask his mother, but nothing happened. In the end George decided to ask Queen Mary himself, to which she exclaimed, 'So that's what Mary has been trying to tell me for the past two months!'[5] Despite their closeness, Mary treated her mother with kid gloves, as Queen Mary was revered so much.[6]

Up until this time, the bride's life had been one of relative seclusion but following the engagement announcement on 19 July 1949 there was a great deal of interest in the earl's fiancée and her every move was photographed and reported. The royal wedding of the year was held on 29 September at St Mark's Church on North Audley Street in the heart of Mayfair.

Marion's dress was made from heavy brocaded silk by a court dressmaker with a square neck and a Romney-style collar. For her bouquet she carried an all-white crescent of gardenias, butterfly orchids, lilies of the valley and stephanotis. As was befitting the child of a member of the royal family, the groom's mother was charged with the task of organising the reception at St James's Palace for some 900 people including 200 tenants from the Harewood estate. Mary generously paid for them to travel from Harewood to London via a special train and to receive a buffet meal at St James's Palace.

The night before the ceremony, women had camped out in North Audley Street to get a good vantage point. Streets around the church had been cleared of traffic and the police cordon attempted to hold back the crowds. The guest list included many illustrious names including the king and queen and Princesses Elizabeth and Margaret, as well as Douglas Fairbanks and Lady Churchill.

The Bishop of Ripon married the couple. Their shared loved of music and of Benjamin Britten was united in the spectacular anthem Britten and Ronald Duncan had composed as a wedding present for the couple, entitled 'Amo Ergo Sum' or 'I love therefore I am'. The score for the anthem was buried in the foundations of the Royal Festival Hall, which was being built at the time. Prior to the wedding and demonstrating the protective feelings he had towards Marion and possibly his concerns over the couple's compatibility, Britten had advised her that she should only marry if she was certain that she genuinely loved George.[7]

The couple honeymooned first in Paris and then Venice, where they stayed in exactly the same hotel that Mary and Harry had chosen in 1922 before moving on to tour Naples, Rome and Capri. With hindsight it is possible that the marriage was ill-fated from the start since Marion and

George were very different and thus never really suited. As George later explained in his autobiography, 'Marion never felt she truly "belonged" at Harewood.'[8] Marion had mainly grown up within towns and cities and so country life was something of a shock to her. It had taken quite a lot of convincing for Mary to agree to move out of her ground-floor rooms and move upstairs to the visitors' suite, complete with dressing room and bathroom. Mary kept her sitting room downstairs and George and Marion repurposed the princess's former dressing room into a sitting room. They added a nursery when their children were born, which was in place of a former bedroom and dressing room on the first floor.

Harewood would always be regarded as Mary's home. Although much of the work was down to servants, Mary continued to take charge of the finances and domestic organisation of Harewood. This role was difficult to relinquish but undoubtedly led to conflict for the new couple. Never one to embrace change, Mary was often heard making disparaging remarks if items were moved or altered. After Harry's death, Mary desperately hung on to the past and maintained tradition, one example being that Christmases were the same as they had been in the 1930s with church, carols, the sovereign's speech and stockings.

As well as royalty and the aristocracy, Harewood was now visited by musical guests such as Benjamin Britten, the pianist Artur Rubinstein, actors, actresses, playwrights, opera stars and conductors. In keeping with George's love of music, there were many concerts and recitals. The newly married couple spent the first years of their marriage travelling a great deal. By 1958 they had made nearly fifty journeys overseas. The couple were able to have some privacy in London; they were given the use of rooms at St James's Palace for a brief time before moving into a house in Orme Square.

George's passion in life was music and he worked to transform the public's perception of opera and make it more accessible, especially to English audiences. In 1950, he became editor of *Opera* magazine and he re-edited Kobbé's *Complete Opera Book* in 1953 and 1976. With his ardent devotion to the performing arts, he became patron of the Yorkshire Symphony Orchestra, director of the Royal Opera House in 1951 and president of the Leeds Film Society. David may have said once of George, the new Lord Harewood, 'It's very odd about George and music. You know, his parents were quite normal – liked horses and dogs and the country!'[9] Clearly, George inherited much of his love of music from his mother. From her earliest days in Yorkshire, Mary was an ardent concert and music lover and had been a patron for the Leeds Triennial Musical Festival since the 1920s, attending many opening nights, frequently inconspicuously, and even after her husband's death, she continued to patronise concerts.

George, like his father, was a cultured man, with a wide variety of interests in many fields. He became chair of the campaign to abolish the death penalty and appeared on a BBC television debate in 1961 declaring that the death penalty was not a deterrent for murderers. From his childhood, George had been a huge supporter of Leeds United Football Club from 1961 onwards and held the position of president of the Football Association from 1963 to 1972.

Gerald appeared to possess more practical skills and interests than his elder brother and had inherited Harry's love of motoring. During the war he had worked as an apprentice in a munitions factory in Yorkshire until he was old enough to join the Rifle Brigade in 1944, where he developed a keen interest in motor racing thanks to his company commander, Tony Rolt, who later won two prestigious victories for Jaguar in the Le Mans twenty-four-hour endurance race. After Gerald's demobilisation he became a member of the West Essex Car Club and acted as a marshal at events. For a brief period, and much to the disapproval of his mother, he attempted to become a racing driver, participating in several rallies during the early 1950s. Fortunately for Mary, this career lasted little more than two years and Gerald recognised that his strengths lay more in administration. Between 1952 and 1954 Gerald worked for Ford as part of their management trainee scheme at Dagenham and learned to be a mechanic. He eventually joined the British Automobile Racing Club and in 1964 became president of the British Racing Drivers' Club, eventually devoting himself to expanding the racing school at Silverstone.

Along with his fondness for motor racing and rally races, Gerald loved practical jokes, which made him very popular among his fellow workers. He shared a passion for jazz with his mother and possessed something like 4,000 jazz records at one stage. He later wrote jazz columns for newspapers and magazines and edited the annual review *Just Jazz*.

Gerald was considered by the press to be an eligible bachelor, and during the 1950s they continually tried to marry him off. Rumoured fiancées included the 19-year-old Felicity Ingleby Mackenzie. At one stage the intense media intrusion and speculation meant that Gerald felt that he had to withdraw from the rally and Concours d'Elegance in which Felicity was to accompany him. In November 1950 he was finally able to participate in the *Daily Express* 48-hour rally. The following year there were again false rumours of Gerald's impending nuptials with Louisa Fens, the 22-year old daughter of a Dutch MP.

Finally, in June 1952, the newspapers announced that Gerald was to marry Miss Angela Dowding, a lady who had acted with ENSA, the Entertainments National Service Association, during the war, touring Egypt and Italy. Much was made of the fact that Angela was five years Gerald's senior and a commoner. The couple had been introduced by the Countess of Kimberley at a ball in 1949 and Gerald had been the first member of the royal family to ask for the new queen's permission to marry. Lady Kimberley commented that 'it was one of those lovely friendships that started that evening at the ball and grew to love'.[10] Angela's engagement ring was rather unusual in its choice of a black pearl and diamond shoulders. The newspapers reported that Angela was an excellent cook and homemaker and had thus endeared herself to her mother-in-law-to-be. Gerald had been encouraged by his fiancée to find a better job and so he was by now a personal assistant to the resident manager of the Feltham factory of David Brown Tractors, who also built Aston Martin and Lagonda cars.

Gerald married on 15 July 1952 at St Margaret's Church in Westminster. Despite the queen's absence, reportedly due to a heavy cold, most of the royal family were present including Princess Margaret and the Duke of Edinburgh. The newspapers interpreted the absence of the queen as a deliberate snub to Gerald and his new bride, and many sensationalised headlines appeared to focus on their romance being akin to the cliché of 'chorus girl marries into royalty', or the supposed link with the affair of his great-grandfather, King Edward VII, with the actress Lillie Langtry, which was not strictly true. The wedding reception was held at St James's Palace and the couple spent their honeymoon motoring throughout Europe. Three years later they moved into Fort Belvedere, David's former home, where he had frequently entertained Wallis. The house had been used as the headquarters of the Commissioners of Crown Lands during the war, but it was now derelict and unloved. The couple renovated the house and gardens with the refurbishment of the interior being exceptionally difficult since there was 'hardly a right angle in the whole house'. Fort Belvedere came back to life in the fifties and it was used for many parties, entertaining at one stage some of the great musicians of jazz including Louis Armstrong and Duke Ellington.[11]

# 20

# Chancellor

To thee on this auspicious Day
Our homage and our thanks are borne
When thou dost first with princely sway
The chief throne of our Academe adorn.[1]

  'Lady Elect of Royal Line', ode for the installation of the chancellor
of the University of Leeds, 9 November 1951

People in the north of England thought of Mary as their own Yorkshire princess. She had endeared herself greatly to the region with her consistent commitment to its charities and organisations. Mary's presence in the region was vital to people's perceptions of the royal family. This was an age when televisions and motor vehicles were considered unobtainable luxuries, transport links were limited, and London appeared to be incredibly far away. Most of the population only saw members of the royal family in newspapers, or in portraits hung in school, if at all.

Throughout the years following Harry's death Mary, in an effort to keep busy and to avoid dwelling on her grief, threw herself into her charitable work with a renewed vigour, and carried out a phenomenal number of engagements. Her main charitable interests continued to be nursing and welfare, but she also began to promote higher education, especially for women.

Mary became a grandmother in October 1950 when Marion gave birth to a son at their London home in Bayswater. He was named after various family members as David Henry George, Viscount Lascelles, and was at the time of his birth thirteenth in the line of succession. He was christened at All Saints Church on the Harewood estate; once again, the church was packed with workers from the estate and family members, many of whom had braved the snow to be there. Along with family members, Benjamin Britten was present to act as godfather. A British Pathé newsreel filmed at Harewood after the ceremony shows Mary proudly holding her grandchild and rocking him quite vigorously to sleep.

Mary loved her grandchildren, who would refer to her as 'Ging Ging'. As was to be expected with Mary's upbringing, she was not demonstrative or affectionate towards them, yet her stern countenance and consistent rebukes over table manners masked a great deal of warmth and an immense sense of fun. Over the next few years she would become a grandmother to five boys. The increased noise of the children exuberantly playing must have been quite a shock to her at Harewood after so much calm and tranquillity. Yet Mary gained much happiness from her new familial role, pretending not to care about their energetic bike races on the terrace or the chandeliers shaking from the boys kicking a football in the nursery, and only occasionally scolding them for running amok in the formal rooms at Harewood. She bought her grandsons a donkey, encouraged them to dress up as soldiers, took them for walks, and her love of collecting small objets d'art and trinkets meant that it was always easy for her grandsons to know exactly what to give her for her birthday.

In January 1951 the Goldsborough estate, which was at the time occupied by a small independent school, was put up for sale. It was hoped that a buyer would continue to use it for commercial purposes. Undoubtedly this distressed Mary, since the home had a great sentimental attachment for her; Goldsborough had been her first marital home and she had lived there when her children were born. This may be why in the early months of the year, Mary suffered from a heavy cold which turned into sinus difficulties. On 10 January an announcement from

St James's Palace informed the public that the princess was indisposed for a short time and needed to rest indoors. Several engagements had to be cancelled. However, the rest did not have the required effect and Mary's condition worsened. By the end of January, a further announcement was made explaining that Mary was suffering from trouble with the mastoid antrum, an air space in the small bone behind the ear. Mary appeared to make progress with treatment and returned to Harewood. However, once home her condition worsened again, and she was still suffering in early February. This necessitated a stay in a nursing home at Queen's Gate, Kensington, for further treatment and Mary spent a brief time recuperating at Marlborough House in the company of her mother. She occupied her old suite of rooms on the first floor, where she had stayed for a time after Harry's death. To ensure a full recovery, Mary flew to Switzerland, accompanied by a small party of five including Viscountess Boyne, for a short convalescent break at St Moritz. She returned on 2 March and two weeks later immersed herself once again in a busy round of engagements.

1951 was to be a busy year for the royal family with the celebration of the Festival of Britain. This would mark 100 years since the first Great Exhibition and was designed to raise the spirits of the nation after the austerity of the Second World War while promoting Britain's contribution to the arts, science, industrial design and technology. The same year, Mary accepted the position of president of the Yorkshire Agricultural society, a position she had previously held in 1937. The society was mostly known for organising the Yorkshire Show every year in Harrogate and it had finally acquired a permanent site to hold the show.

Mary abhorred litter and would obsessively pick it up and chastise anyone seen to drop it. She was known to walk around the Harewood estate spiking litter on to her walking stick. In 1950, speaking to the York Georgian Society, of which she was president, she expressed her hatred of having to dispose of paper bags, sweet wrappers and bottles discarded by visitors to Harewood. Mary urged people to dispose of litter correctly, especially in beauty spots, to make Britain look tidier during the 1951 Festival. She believed that not only would this enable overseas visitors to see this country at its best but it would also add to the pleasure of the people who lived in it. She continued to raise her concerns in 1952 at a national conference of the Council for the Preservation of Rural England in Harrogate, telling the delegates that in the course of her travels throughout the country she saw much litter and untidiness: 'I must tell you that paper bags and broken glass have much the same effect on me as a red rag to a bull.'[2] Highlighting this cause must have influenced the Women's Institute, which, led by its chair Lady Elisabeth Brunner, passed a resolution in 1954 to 'Keep Britain Tidy'. Thus began a nationwide initiative that continues today.

Another cause which Mary felt passionately about was the blood donor service. It has already been shown how she supported the service during the war. On 3 April, at a celebration to recognise the achievements of long-serving blood donors and wearing a scarlet and black gown and a mortarboard of a fellow of the Royal College of Surgeons, Mary spoke about the urgent need to give blood to save lives. In her speech Mary recognised that more young people needed to come forward to donate and expressed her belief that such celebratory events acted as a stimulus to encourage new people to volunteer.

A week later, on 10 April, Mary was honoured with the freedom of Harrogate, to acknowledge the affection the people had for the princess as well as 'in recognition of the eminent services rendered by her to the borough'.[3] Twenty-three flowering chestnut trees were planted alternating between white and pink on either side of the Leeds Road into Harrogate, which Mary always took when driving from Harewood and part of it was renamed the Princess Royal Way. The ceremony was held in the Royal Hall packed with civic dignitaries, MPs, army apprentices and members of the band of Royal Signals, the Bishop of Ripon and hundreds of schoolchildren. The mayor thanked Mary for the way in which she had 'woven her personality into the very fabric of our national life, providing an example of devoted and unstinted service for others'.[4] As she received this honour, Mary expressed her love of Yorkshire:

> Yorkshire has become such an integral part of my life that it would be a great sorrow to me to contemplate making my home elsewhere … Since I became a Yorkshire woman … it has grown very dear to me

and from the very early days, I have known the people of Harrogate and have looked upon them as my friends. Yorkshire people do not give their friendship lightly, ill-advisedly or wantonly, but once given, it is true and lasting.[5]

During the same week, in New York, David as the Duke of Windsor published his memoir, *A King's Story*. David explained his rationale behind the abdication, stating that he could not have continued to remain king without the support of Wallis. He believed that their subsequent happiness together justified his actions. Many of the more sensationalist newspapers focused on David's unsuitability to be king because of his dislike of pomp and ceremony. Furthermore, there was much criticism of the duke for what many considered to be a crass publication. One newspaper said that 'silence would better have matched that regal dignity of his parents'.[6]

Mary completed a five-day tour of Carinthia in Austria in July 1951 to present new colours to the West Yorkshire regiment and meet members of the Austrian and Carinthian governments. This was a successful visit in which Mary made an impression on her hosts not just because she spoke fluent German but also because of her kindness and generosity. She went shopping in Klagenfurt and presented her host Colonel Roberts with a leather wallet and even posed for photographs with Italian tourists. Mary climbed the 6,000ft of the Kanzel Mountain accompanied only by three ladies in her party. As part of her tour, Mary flew to Germany to visit British military units on the Rhine including hospitals, canteens, camps and women's units. There was an oppressive heatwave and yet Mary insisted on sticking to her schedule as much as possible, with only one cancellation.

Tertiary education for women continued to remain a cause championed by the princess. As early as July 1923 Mary had contributed £100 to a £10,000 fund to support four women attending Oxford University. This was, according to the newspapers, 'a striking refutation of the oft-made assertion that women are not interested in the education of their own sex'.[7]

By 1951, Mary had received three honorary degrees: Doctor of Law from Leeds in 1925, Doctor of Law from Sheffield in 1926, and Doctor of Civil Law from Oxford in 1930. Mary had always supported the University of Leeds, attending many degree ceremonies, and she had been present at the opening of the university's Brotherton Library. She had patronised informal occasions such as music concerts and was well known within the university community. The position of chancellor fell vacant when the nineteenth chancellor, the Duke of Devonshire, died. The vice-chancellor, Mr C.R. Morris, had approached the princess and asked if she would consider the position. Mary immediately said that she would have to consult the king. Consent was given and Mary accepted the position. She was to be the first female chancellor of a university in Great Britain. The only other member of the royal family who held a chancellorship in the British Isles was Prince Philip, Duke of Edinburgh, at the University of Wales. The pro-chancellor said, 'I think that it is a gracious act by her which will give immense pleasure to all who are associated with this university ... and ... to the wider public of Yorkshire'.[8]

Alderman Mrs Kathleen Chambers, a member of the University council and the first female Lord Mayor, maintained that the appointment of Mary as a chancellor would serve as an inspiration and encouragement to female students. During the 1950s, the importance of women in the academic world was starting to grow, particularly those in towns and cities. At this time, the university teaching staff were striving to make the university one of the leading establishments in the country to rival Oxford and Cambridge. It had been founded in 1909 and by 1951 had over 3,000 students; it had started to undergo an ambitious programme of extensive building work to increase the size and facilities. Joyce Mather, a reporter, who had met the princess on many occasions, explained in the Yorkshire Post why Mary deserved such an honour:

> During the War, the Princess was tireless in her efforts for the WVS ... and for women in the Forces. She concerned herself with every aspect of the training and work of the ATS of which she was Controller. She put in long arduous hours visiting remote camps, barrack squares and on other duties ... For contrast there is the picture of the Squire's lady cycling round the village of Harewood, helping in the salvage

campaign. Nothing was too small … the Princess knitted and sewed and was an enthusiastic supporter of the Blood Transfusion Service, showing the way by giving her own … On the social side, the presence of the Princess ensures the success of every important function in the country … The Princess will be the first woman to hold such an office in Great Britain. Yorkshire men and women feel she has earned it.[9]

On the day of the installation, large crowds gave a great ovation to Mary as she arrived at the University of Leeds with a guard of honour provided by the training centre of the Royal Signals. During the ceremony the university's music society sang a special ode written for the occasion which made much of the significance of the appointment of the first female chancellor. Representatives from all over the country descended upon Leeds for the occasion. Mary awarded several honorary degrees including one for her sister-in-law, Viscountess Boyne, who was among seven other women including Dame Hilda Lloyd, the president of the Royal College of Obstetricians and Gynaecologists, a body composed predominantly of men.

The newspapers again made much of the sheer number of women awarded honorary degrees that day. Members of the university training corps formed a guard of honour lining the steps to the main entrance of the new Parkinson building, which Mary opened. She unveiled two war memorials of carved Portland Stone flanking the main doors leading to the Brotherton Library. Between the two ceremonies, a luncheon for 200 was given by the Lord and Lady Mayoress of Leeds. Mary was followed around during the day by an 8-year-old boy, Richard Hamilton-Russell, a cousin of Lord Harewood, as her page in an outfit of green box cloth, gold braided with white leggings. A page was needed since her robes were estimated to weigh 30–40lb. Clearly all the lengthy speeches of the ceremonies were taxing for a small boy of 8: in several of the photographs of the day, he can be seen falling asleep.

The newspapers made much of the dignified occasion and it was considered one of Leeds's most impressive occasions by the *Yorkshire Post*, although it must have been quite an ordeal for Mary, who played the 'central role with her usual dignity, charm and a happy, smiling, grace'.[10]

That evening, when Mary returned to Harewood, she posed on the terrace in her robes for the press to photograph her. Her gardener Geoffrey Hall relates in his memoirs how he wanted to take a photograph of her but by the time he had returned home to collect his camera, the princess had already finished and taken off her robes. When Mary realised that the gardener was disappointed to miss this photo opportunity, she agreed to put the robes back on and posed indoors near the staircase for him. For Geoffrey, this kindness was 'typical of the way she would treat her staff'.[11]

In an article entitled 'Women's Rights Conquer Man's World'[12] the *Hartlepool Northern Daily Mail* spoke of the pivotal year of 1951 being significant for a range of firsts for women. Along with the first female coroner, the first woman appointed as president of the Institute of Landscape Architects, the youngest woman to take ministerial office and the first female pilot, the newspaper compared Mary's appointment as the first female chancellor to 'a gigantic stride over the Century since the days when Queen Victoria was bemoaning the wicked folly of women's rights'.[13] Furthermore, these appointments showed 'the gradual lessening of the gap of inequality'.[14] For Mary, becoming the chancellor was one of her greatest achievements.

# The Deaths of George VI
# and Queen Mary

A cruel and sad blow.[1]

    Letter from Princess Mary to Lord Middleton, 29 March 1952

In April 1949 Mary wrote to her mother: 'Am so distressed Bertie should have a fresh worry through David. Why cannot he leave him alone; undoubtedly, she is egging him on. But Bertie must be firm.'[2] The mention of the 'worry' refers to the last attempt David made to have his wife given the title of Her Royal Highness. In 1937 when they had married, David was furious that Wallis would not be granted this. At the time he had consulted the lawyer William Jowitt, who told him that the Letters Patent issued by the king during this period, giving the title to David but not to Wallis, were insignificant and there was no legal reason for Wallis not to have the title. William Jowitt became Lord Chancellor in November 1949 and David used this as an opportunity to consult him again to try to reverse the decision. This happened during a period of considerable stress and anxiety for the king, who was suffering from serious illness.

Bertie had experienced an obstruction to his circulation through the arteries of his legs in 1948. The king agreed with his doctors to rest and not to undertake any public engagements for a while. However, the condition failed to improve and in order to avoid the possibility of gangrene developing, an operation was carried out to relieve the obstruction in March 1950. Bertie had been a heavy smoker for much of his life and it was no surprise when he developed lung cancer; in September 1951 part of his lungs were removed. To his family, he seemed to be recovering well. The full truth of the king's condition was kept from the public, who were instead informed that the king had recovered rather miraculously. However, the king's doctors were aware that his heart could stop at any point. He was living on borrowed time. A tour of Australia which had been scheduled for the beginning of 1952 was cancelled with the idea that Princess Elizabeth and Prince Philip would instead take the place of the king and queen. The king was expected to take a private convalescent cruise in March and April visiting South Africa.

Mary suffered from an attack of fibrositis towards the end of January 1952 and it was announced that she planned to convalesce at St Moritz in Switzerland for a fortnight. Before she could leave, events took a tragic turn when on Wednesday 6 February Bertie died in his sleep at Sandringham at the age of 56 from a coronary thrombosis. The news was an unexpected and terrible shock, not just for the family but the country as a whole. Mary was at St James's Palace when she was informed. She agreed to delay her trip, although she was advised by doctors to go as soon as she could. Mary's first thoughts were of her mother and how Bertie's death would undoubtedly distress her.

In a letter to Guy, Lord Middleton, Mary expressed her feelings over the man who was both brother and sovereign:

> The King's death is a cruel and sad blow to us all but the knowledge that thousands, even millions, are sharing our sorrow is a great comfort – For his sake one is so thankful he had those last few happy weeks in his beloved Sandringham.[3]

Bertie's daughter Elizabeth was now queen, and she immediately flew back from Kenya. Mary's son Gerald flew home from Barbados to attend the funeral. The Duke of Windsor was in New York when he learned of the news through newspaper reporters. He issued a press statement expressing his shock and disbelief and came to England on the *Queen Mary* liner, staying with his mother at Marlborough House.

He had come alone, having been informed that Wallis would not be welcome. Nonetheless, the couple were optimistic that a new monarch might finally signal a period of reconciliation. Wallis wrote to David and hoped that he could 'make some headway'[4] with the queen mother and the new queen, whom Wallis spitefully nicknamed 'Cookie', on account of her dumpy figure, and 'Mrs Shirley Temple Junior', since Princess Elizabeth when young bore a similarity to the child star. David found his reception from his family 'correct and dignified'.[5] Encouraged by Wallis to try to seek a way to bring him back into the family, David had tea with the now dowager Queen Elizabeth and her daughter, the new Queen Elizabeth. However, he soon learned that no such reconciliation was to take place and that much to his chagrin, the allowance he had received from his brother Bertie would be withdrawn by the new monarch.

The body of King George VI was taken from St Mary Magdalene Church at Sandringham to lie in state at Westminster Hall. Here David, Mary and their mother went to pay their respects for a quarter of an hour, standing motionless with their heads bowed, before returning together to Marlborough House. Some 300,000 well-wishers queued for hours. On 10 February, Westminster Abbey had one of the largest congregations it had known for morning prayers as many, including Mary, turned out to hear the Archbishop of York describe the dead king as the 'monarch who did not spare himself'.[6] Some members of Harewood staff, including Blades, the butler, and Mrs Delaney, the housekeeper, were permitted to visit Westminster Hall and a further service was held at Harewood church officiated over by the local vicar, Rev. Griffith. The Harewood estate residents sent a wreath to Windsor.

The king's funeral was held on 15 February and he was interred in the Royal Vault until 1969, at which point he was placed in the George VI Memorial Chapel inside St George's Chapel, Windsor. The funeral demonstrated a great outpouring of sorrow and affection for the late king. The funeral service was of moving simplicity, during which the women were so heavily veiled that for some, it was difficult to tell which figure was the Princess Royal and which the queen. Mary rode in the state carriage following the coffin with the new queen, Queen Elizabeth the

Queen Mother and Princess Margaret. Queen Mary did not attend since it was felt that the funeral would be too much of a strain for her. Instead she stood at a window in Marlborough House watching the procession. The dukes of Gloucester, Edinburgh, Kent and Windsor followed on foot. For Queen Mary, this was the third child she had outlived. Her sorrow was overwhelming. Mabell, Lady Airlie, was with Queen Mary during the funeral. 'The queen whispered, "Here he is," and I knew that her dry eyes were seeing beyond the coffin a little boy in a sailor suit. She was past weeping, wrapped in the ineffable solitude of grief.'[7]

Queen Mary celebrated the auspicious occasion of her eighty-fifth birthday in May 1952. She lunched with Mary at Marlborough House and some of her children and grandchildren; two of her great-grandchildren, Prince Charles and Princess Anne, came to see her. David arrived a day later and was to stay with her for a few days.

Towards the end of June, Mary paid a short visit to Lisburn in Northern Ireland on behalf of the Red Cross. This would be her first visit to Ireland since the war, and although the stay was a mere three days, Mary had a tight schedule of engagements to fulfil. She presented colours for the Red Cross and paid a visit to the dowager Marchioness of Londonderry, a noted socialite and writer who had been an active member of the WVR (Women's Volunteer Reserve) during the First World War. In addition, Mary inspected a parade of the Women's Royal Army Corps, carried out numerous social functions including a tea party with American servicemen, attended a service of thanksgiving, and visited Mountstewart, Belfast, County Antrim and Londonderry. Mary received purses to the value of over £4,000 for a YMCA Centre for the Royal Naval Air Station for which she received yet another gift of Irish linen. Throughout her stay the crowd gave Mary a warm welcome.

In the New Year's Honours List of 1953, Mary was made a Member of the Royal Red Cross (First Class). The New Year also brought with it the prospect of a royal tour for Mary to Trinidad, sailing in the oil tanker *Regent Hawk*. She would visit Tobago, British Guiana and Barbados.

The new year would see many changes in the royal family and their commitments. With the Queen and the Duke of Edinburgh undertaking a lengthy tour of Australia and New Zealand, it was announced that Mary and her sister-in-law the Duchess of Gloucester, who was married to Prince Henry, Duke of Gloucester, would be taking part in far more engagements from the new year onwards. Their list of duties would be lengthy.

Mary set sail from the Clyde on 24 January, and the programme for the tour was a packed schedule without a day off. Mary arrived on 9 February in the Port of Spain to be met by excited crowds and the governor of Trinidad, Major-General Sir Hubert Rance. She took the salute of the Police guard of honour before meeting many representatives from the Red Cross. As she drove in an open car through the streets, waving to the hordes of crowds on the route to Government House, she was greeted everywhere with the same enthusiastic and cheering crowds. The following day Mary attended an official dinner at Government House. She saw the West Indian premiere of the film *The Lady with the Lamp* about Florence Nightingale and visited a farm in St Joseph's where she saw palms planted by her father in 1880. In Georgetown Mary had five engagements in a day. She visited the cathedral, a museum, a library, the botanical gardens and a convalescent home. Her speech to Red Cross units once again championed the importance of donating blood and she detailed her own experiences. Mary's tour was considered a huge success with the only slight annoyance being when a few men, who were thought to be communists, waved placards telling the princess to go home. As tokens of their affection in Guiana, Mary was presented with many souvenirs including a brooch made from a nugget of Guiana gold. So immense was the number of gifts that Mary feared she would 'go away with a swollen head'.[8]

By February 1953 the elderly Queen Mary was struggling with her health. She had been confined to her room since late 1952 with a troublesome cough. Lady Airlie was one of the few fortunate people permitted to see her: 'I was conscious of the perfection of everything around her; the exquisitely embroidered soft lawn nightgown … the immaculately arranged grey hair. Her face had still a gentle beauty of expression; no trace of hardness as so many faces have in old age, only resignation."[9]

In the midst of her successful tour, Mary received news that Queen Mary was struggling with a recurrence of gastric trouble. It was not possible to operate on the queen because her heart was not sufficiently healthy. Her condition must have appeared serious, since Mary made the decision to cut short her tour by ten days to return on 5 March and David, who was in New York, was called back to England by Queen Mary's physician, Sir Horace Evans, who believed that she wished to see her eldest son. Mary decided to make a detour via New York so that she could return with David on board the *Queen Elizabeth* liner. It was during this stay in New York that a momentous occasion occurred when Mary met Wallis for the first time. Mary's initial feelings of embarrassment were soon dissolved by Wallis's great charm and they later posed for photographers. Mary was only the second person in David's direct family to meet Wallis since the Duke and Duchess of Gloucester had met her briefly in Paris in 1938.

As soon as they embarked on the return to England, reports indicated that there was a slight improvement in Queen Mary's condition. David was struggling to be away from Wallis. His ostracism from his family had made him totally dependent on his wife. He sent her a letter from the ship:

> The bulletins from Marlborough House proclaim the old lady's condition to be slightly improved! Ice in place of blood in the veins must be a fine preservative … Mary seems to have become more human with age and has revealed a few interesting family bits of gossip.[10]

Even though the arrival of Mary and David at her bedside appeared to have lifted her spirits, Queen Mary was dying, and her physicians were aware that she could die in her sleep or remain in such a condition for several weeks. David found his enforced separation from Wallis unbearable and he tried to keep himself busy, seeking out furniture for his new home in the Bois de Boulogne. Mary continued to visit her mother daily at Marlborough House and deputised for her at a prior engagement of a meeting of the presidents of the Queen Mary's London Needlework

Guild. Bulletins continued to be released stating that Queen Mary's condition had worsened.

Queen Mary survived for a fortnight after Mary and David's arrival. On her final evening, she asked to have a book concerning India read aloud to her, clearly reminiscing about the great Delhi Durbar of 1911, a spectacular and dazzling event that had marked the coronation of George V as emperor in India and Queen Mary as his empress. George Lascelles later revealed that his grandmother had 'never got over the beauty of it'.[11] By Tuesday afternoon the queen, unconscious from sedatives and painkillers, was visited by the Archbishop of Canterbury who had come to pray for her. Queen Mary finally died in her sleep on the evening of 24 March 1953, with her daughter at her side, a few weeks short of her eighty-sixth birthday. It was reported in the news that Queen Mary had never been able to overcome the grief of losing her son Bertie. The close family gathered at Marlborough House the following morning. David was incredulous as well as bitter that even in her last moments his mother had failed to accept Wallis as his wife. Yet at the same time, he mourned the passing of his mother, signifying the end of a generation and reminding him that he no longer had any 'part in the Royal Family beyond Burke's Peerage or Who's Who'.[12]

Queen Mary left strict instructions that her death should in no way postpone the coronation, due to take place on 2 June 1953, or that there should be too long a period of mourning. However, her funeral needed to be one befitting of a queen consort. Her body lay in state in Westminster Hall for two days and was later taken to St George's Chapel, Windsor, where the service, led by the Archbishop of Canterbury, was broadcast by the BBC. Queen Mary was laid to rest next to her husband. Later in the day, a service of memorial was held at St Paul's Cathedral. As was to be expected, Mary felt the loss of her mother more than anyone, particularly since they had become close companions following Harry's death. Mary struggled to write letters thanking people for their sympathy. In a typed letter to Dame Rachel Crowdy, Mary wrote, 'I am deeply touched by your most kind sympathy in my great sorrow … It is a great comfort to me to realise what universal love was felt for my mother, and to know how many friends are sharing my grief.'[13]

Out of respect for the former queen, many churches held remembrance services. One was held at the Queen's Chapel of the Savoy on 29 March 1953, during which Kenneth Rose, the biographer and historian, remarked in his diary that David was seen to look 'very miserable and, as at last funeral, he looks about constantly'.[14]

Before returning to Wallis, David went to look over Marlborough House with Mary, to 'show her the kind of things I should like to have when they begin disposing of Mama's personal possessions ... of course I'll be at a disadvantage when the division is made and the "vultures" will have had first pick'.[15] Despite his bitter sentiments towards many members of his family, declaring them to be 'a seedy worn out bunch of old hags',[16] David still found his sister 'quite sweet and human on the whole'.[17]

The coronation of Elizabeth II had been fixed for 2 June at Westminster Abbey. David may have originally believed that he would be invited but after Queen Mary's funeral he had resolved that it was better that he did not attend. Furthermore, Sir Alan Lascelles notified the Duke's lawyers that he would not be welcome. David prepared a statement to the press explaining that it would go against royal tradition for a previous monarch to attend the coronation of another, although the presence of Queen Elizabeth the Queen Mother was permitted just as Queen Mary had attended the coronation of George VI in 1953. This would be the first coronation televised by the BBC and it took over fourteen months to prepare.

Five days before the coronation, Mary attended a garden party for 7,000 guests at Buckingham Palace and thousands of people turned out to witness rehearsals at the abbey, desperate to catch a glimpse of the royal family, causing difficulties for the police who were attempting to control the crowd. The event provoked much excitement for the nation, and they organised street parties with mock coronations; some households were even fortunate to be able to watch the event on a tiny black and white television screen to celebrate. Mary was no longer of the same generation as the monarch and undoubtedly the new queen had much respect for her aunt since Mary played a central role in the coronation. The death of Queen Mary had given Mary a place as one of the more stately members of the family who knew much about royal traditions and precedents. In the films and photographs of the day, Mary was seated in between the queen mother and Princess Marina. Mary was incredibly proud of her coronation attire as well as all her magnificent jewels. For this occasion she chose to wear the diamond diadem tiara swopping the diamond centrepiece for an impressive sapphire. As a touching tribute to Harry, she wore a matching necklace of sapphires and diamonds; it had been a gift from him to mark the occasion of their wedding.

The pomp and pageantry of the coronation had given Britain some much-needed cause for celebration during the period of post-war austerity. As the new queen embarked on a lengthy six-month Commonwealth tour in late November 1953, encompassing Australia, Asia, Africa and the West Indies and covering more than 40,000 miles, it fell to many other members of the royal family, including Mary, to continue to deputise for and support the monarch. Mary was appointed a counsellor of state along with her son George, and throughout this period she maintained a hectic schedule of engagements. Towards the end of the coronation year, in October, Mary was rewarded for her commitment to the north of England by being accorded the honour of the freedom of Ripon in recognition of her 'eminent and devoted services to the city'.[18] Mary was met at the city boundary by the mayor of Ripon and she inspected a guard of honour of the Royal Engineers who also received the freedom of the city on the same day.

In her address Mary spoke of her pride in being part of Yorkshire life:

I thank you for the … honour you have done me today. I am already proud to be on the roll of Freemen of Leeds, of Harrogate and of York. Each has a character of its own – Leeds, a growing industrial city with a young university of which I take great pride in being Chancellor. Harrogate, a borough centred round its spa, offering healing and health to many visitors. York, a medieval city watched over by the glorious Minster and with modern industries springing up to give it life and new vitality. And now today Ripon – a city full of history and ancient tradition … I have spoken often of my love for Yorkshire how it has grown with the years. Since I married a Yorkshireman 31 years ago, I have spent the greater part of my life in this county and have learned to appreciate the sterling qualities of the people ... The honour you have paid me today forges yet another link in the chain of my affection for Yorkshire. May I assure you that it needed no rowels to spur me on my journey here to receive the gift which I treasure more deeply than I can find words to express.[19]

To commemorate the occasion, Mary was presented with an illuminated scroll and an inscribed clock, barometer and thermometer.

Mary's following engagement was to open the three-day York Festival of the Home: an event notable for having the largest gathering of members of the Mothers' Union in the north of England. The Mothers' Union was a Christian organisation that aimed to provide support for those experiencing adverse times. This event was exceptionally nerve-wracking for Mary since she had to give a speech over a loud-speaker to a packed crowd of over 2,000 members, some accommodated in an over-spill room. Mary's speech concerned the role of the Church in sustaining the family unit and furthermore it demonstrates her commitment to the philosophy of Christianity, as well as the importance of family life:

There are times when it seems to us as though the Church were out of touch with everyday people and events. The answer is that we are the Church, and the part the Mothers' Union can play in modern life has never been greater ... One of the chief causes of rising crime among the young is the lack of religious teaching in the home. This the Mothers' Union can remedy by the inculcation of Christian principles and this Festival, by its exhibition, and wide range of lectures, will enable members to fit themselves further for this vitally important work.[20]

In the later months of 1953, and in a bid to keep herself from dwelling over her mother's death in the build-up to Christmas, Mary was exceptionally active, attending the opening of parliament, visiting Blackburn, assisting the women of Queen Mary's London Needlework Guild, as well as purchasing Christmas gifts from a Disabled Ex-Servicemen Sale in Chelsea, receiving purses for the YMCA in Dewsbury, attending the Harrogate Chrysanthemum Show, opening the Painted Fabrics Christmas sale in Sheffield and installing new gates at Harrogate Ladies' College. During her trip to Harrogate, Mary presided at the jubilee meeting of the local branch of the National Society for the Prevention of Cruelty to Children and spoke of the importance of undertaking voluntary work:

> Many people, nowadays, are of the opinion that as the State assumes more and more responsibility, much of the voluntary arrangements, voluntary associations and voluntary services may be brought to an end. That is a view with which I for one profoundly disagree. I think it is right and proper we should be leading the world in the development of social services. But it seems to me that it is just that development which makes voluntary effort not less important but more so. Because … we are coming constantly upon problems with which only voluntary effort can deal.[21]

In the last months of the year, Mary addressed delegates of the women's section of the British Legion and paid tribute to their work. She attended the Not Forgotten Christmas party where she continued a tradition, by now over thirty years old, of distributing Christmas cakes. She attended a further party for the Royal Signals, a meeting of the council of the British Red Cross and agreed to become the president of the National Rose Society. She returned to Harewood for Christmas with her sons and their families; George and Marion's second son, James, who had been born in October, was christened at Harewood just after Christmas.

The new year commenced with a visit to Murdostoun Castle in Lanarkshire, where Mary carried out several engagements. She was especially touched when attending a church service to learn that her mother's favourite hymn was to be sung, 'Oh love that wiln't not let me go'. The University of Leeds celebrated the fiftieth anniversary of the granting of its charter in April. As its chancellor, Mary attended many events to mark this occasion including a ball and the conferment of an honorary degree of Doctor of Law to Queen Elizabeth the Queen Mother. Although Mary was always treated in the north with much respect, warmth and affection, it is interesting to compare the crowd's reaction to the queen mother, which appeared to be far more animated and vociferous. This undoubtedly had much to do with Queen Elizabeth's position as a former consort to the king, as well as her perpetual sunny disposition. Mary was perceived as being far more solemn and staid. Yet the queen mother's acceptance of the degree certainly grew from Mary establishing the new custom for female members of the royal family to receive a degree, thereby normalising the position of women in tertiary education.

Mary paid a further visit to Scotland in May, completing a round of engagements for the Royal Scots, the Royal Signals and the Women's Royal Army Corps, along with the British Red Cross before receiving the honorary degree of Doctor of Law from St Andrew's University. Realising the significance of her award as a woman, Mary stated, 'I am a delighted recipient of an honour which has been bestowed in the past upon men of the highest eminence in the worlds of learning and public affairs.'[22]

Mary was certainly making an impact with her work in the field of tertiary education as two days later on 12 May, she received a further honorary degree from Lord Woolton at Manchester University. The dean of the Faculty of Theology, Professor Manson, said in his address regarding Mary's position as chancellor of Leeds:

It is but three years since she accepted the invitation to Chancellorship and in that brief space she has carried out the formal duties of her office with such grace and dignity and shown such a keen and lively interest in all that affects the welfare of the University, that she has secured not only the respect due to her position but also the firm confidence and affectionate regard of the whole academic community. HRH has never sought to evade the obligations that go with Royalty, she accepts and fulfils them readily and graciously … our honorary doctorate will be … a tribute of gratitude and high regard offered to herself.[23]

# 22

# A Family Affair

Baby secret shocks London.[1]

*Sydney Sun*, 3 January 1967

It was to prove to be a fateful night in January 1959, when George, Earl of Harewood, found himself stranded for some time at Milan airport. He was returning from a meeting with the renowned opera singer Maria Callas, having failed to convince her to agree to extra performances at the Royal Opera House in Covent Garden. While waiting in the Air France lounge, he inadvertently came across Patricia Tuckwell, an elegantly beautiful former model and violinist who was also known as 'Bambi'. The earl offered to carry Patricia's bag and they soon discovered that Miss Tuckwell's brother, Barry, was a friend of his. They connected instantly as if they had known each other for years and never stopped talking during their flight. For the earl, it was love at first sight. This seemingly innocuous meeting was to change the entire course of his life and impact upon his marriage, his children and his mother, more than anyone could ever have imagined.

Over a decade later, the year of 1967 opened rather sensationally in Australia, with newspapers dedicating their front pages and many column inches to the private life of a fellow Australian who was involved in what the *Daily Mirror* of Sydney declared to be a 'Scandal over Queen's

Cousin'.[2] George was to be divorced by his first wife Marion on the grounds of his adultery with Miss Patricia Tuckwell, whom he intended to marry as soon as possible since they already had a son, Mark, born out of wedlock in July 1964. The British *Daily Mirror*'s front page was slightly less tempered: 'The woman I want to marry by Lord Harewood'.[3]

At the time George was eighteenth in the line of succession to the throne. He knew that the papers were about to break the story and therefore decided that it would be provident to issue a prepared statement through his lawyers, Bircham and Co:

> We have recently, on Lord Harewood's behalf, accepted service of divorce proceedings, whereby Lady Harewood petitions for divorce on the grounds of her husband's adultery ... Lord Harewood will not defend these proceedings and he and Miss Tuckwell would wish to marry if and when they are free to do so.[4]

Of course, much was made by the newspapers of Miss Tuckwell's attractive and glamorous appearance.

George and Marion's divorce was finalised two years after Mary's death, but the events leading up to it had occurred for over a decade. Similarly, George and Patricia's relationship and living situation had been an open secret among many friends and family members. The affair gave Mary obvious concern in the later years of her life. With her tendency to internalise her anxieties, it no doubt affected her health. She must have yearned for Harry and his sound judgement and advice during such onerous times, in addition to his strength to sustain her. Evidently, living in close proximity to Marion and George at Harewood, Mary was fully aware of difficulties in their marriage, especially with the couple spending more time apart as their marriage unravelled. However, Mary never spoke to anyone about the matter; that was not her way. The only time Mary had even discussed the affair remotely with George was when she asked him, rhetorically, 'What will people say?'[5] As a doting grandmother to four boys, it might be difficult to comprehend why she never met her youngest grandson, Mark, despite being aware of his existence. Yet for Mary, this was part of her coping mechanism. She simply swept aside any mention of the situation and when her son tried to speak to her about it, she refused to be drawn into any discussion. Mary always dealt with family crises in this way; she compartmentalised, and it enabled her to avoid conflict. In the same way that she was able to separate her relationship with David from the act of his abdication, she separated George from the affair. She may not have enjoyed a close relationship with Marion, but she had no desire to take sides. Mary did not live to witness the divorce, and this undoubtedly spared her considerable emotional upset.

If Mary had taken the time to learn more about her son's relationship with Patricia, she might have realised that there had been no malicious premeditation to the affair. From the outset, and almost despite his instant attraction towards Patricia, George's intentions had always been honourable, wanting to include her in his and Marion's social circle. George had never set out to hurt Marion and his children.

Patricia had been born in Melbourne in 1926, the daughter of an organist, Charles Tuckwell. She pursued a career as a violinist within the Sydney Symphony Orchestra. As a young woman she worked as a model, hence the nickname Bambi. Patricia was said to be so beautiful that many people would attend concerts in which she played merely to look at her. In the 1940s her modelling work led to her becoming the muse of photographer Louis Athol Shmith, famous for his stylish portraits. The couple were married in 1948, although the marriage did not last long.

With her incredible beauty and her shared passion for music, George found it impossible to ignore his love for Patricia. Over time, she started to feel the same and both realised how utterly impossible the situation had become, since neither wished to upset Marion and the children and break up their home. George asked Marion for a divorce but she refused, believing that Patricia would ultimately tire of George. However, the affair continued until Patricia, understandably suffering from the turmoil of such a situation, decided to go home to Australia, where she wrote explaining that it would be too painful for all parties if she came back. Inevitably, he was devastated and begged her to reconsider, declaring that he could not imagine his future without her. Patricia conceded and returned to England. In his memoir, *The Tongs and the Bones*, George addressed the situation candidly and offered much self-analysis. He clearly felt overwhelming guilt. For him, the marriage to Marion had broken down since 'we failed too regularly to overcome the small misunderstandings and breakdowns of communication that occur in any married life but allowed them to grow into issues where no true issue should have existed'.[6]

At the 1964 Edinburgh Festival, which was to be George's last as director, there was much dishonour for the earl when Marion slapped Patricia's face 'with much invective in front of everyone present'.[7] It was this humiliating incident which resulted in George losing his position as director of the festival and he was forced to resign as chancellor of the University of York.

George's inner turmoil was compounded by the fact that he had few people to counsel him because most friends understandably took Marion's side. Mary's disapproval and determined refusal to discuss the situation did not help either. In an attempt to 'see my position with greater clarity',[8] he sought the advice of psychoanalysis. Well-meaning friends encouraged him to do so, naively confident it would enable him to see the huge mistake he was making and return to his wife. However, the psychoanalysis made the earl more resolved than ever to seek out happiness with Patricia and so he finally informed his sons of his decision and left Marion. Eighteen months later, Marion agreed to the divorce.

The decree absolute was granted in July 1967. The month prior to this, David and Wallis were finally permitted to attend a royal event at Marlborough House, when a plaque was unveiled in tribute to Queen Mary. George attended on his own, while his brother Gerald was accompanied by his wife, Angela. Queen Mary had been so against meeting Wallis, and yet at an occasion to celebrate the former consort's life, when the ink was just drying on the first royal divorce, here was at last a public acceptance of the Duke and Duchess of Windsor.

For a considerable time the gossip columns featured stories concerning George and his new partner. He was the black sheep of the family and considered a 'Royal Maverick'.[9] Much was made of the so-called shunning of the earl by the royal family. However, as with many of the sensationalist headlines concerning Mary and her family, this was not entirely the truth. It is true that as the head of the Church of England, which did not at the time sanction divorce and remarriage, the queen could not be seen to approve of her cousin's divorce and remarriage. George's divorce must have given the queen great anxiety, especially since there was a child involved. In the 1970s, George felt aggrieved that he was not invited to the Duke of Windsor's funeral and despite giving Princess Anne and Captain Mark Phillips a generous wedding present he was not invited to the ceremony at Westminster Abbey in November 1973. This alleged banishment continued until 1977 when the *Daily Express* reported that the queen had finally ended the rift by giving George a salutary kiss at a public event. George was considered to have been forgiven in time to attend the wedding of Prince Charles and Lady Diana Spencer in July 1981 with his wife Patricia and the queen honoured him further with the award of KBE in 1986. Over time, George's perspective on the matter mellowed and in an interview he gave to Yorkshire Television in 1982,[10] he claimed that he had never felt totally ostracised. He stated that the reason he had not taken part in royal events was mainly because he never considered himself to be a member of the royal family. Like Mary, he had always suffered from a certain timidity.

George and Patricia were eventually married in New Canaan, Connecticut in 1967 at the home of friends, with the queen's permission. The Royal Marriages Act forbade George from marrying in a registry office and since both he and Patricia were divorced, neither could marry in church. Mary died before seeing the culmination of the affair and this clearly would have continued to trouble her, since she had been brought up to believe that divorce was against the Christian teachings of marriage. However, during the war, Mary had nearly lost her son when he had been a prisoner of war and in the same way in which she softened in her views towards David, she would undoubtedly have felt greater empathy for her son, as well as understanding his need for personal happiness. Times were beginning to change, albeit gradually, and just as Christian principles of life were being questioned then so too were societal norms. It would not be long before royal divorces became more accepted with that of Princess Margaret in 1978 and the subsequent divorces of Queen Elizabeth's children in the 1990s. It must have given the 7th earl much consolation that he remained happily married to Patricia until his death in 2011. Obituaries of the 7th earl had much in common with his mother's: his inherent shyness, kindness, wit and lack of formality and royal hauteur, with the focus more on 'what he achieved, rather than who he was'.[11]

In 1973 Marion remarried at Paddington Registry Office. Her choice of husband this time was Jeremy Thorpe, the leader of the Liberal Party, who in the 1950s had been considered a bright star among politicians because of his persistence and willingness to tackle issues for his North Devon constituency. Jeremy had a 3-year-old son, Rupert, from his first wife, Caroline, who had tragically died in a car accident not long after the Liberals had suffered a humiliating defeat in the general election of 1970. Thorpe took time out to mourn his first wife and returned to politics in 1972. In 1979 Thorpe was accused of conspiracy to murder Norman Scott, and Marion accompanied Jeremy every day to the court trial. Thorpe and Scott had been in a relationship in the early 1960s. Although Thorpe was acquitted, his career was over. Marion remained with Thorpe until her death in 2014.

Mary's younger son, Gerald, was involved in a similar situation, although it received minimal publicity since he led a relatively secluded life. In the early 1960s, Gerald began an extramarital affair with Elizabeth Collingwood, an actress. He was still living with his first wife, Angela, when Elizabeth gave birth to a son in 1962. At this point Mary was still alive but she was never aware of Gerald's secret life. The revelations were only made public in 1978, when Gerald divorced Angela and married Elizabeth in Vienna. By this time Gerald and Elizabeth had been together for over twenty years. Angela continued to remain on good terms with the royal family and was often invited by the queen into the royal enclosure at Ascot until her death. She was given a grace and favour home in the Great Park at Windsor

# 23

# Later Years

She travelled extensively in the Commonwealth and did much to strengthen the links which bind us together.[1]

*Belfast Telegraph*, Wednesday 31 March 1965

Although Mary never truly got over Harry's death, over time she learned to live with it and the atmosphere at Harewood was again one of happiness and laughter. In 1953, Neville Ussher, who had previously served as aide-de-camp to Lord Athlone, became the manager of the estate and eventually a great friend to Mary. When Neville first arrived at Harewood, Mary seemed somewhat wary of him, yet within six months, she would not even sharpen a pencil without first consulting him and he remained a loyal friend and estate manager until her death. There are many accounts of amusing stories concerning the Princess at this time. Such as when housekeeper Olive Clark, a rather fussy woman, decided to feed some pigeons on the roof of Harewood, resulting in an outbreak of scores of pigeons and an unfortunate abundance of bird droppings on the house. Mary asked Neville how they could deal with the issue, who suggested that an air gun would prevent damage to the house. Mary, Neville and his young son, Christopher, went to shoot the pigeons, unaware that Olive was watching them. Olive called the RSPCA and reported that the Princess Royal, her estate manager and his son were killing the birds. Later Neville received a phone call from the RSPCA concerning the cull and mentioning that the charity had been placed in rather a delicate position since the Princess was in fact a patron of the charity. The incident subsequently led to much amusement for the princess.

When Mary was born in 1897, the British Empire was at its peak as the foremost power in the world, with Queen Victoria reigning as empress and a population exceeding 400 million. As Mary entered the seventh decade of her life in the late 1950s and early 1960s, and the gloom of post-war austerity lifted, many nations were seeking independence from the empire with most forming part of the British Commonwealth of Nations. Life expectancy during this period was much lower than today; Mary would have been considered elderly by this time and more suited to retirement. However, the last ten years of her life were characterised by an energetic schedule of tours and engagements in which she represented the queen.

Mary had always been fond of Canada, with its welcoming people and vast diverse landscape; she maintained strong links with the country since she was colonel-in-chief of two Canadian regiments, the Canadian Scottish and Royal Canadian Corps of Signals. A planned short trip in autumn 1955 to visit these regiments swiftly snowballed into a hectic month-long tour encompassing Quebec, Montreal, Ontario, Niagara Falls, Ottawa, Toronto, Winnipeg, Victoria and Vancouver. Mary travelled on board the Canadian Pacific liner, *Empress of France*. A spokesperson for Canadian Pacific stated that Mary had requested, in her typical fashion, that 'no fuss'[2] should be made for her journey except for a few coats of paint speedily made to the state rooms she would occupy. Mary arrived in Quebec to be met with a 100-man guard of honour and a twenty-one-gun salute; she proceeded to Laval University, where she accepted a further honorary doctorate.

The promotion of higher education and overseas service units justified a four-day visit to France in April 1956. Mary arrived in Paris on 22 April to visit the central European headquarters of the Allied forces at Fontainebleau and was received by Marshal Juin, the commander-in-chief, and the celebrated diarist Cynthia Jebb, later Lady Gladwyn, whose husband was the British ambassador to Paris. Lady Jebb writes of the rather unexpected manner in which Mary arrived, giving an insight into what is what like for those involved in receiving the princess:

> The Princess Royal emerged, in full military uniform. This masculine-looking figure … came briskly down the steps in her solid low-heeled shoes … leather gloves in her hand, her chest resplendent with decorations, her lady in waiting carrying her handbag, and saluted the astonished company.[3]

In view of the lack of the formality and pomp accorded to other members of the royal family, the large bouquet that had awaited the princess appeared rather superfluous. As Lady Jebb drove back to the embassy with Mary, she was amazed by how often and conscientiously Mary saluted the greeting crowds. Throughout the journey, Mary gave the impression of being incredibly shy and ill at ease. She seemed to resemble both of her parents, yet with grey hair and unbecoming clothes with no make-up, she looked most unlike what one would expect of a princess. Lady Jebb realised that:

> One begins to be aware of her sincere and good character and her many other merits. She is, above all, very conscientious and will always do the right thing. This shines out in her so strongly that … I was aware that this visit was going to be much more simple than that of the Queen Mother. In lieu of charm, here was a person who was anxious to help, brought up in the old school, well-educated, intelligent, well-read, aware of what is going on in the world and forming a sensible judgement on it all.[4]

Lady Jebb soon warmed to the princess, especially when her small dachshund took an instant liking to Mary. A couple of days later, on Mary's fifty-ninth birthday at a ceremony at the Opera House in Lille and wearing the gold-braided green robes of chancellor of the University of Leeds, an honorary doctorate was conferred upon her. Mary made a brief speech in French, demonstrating her perfect grasp of the language.

In response to the end of the Second World War and the emergence of the new Commonwealth, royal overseas tours began to hold greater significance in the mid-twentieth century. Mary conducted an official twelve-day tour of Nigeria in November 1957. Such tours inevitably required extensive planning and preparation as well as consideration of finances for the public purse. It was necessary to give careful thought to any possible political and diplomatic difficulties. The matter of the rivalry between east and west Nigeria needed to be treated with sensitivity to ensure that one side did not feel favoured over the other. The president of the east was Nnamdi Aziwike of the Yoruba people, who would later become known for his role as the 'Father of Nigerian Nationalism'. Obafemi Awolowo was the premier of the western region and was a proponent of federalism.

The tour had several aims. Africa in the 1950s was characterised by an increasing belief in independence and Mary's presence would hopefully ensure that Nigeria's move to independence would run as smoothly as possible. The first session of the Nigerian Constitutional Conference had already taken place in autumn 1957, during which an undertaking had been given by the British government that if during the first few months of 1960 the newly elected Nigerian legislature passed a resolution asking for independence, this would be agreed and a bill would be introduced to parliament in October 1960. However, Mary's attendance in Nigeria did not form part of independence ceremonies. These were carried out in 1960 when Mary's niece Princess Alexandra, the daughter of George and Marina of Kent, represented the queen. Higher education was a further purpose of the trip and part of Mary's role involved opening two universities: the University College Teaching Hospital in Western Nigeria and the Nigerian College of Art, Science and Technology in the Northern region of Zaria.

As well as marking the introduction of self-government in western Nigeria, Mary wished to visit the Nigerian branch of the Red Cross, present colours at Lagos and see Nigeria's largest river port city, Onitsha. It was rare for a princess to travel so extensively on her own in those days for official or non-official visits, and in doing so Mary set the precedent which many later followed, most notably Princess Margaret and Princess Anne. The Queen had already visited Lagos in Nigeria in 1956 and had received an affectionate welcome, suggesting a good omen for any subsequent royal tours. Furthermore, the role of an aunt in Nigerian families was considered as someone with high authority; thus it was hoped that equal affection and loyalty would be shown to the Queen's aunt.

The Ministry of Home Affairs building was turned into a hotel for the purposes of accommodating Mary, her staff, British MPs and the press. Chief Obafemi Awolowo, the premier of western Nigeria, recognised the importance of film at such a significant event. Therefore, an eighty-five-minute colour film of the princess's visit was recorded by the Department of Information Services celebrating the changes in Nigeria rather than dwelling on colonialism or anti-British sentiment.

Mary undertook the 3,500-mile trip in a specially chartered Argonaut aircraft on 13 November. The flight stopped over in Malta and Tripoli before arriving at Lagos airport for a short stay of three days. On arrival at Lagos, she was received by the governor-general, Sir James Robertson, Prime Minister Alhaji Balewa and a large crowd of spectators. Mary inspected a guard of honour by the 4th Battalion of the Queen's Own Nigeria Regiment and was introduced to ministers, members of the consular corps and town council officials.

Mary's successful tour encompassed a visit to the Ibadan racecourse to attend a children's rally, where 17,000 children were each given a white handkerchief promoting self-government to wave. The response for the princess was tremendous and the children welcomed her with a song in Yoruba as she stood in an open-topped jeep, waving to the crowds. Mary commemorated the occasion by planting a tree in the grounds of the new Government House and a speech was given by the premier. Further engagements included seeing the legislature, opening new Red Cross headquarters and inspecting the 4th Battalion Nigerian Regiment.

The University College Teaching Hospital in Ibadan was one of the most expensive projects ever undertaken in Nigeria, costing over £5 million. The hospital was affiliated with London University, which had given accreditation to the hospital's clinical course. Once more, excited crowds of people turned out to see Mary open it and her speech stated that 'a modern hospital is a complex organisation and requires ... the highest degree of harmonious collaboration between the many varied departments and services which constitute it'.[5] The tour was only slightly disrupted at Ibadan, when a 20-year-old local Nigerian man broke through a police cordon and threw a letter into Mary's car, claiming to be seeking her help.

Mary always researched her visits and tours extensively, something that was apparent to the people she met from their conversations with her. The packed schedule of engagements, coupled with the stifling heat, would have been demanding for a younger member of the royal family, let alone one who was at 60 considered elderly by the standards of the day. Hence it was not surprising that Mary had to cancel several of her planned engagements as she was suffering from a mild illness. She later wrote to Lord Middleton that she had been unwell prior to the trip and, with the heat, had really found it exhausting. Yet she considered her visit an immense success and was captivated by the culture and sights of Nigeria.[6] An amusing incident occurred during an evening function when Mary wore a tiara. She noticed that moths and flies, which had been attracted inside by the acetylene lamps, had decided to settle in her hair. It was only when eyes were no longer on herself that Mary later told a friend she could 'have a good scratch'.[7]

Mary was unable to shake off the illness and when she returned home in June 1958 her doctor diagnosed overstrain and advised a convalescence period of two months, during which she took a brief holiday in Balmoral. Of course, it was stressed that this was a work convalescence, since nothing would prevent the princess from honouring her race meeting engagements.

If Mary had found the tour of Nigeria demanding, her next foreign visit of three months in the West Indies and British Honduras in 1960 was to prove even more taxing. The tour had originally been envisaged as a private cruise of rest and relaxation aboard the royal yacht *Britannia*. However, as was often the case with planned short visits, this did not happen, and in February 1960 she set foot in the West Indies with the purpose of meeting 'people establishing a virile new dominion'.[8]

Established in 1958 as a means of creating an independent political unit, the West Indies Federation experienced many difficulties, not least because of the size of its population and issues with financial arrangements. In May 1962 it collapsed and eventually re-emerged as nine sovereign states and four British overseas territories. The list of places Mary stopped at on her tour reads more like an atlas than the itinerary of a 62-year-old princess: Barbados, British Guiana, British Honduras, Trinidad, St Vincent, St Lucia, Dominica, Monserrat, Jamaica, Montego Bay and the Cayman Islands. It is even more impressive that during this relentless tour Mary inspected Girl Guide units and participated with them in camp-fire ceremonies; she opened playgrounds; attended banquets and civic receptions; held lunches on board *Britannia*; carried out visits to schools, hospitals and homes for the blind; inspected and tasted local produce; visited banana and sugar cane farms; and listened to and even conducted a steel band in British Guiana. In Layou, Mary met children cheering and waving breadfruit leaves as she passed under banana arches. In Kingston, Benjamin Marson took great pride in showing Mary his highly polished, immaculate Princess Mary Gift Tin from the First World War complete with its contents. On her return to Portsmouth in April, there was much amusement when the Royal Marines band on board played a selection of calypso tunes to welcome Mary home.

The fifteenth Commonwealth state to emerge was Trinidad and Tobago, and celebrations were scheduled for August 1962. Once again Mary would represent the queen as head of state, accompanied by a delegation of five men representing the British government. This tour was extensively covered in the press from Mary's arrival at Piarco Airport on 28 August 1962, where she was met by the first Prime Minister, Dr Eric Williams, and the governor-general and his wife, Sir Solomon and Lady Thelma Hochoy. Lady Hochoy found much to discuss with the princess, since she had been so touched by the poor treatment of disabled children in Trinidad and Tobago that she had established a school and residential home to care for them. Mary's first undertaking was to open the new million-pound West Indies air terminal followed by an inspection of the Trinidad and Tobago Regiment. Despite the rain, continual cheers and much enthusiasm met the party along the route as they drove the 20 miles to the residence of the governor-general.

In view of Mary's packed schedule, her first full day in Trinidad was left free of engagements to give her sufficient time to recover from the flight. The following day she attended the first major independence celebratory event when over 20,000 children sang to her at a rally and she watched dances from a wide range of countries to signify the multicultural diversity of Trinidad. As before in Nigeria, Mary drove slowly around a stadium in an open car waving at the crowds.

A historic ceremony marking the end of 165 years of British rule was held on 30 August at midnight at the seat of government, the Red House. The Union Jack flag was lowered and a new flag of black red, and white colours of independent Trinidad was hoisted in its place whilst a multi-denominational group of religious leaders offered prayers to guide the new nation. The following day was particularly hot and humid, yet Mary maintained her dignity and solemnity as she handed over the constitutional instruments of independence at the first state opening of parliament. This was an occasion steeped in pageantry and depicted in the press as 'in the Westminster tradition'.[9] Much like the British state opening of parliament, judges, the speaker and members of both houses waited for three knocks at the chamber door to denote the arrival of the royal party. In her speech given as she sat on the throne, Mary vowed to ensure the closest possible association with all countries of South America and the Caribbean, and she included a message from the queen welcoming the country to the Commonwealth of Nations. That evening Mary attended a state banquet and stood on the roof of the Hilton Hotel to watch a magnificent firework display.

Mary undertook two further tours of her beloved Canada. The first was to Quebec, Ontario and British Columbia in 1962 as a result of a request to award new colours for the Canadian Scottish Regiment. In another first for Mary, she became the first royal to fly to Canada via the Polar route on a fifteen-hour flight. There, she received yet another first; this time the honour of becoming the first woman and the seventh honorary bencher of the Law Society of Upper Canada. Previous recipients included her grandfather Edward VII. The newspapers in England contained scant details of Mary's tour. However, it had been a great success for the princess, and it is an indication of her modesty and graciousness that she would always recognise the support of her staff on overseas visits. In a letter Mary wrote to her lady-in-waiting at the time, Dame Mary Colvin, she acknowledged those who had accompanied her: 'I could not have carried on without the liaison and backing of my staff. At times I was very busy, but I know I could rely on you all and this helped very much indeed.'[10] Similarly, after every tour and engagement, Mary would religiously write to her hosts to thank them for their hospitality. She would mention every activity she had seen and explain its impact on her. In particular Mary frequently commented on the smartness of uniforms.

In September 1964, Mary embarked on a nine-day tour of Newfoundland, travelling on *Britannia*. She wished to visit the Royal Newfoundland Regiment, to accept an honorary colonelcy and to commemorate the fiftieth anniversary of the departure of the first contingent of the regiment from St John's to the First World War battlefields. Furthermore, Mary hoped to strengthen ties between the regiment and the Royal Scots. This tour included thirty-seven engagements culminating in a special convocation at the Memorial University of Newfoundland to receive an honorary degree of Doctor of Laws, for which she received a resplendent scarlet robe and black velvet cap. During her tour Mary met many veterans, planted trees, held several inspections of guards of honour and took the salute for regimental parades. The student newspaper *The Muse* recorded Mary's visit when she had unveiled a 6ft plaque in the Arts Building donated to the university by the Royal Canadian Legion, intended to serve as a reminder to future students of the university that their opportunities had been made possible owing to the bravery of the Newfoundlanders who had served in the First World War. This was to be Mary's last visit to Canada. As she embarked before the return journey home, she was seen to look back with a slight tear in her eye. She was probably aware at this stage that she had health difficulties with her heart and the tear may have come with the realisation that she would never see the country again.

1964 was to prove to be one of Mary's busiest years for engagements. As *Australian Women's Weekly* reported in March 1964, the queen,

Princess Margaret and Princess Alexandra were all expecting babies. The queen mother was convalescing after an illness and so it fell to Mary to take on many engagements in their place. This included the distribution of Maundy money on 26 March at Westminster Abbey to thirty-eight men and women on behalf of the queen; this was (and still is) an annual tradition in which the sovereign donates special coins to the elderly as a commemoration of Jesus washing the feet of his apostles at the Last Supper. A Westminster Abbey official attempted to instruct Mary on how to carry out the ceremony and soon realised that she knew exactly what to do, having seen her parents carrying out the same ritual several decades before.[11]

Mary's next engagement was Lusaka for the independence ceremony of Zambia on 24 October 1964. Zambia was the ninth African dependency of Britain to attain independence. Mary arrived in Lusaka on 22 October to see a city bedecked in the red, black, green and orange colours of the Zambian flag. At midnight on 23 October, in the company of the last governor, Sir Evelyn Hone, and the new president, Kenneth Kaunda, she witnessed the lowering of the Union Jack after seventy years of British rule. The following day, Mary handed over the instruments of independence to Kaunda on behalf of the queen and read a message from Her Majesty. The new president was sworn in just as, on a hilltop, a huge copper kettle fire burned, representing the birth of the new republic. Mary was incredibly touched when the people of Lusaka awarded her the freedom of the city and in return she told them that it was an occasion that she would always remember.

As a new year opened, Mary showed no signs of slowing down. There were many commitments, especially in the north of England, including a regimental dinner at the Carlton barracks for the Leeds Rifles and a conference for the Women's Royal Army Corps in York. Mary attended the state funeral of Winston Churchill at St Paul's Cathedral on 30 January; on 13 March she travelled to Sweden to represent the queen for a final time at the funeral of Queen Louise of Sweden in Storkyrkan in Stockholm. Louise was the daughter of Prince Louis of Battenberg, who had renounced all of his Germanic titles during the First World War; she was also the sister of the first Lord Mountbatten of Burma and the aunt of Prince Philip. Thousands of people gathered along the route to Stockholm Cathedral to pay their respects to the queen, who was buried in the royal cemetery on Karlsborg Island in Solna.

For some time, Mary had been contemplating a move to Sandringham. Doctors had advised her this might improve her health and suggested that she begin to take life at a slower pace. This idea may have been prompted by the need to distance herself from Harewood before people became aware of her son George's divorce and remarriage. Yet Harewood had been her life for over forty years and the people of the north had such a sense of ownership over their northern princess that any move would have caused major upheaval along with a sense of loss throughout the region.

A few days after Queen Louise's funeral, Mary visited her brother David in hospital in London, where he was recovering from three operations for retinal detachment of his left eye. She took him some flowers and spent over three-quarters of an hour speaking to him and his wife. It was hoped that now 'Mary would do much to draw the Duke and Duchess of Windsor back into the family circle'.[12] Sadly, it was to be a final farewell to the brother she had supported and favoured throughout their lives; one who, unlike Mary, had never been able to accept the responsibility of his royal duty. In this respect, he could not have been more of an antithesis to her.

Mary had been experiencing some difficulties with her heart for a while and her family had failed to exhibit much concern for her complaints because she had often suffered from illness after periods of intense stress and activity. She was merely advised not to overexert herself. Whether the frequent and demanding royal tours she embarked on in her later years had any impact on her health is uncertain.

Mary regularly walked within the Harewood estate every day, completing a circuit of about 2 miles around the lake. Sometimes she would be accompanied by her lady-in-waiting and other times she would be alone with her dogs. Her gardener Geoffrey Hall believed that after Harry's death Mary was frequently lonely, and she would therefore make a point of stopping on her walk to speak to him about the latest plants or garden work. One day, on 28 March 1965, all of her grandchildren were at home for the Easter holiday and, with Mary and George, they went for a stroll after lunch. At some point near to the lake, Mary tripped and fell, and her son helped her to a bench while the children ran to get someone to come in a car. As her son later poignantly related in his autobiography:

> I supported her while the boys ran off ... There was no apparent crisis and I had no idea that in the quarter of an hour which intervened before the car came, she had died quite peacefully in my arms. Somehow the shock was cushioned by the lack of struggle involved ... I suppose she would have wanted that, as although she liked her due, she also disliked fuss and bother – of any kind.[13]

It was not just the family who were upset by her death; it was 'a black and distressing day'[14] for all the residents on the estate. The princess's presence at Harewood had always given an additional element of 'dignity and respect'.[15] Mary's death meant that 'something not wholly tangible disappeared ... it was not simply the loss of a beloved parent ... I missed her as a grown-up misses someone in whom he has always found a point of certainty. Harewood was her home and ... very much her creation'.[16]

The Times recorded that 'Yorkshire's own Princess'[17] had died of a heart thrombosis. The sad news of her death was soon passed onto the queen at Windsor Castle. David was notified whilst at Claridge's while recuperating from his eye surgery. As soon as Prime Minister Harold Wilson was informed, he sent a message of sympathy to Mary's sons. The court would be in mourning for a week until 3 April and flags were flown at half-mast.

In its obituary of Mary, The Times headline could not have summed up her life more accurately than it did by pronouncing it 'active, unobtrusive and purposeful'.[18] It called Mary 'a true Englishwoman'[19] who had 'inherited the shyness and reserve'[20] of her mother:

> Her knowledge of racing and enjoyment of a race meeting were outstanding ... she was assured of an honoured and distinguished welcome at the York races. ... The Princess Royal had a fine knowledge of the arts and of history. Her natural reserve made her public duties ... more

onerous than was the case with many members of the Royal Family; but she overcame this and served the nation especially in Yorkshire where she was dearly loved with a constant and rare fidelity.[21]

According to the *Birmingham Daily Post*, Mary was the 'Princess with the Common Touch'.[22] Her position in Yorkshire was 'a kind of territorial representative … she never did seek the limelight, though it sometimes caught her, but she lived a life of unassuming goodness and service'.[23] Throughout the country there was a genuine outpouring of grief that the life of such a gracious lady had been cut short so suddenly. Newspapers contained many stories of Mary's acts of kindness towards people.

The Prime Minister paid tribute to the princess in the House of Commons and spoke of her devotion to duty and her contribution to strengthen national life: 'She was loved and respected, and there is no need to look for the reason: she personified everything which to all of us simply seemed to be good.'[24] The Archbishop of York stated that 'the people of Yorkshire regarded her as, in some ways, especially their own for she identified herself with so many of their interests and constantly responded to calls for help in all kinds of good works'.[25] On a more personal level, Scobie Breasley, one of her jockeys, told the press, 'She was one of the most charming people … always very sweet and pleasant and … made you feel at your ease.'[26]

In the House of Lords on 30 March the Lords spoke of Mary's legacy. The Earl of Longford echoed the sentiments of everyone towards the princess when he said that 'the war gave her many opportunities for activities which soon became the pattern of her life – a life spent to a degree exceptional even for the Royal Family, in public service'.

Mary's involvement in any cause she took up was never perfunctory and she was never content to be anything like a figurehead. She was naturally shy and reserved, and if some who did not know her found her at first a little formidable, they soon discovered that she had a deep feeling for people, a great sense of humour and a formidable grasp of the details and the essential purpose of any cause that she espoused. Stella, Marchioness of Reading said that 'she put much more into life than she took out.'[27]

According to her wishes, Mary's funeral was held at All Saints Church, Harewood, on 2 April. It was attended by many members of the family including the queen and queen mother. David was still recuperating from his operation in London. Some news reports suggested that Mary's death had occurred at 'the very moment in history when softening hearts in the royal family had drawn the Duke and Duchess of Windsor into their tight circle'.[28] On the morning of the funeral, Mary's gardener took responsibility for over 100 floral arrangements and tributes which had been sent from all over the world. Many of these were spectacular displays; however, in addition there were small posies of flowers from the members of the estate, who were not wealthy, showing how Mary had touched the lives of ordinary people. A simple funeral service was conducted by the Archbishop of York, during which he spoke of Mary's devotion to duty and her deep love of Yorkshire and its countryside. Her body was laid to rest in the 200-year-old family vault.

On the same day as the funeral, a memorial service was held in Westminster Abbey, attended by members of all the organisations with which Mary was associated as well as such dignitaries as Lady Churchill, Lord Mountbatten, Harold Macmillan, Lord Attlee, Prime Minister Harold Wilson and the Duke and Duchess of Windsor, attending a public event in Britain together for the first time. As was befitting of a Yorkshire princess, memorial services were held in Leeds on 2 April and at York Minster on 7 April.

When Mary's personal standard was lowered at Harewood House for the very last time, it signalled not just the end of an era for the estate and the people of the north, but the close of a life for someone who had contributed so much to the founding and principles of a modern monarchy, and to the emergence and survival of the House of Windsor.

# 24

# Legacy: A Purposeful Life

Hers was truly a purposeful life, dominated by a strong natural reserve ... controlled by her belief in the obligations of her birth right. She had only one standard – the highest.[1]

Baroness Swanborough, House of Lords, 30 March 1965

When I began writing the story of Mary's life, an eminent royal biographer suggested that I would struggle to find enough to write about her; much of her life seemed to have passed by rather unremarkably. Only two biographies have ever been written about Mary, both now out of print. The first was by Mabel Carey in 1922 to mark the occasion of her marriage; a second was undertaken by infamous trickster Netley Lucas, under one of his many pseudonyms of Evelyn Graham. Carey's book was written in a long-gone age when the royal family were treated with reverence and surrounded in secrecy; it was not therefore wholly reliable as a source. Graham's claimed to have royal cooperation but was little more than a rewrite of the first, coupled with some added articles from newspapers. As a result of this, over the years there has been much rumour and gossip about Mary's life. Her supposed arranged marriage to a cold and detached man. Her refusal to attend events because of her brother's exclusion. Her unhappy life. Her unhappy childhood. Much of it was based on speculation and gossip and very little was true.

It was not easy to find material concerning Mary's life and for a time it required a great deal of creativity and much thinking outside of the box, along with the kindness and generosity of many institutions and people. Mary's diaries, like Queen Mary's, are rather bland and devoid of opinion, with a strong reliance on the weather and her health. In addition, Mary was inherently shy and retiring by nature. Her private life rarely made headlines. Mary did not possess the charm and cheerfulness of her much more popular contemporary, Queen Elizabeth the Queen Mother. She was not as glamorous or elegant as other princesses such as Princess Marina, and later Princess Margaret. According to Cecil Beaton she had a 'determined lack of style'.[2] In many ways, she was as far removed as possible from pre-conceived ideals of what a princess should look like and how she should act. As one MP said of her: 'There are two characteristics I always felt about the Princess Royal. One was her dislike of fuss … the other was her very strict interpretation of duty.'[3] It was the former which meant that much of her work passed largely unnoticed in the press. Fortunately, Mary was a habitual letter writer and it was not long before I felt that I was facing a monumental avalanche of material. I soon began to realise the colossal amount of work that Mary had undertaken in her almost sixty-eight years, both publicly and privately, demonstrating longevity of commitment. One example, of which there are many, is to be found in her letters to Dame Mary Tyrwhitt, director of the ATS and WRAC. These exemplify Mary's dedication to the ATS and show the extent to which she involved herself in patronages over many years from discussing the buttons on their uniform through to caring for personnel who were struggling with illness. In every engagement, no matter how brief, she showed the same level of sincere interest to ensure that all felt valued.

As a daughter and a princess rather than a prince, Mary could easily have sat back and done very little. Yet from a young age she had an inherent need within her to help people, coupled with a true social conscience. She was genuinely enraged by the struggles of those less fortunate or the lesser members of society at the time: the poor, the sick and children. She had learned from her mother and, by extension, her grandmother

Princess Mary Adelaide, the importance of being more than a mere figurehead for charities. Her attachment to any charitable cause was never perfunctory. Following the welfare reforms that emerged in the early twentieth century, George V had needed to reinvent the monarchy and make the royal family more visible. Moreover, he understood that in order to survive, the monarchy needed to serve its people rather than rule them. He understood the importance of royal tours, especially in industrial areas. If anyone personified George V's model of monarchy, it was Mary, who dutifully followed her parents' example and, in many ways, set the prototype for royal patronage that is still followed by the royal family today.

When Mary married and became the wife of a very wealthy man, who lived out of public gaze in Yorkshire, she could have retired and lived quite happily carrying out very few engagements. Similarly, following the death of her husband, one would have expected her to retreat to nurse her grief rather than undertake a demanding round of royal tours that many younger royals would struggle to complete today. At the time of her death, Mary was the patron of over fifty organisations and held twelve honorary positions in the armed services. Many of these organisations are still in existence and continue to be patronised by the royal family, such as the Red Cross, the YWCA and the YMCA and the British Legion. Mary was not afraid to take on contentious causes or those which had largely been neglected since they were not considered appropriate. In an age when the full horrors of post-traumatic stress were not yet understood, she was one of the first royals to understand the need to rehabilitate servicemen who had lost limbs through armed combat and the vital importance of supporting their families. Mary was more than happy to lead by example and to do so diligently. This can be seen in her work with the campaign to give blood in 1941, when she volunteered to give her own pint of blood in front of the press; her work serving in canteens; knitting comforts for soldiers; and in her continual lifetime campaign against litter. Similarly, by its very nature, nursing is a caring and hands-on profession. It is no wonder that Mary trained as a nurse given her propensity to roll up her sleeves and carry out manual work. From 1926 onwards, Mary resolved to visit every hospital in the country. Her hands-on experience of nursing gave her a unique understanding of the profession, the work of hospitals and enabled her to play an active role in the General Nursing Council.

Mary may not adhere to modern definitions of a feminist. She was never political, since as a member of the royal family she had been taught to communicate only on an uncontroversial level. Yet in some ways, I believe that she was a feminist, since she stressed the importance of creating equal opportunities for girls and women in many areas. Many of the causes she championed focused on women: their health, education and ensuring an equality of opportunity for all. Many challenged the norm regarding female stereotypes. As one newspaper wrote in 1952, she was among a group of pioneering women who helped to lessen 'the gap of inequality'.[5] Her position as a champion of equality should now be acknowledged. Having experienced a broad education, which was considered at the time to be a break from tradition, she championed the need for girls to be educated, especially in tertiary education as well as vocational training and employment programmes. As early as 1929, Mary opened a new building at Battersea Polytechnic for Women. More significantly, she showed with her work with the ATS, the Red Cross and the WRVS the importance of women's role in war work, their contribution in defeating the Nazis, and more significantly the importance of women having a career outside of the home. Mary's life was characterised by many firsts for a woman and a member of the royal family. She was the first female chancellor of a university and the first royal woman to receive the honour of the freedom of Edinburgh. She received eleven honorary doctorate degrees during her lifetime. In 1932, when Mary was given the freedom of the city of Leeds, her husband gave a speech championing the importance of the role of women in the world, signifying his own commitment to the importance of women in public life.

During nearly forty years of public service, Mary's financial support from the civil list remained the same at £6,000 per annum. This suggests that many of her engagements were partially financed by herself and her husband. Mary frequently donated personal items of cash, jewellery and furniture to worthwhile causes, especially during both world wars.

Giving her support to any fundraising was an automatic guarantee of its success. This can be seen in her ability to fundraise for the Princess Mary Tin, which is still remembered over a century later, as well as her work with the Five Sisters' Window in York Minster. Likewise, she took an active role in campaigns for clothing, ambulances and canteens.

Mary's life was defined by the period in which she was born. She lived during the reigns of six monarchs: Queen Victoria, Edward VII, George V, Edward VIII, George VI and Elizabeth II. The magnificent occasion of her wedding ceremony lifted the gloom of life after the First World War. She lived through both world wars and saw the metamorphosis of the British Empire into the Commonwealth. The interwar years saw periods of economic depression and unemployment. Much of her work arose from these significant events, which sparked many charitable patronages that soon became part of her life. Mary witnessed many key historic events including Edward VIII's abdication. In her response to the abdication, we see many traits typical of Mary: her love for her family, her devotion to duty and her commitment to the monarchy. Mary was always seen as the peacemaker in the family and at times her patience with David must have been pushed to its limits. Yet she kept in touch with him throughout their lives and consistently gave him her love in the same way that she remained supportive of her brother Bertie during his reign as George VI. Mary was the glue which held the family together and she was the link to the past for a new generation of royalty.

In an age before television and improved communications, it was rare for royalty to travel to the north of England to conduct engagements and few people in this area had experience of the royal family. Prior to Mary's arrival in Yorkshire, there was little regard for charitable causes in the north. When she married Harry, it is doubtful that she had ever envisaged setting an agenda for raising the profile of the north; however, by living there Mary made the royal family's presence a habitual daily occurrence, rather than something that happened once every so many years. Whenever she visited any town or city in the north she was greeted with much warmth and affection; speeches given by dignitaries welcoming her frequently spoke of her devoted service to so many local charitable causes. Mary did much to dispel the myth of royalty. Unlike Princess Margaret, she was not royal in a regal or pompous way, only in a gracious and benevolent manner. That is not to say that Mary disliked the tradition of monarchy; when she became a senior member of the royal family she had a comprehensive knowledge of royal tradition and ceremony. Mary began traditions of her own, which are now common-place, most notably the tradition of honouring the war dead with a royal bride's bouquet. On a personal level, Mary immersed herself fully in the life of a resident of a country estate. She bred cows, grew roses, attended many race events, inaugurated riding trials and contributed to the artis-tic and cultural aspects of life in and around a stately home.

It is imperative not to forget the impact on the princess's health of her many engagements. In one day, Mary might visit at least five or six different organisations. As the nature of her visits changed, she was frequently called upon to give speeches, something far from easy for someone so shy and socially awkward. Frequently after a period of relentless engagements, Mary would become unwell and forced to take a prolonged period of convalescence. Whilst overexertion is not a quality we would necessarily associate with royalty, it does show Mary's com-mitment and how hard she worked.

We look at our modern princes and princesses and seem to think that their work is somehow innovative or unique to our times: their support of unfashionable causes, their ability to empathise with the public, their royal tours and patronages, their charitable donations and fundraising. Mary was carrying out such work nearly a century ago and so it is cer-tainly not a modern phenomenon. Similarly, without the groundwork that Princess Mary covered, it is doubtful that the public life of the monarchy would have evolved to the extent to which it has now. When Mary died in 1965, she left behind an exemplary body of work, char-acterised by a wide range of interests and a commitment to the highest possible standards. The work she did was not carried out to gain any reward, although undoubtedly she did gain admiration, affection, loy-alty and respect. In his tribute to the princess, Sir Alec Douglas-Home stated that she 'personified everything which to all of us simply seems to be good'.[4]

In my research, I have found much to dispel the many false rumours surrounding Mary's life and, in the process, I have found one unerring truth. Of all the people who met or encountered Mary, in both her personal and public life, there is not one who ever saw fit to criticise or condemn her. Perhaps this is her single most significant achievement as Princess Mary, Britain's first modern princess.

# Notes and Sources

## Chapter 1

1. RA VIC/MAIN/QVJ (W) 25 April 1897 (Princess Beatrice's copies).
2. RA VIC/MAIN/QUV 22 June 1897 (Princess Beatrice's copies).
3. Windsor, Edward, Duke of, *A King's Story: The Memoirs of HRH The Duke of Windsor KG* (London: Cassell, 1951) p. 9.
4. Ross, Janet Ann (Duff-Gordon), *The Fourth Generation: Reminisces* (London: Constable, 1914), p. 62.
5. *The Journal of Benjamin Moran 1857–1865*, vol. 1, p. 93, cited in James Pope-Hennessy, *Queen Mary (1867–1953)* (London: George Allen and Unwin, 1959) p. 32.
6. Ross, *Fourth Generation*, p. 213.
7. Kinloch-Cooke, Clement, *A Memoir of Her Royal Highness Princess Mary Adelaide, Duchess of Teck. Based on Her Private Diaries and Letters* (London: John Murray, 1900), p. 6.
8. Ibid., p. 131.
9. Ibid., p. 197.
10. Warden, Alex J., *The Gentlewoman's Royal Record of the Wedding of HSH The Princess Victoria Mary of Teck and HRH The Duke of York* (London: Unwin Brothers, 1893), p. 6.
11. Ross, *Fourth Generation*, p. 213.
12. Kinloch-Cooke, *A Memoir of Her Royal Highness Princess Mary Adelaide*, p. 235.
13. RA VIC/MAIN/QVJ (W) 5 December 1891 (Princess Beatrice's copies).
14. Pope-Hennessy, *Queen Mary*, p.194.
15. Vincent, James Edmund, *His Royal Highness Duke of Clarence and Avondale: A Memoir* (London: John Murray, 1893) p. 39.

16. Arthur, George, *King George V: A Sketch of A Great Ruler* (London: Joseph Cape, 1929) p.18.
17. Queen Victoria, letter to Mary Adelaide in Pope-Hennessy, *Queen Mary*, p. 208.
18. Princess May's diary, cited in Pope-Hennessy, *Queen Mary*, p. 210.
19. RA VIC/MAIN/QVJ (W) 14 January 1892 (Princess Beatrice's copies).
20. RA VIC/MAIN/QVJ (W) 15 January 1892 (Princess Beatrice's copies).
21. Jack the Ripper Tour. *A Walk Worth Investigating*, www.jack-the-ripper-tour.com/generalnews/death-of-the-duke-of-clarence/.
22. Letter from Duke of Teck to Princess Amélie, cited in Pope-Hennessy, *Queen Mary*, p. 236.
23. Dundee Courier Weekly, 6 September 1892, p. 6. This and all subsequent references to newspaper articles may be found at the British Newspaper Archive.
24. *Lloyd's Weekly Newspaper*, Sunday 12 February 1893, p. 1.
25. Pope-Hennessy, James, *The Quest for Queen Mary* (London: Zuleika, 2018) pp.137–8.
26. RA VIC/MAIN/QVJ (W) 6 July 1893 (Princess Beatrice's copies).
27. RA VIC/MAIN/QVJ (W) 6 July 1893 (Princess Beatrice's copies).
28. Queen Victoria to Victoria, Princess Royal, Empress Frederick, cited in Pope-Hennessy, *Queen Mary*, p. 272.
29. Nicolson, Harold, *Diaries and Letters 1930–1964*, ed. S. Olson (Harmondsworth: Penguin, 1984), p. 342.
30. Pope-Hennessy, *The Quest for Queen Mary*, p. 187.
31. George, Duke of York to Mary, Duchess of York, cited in Pope-Hennessy, *Queen Mary*, p. 280.

# Chapter 2

1. Arthur, *King George V*, p. 52.
2. Ibid., p. 55.
3. Rose, Kenneth, *King George V* (London: Weidenfeld and Nicolson, 1983), p. 39.
4. Windsor, *A King's Story*, p. 6.
5. Airlie, Mabell Countess of, *Thatched with Gold: The Memoirs of Mabell Countess of Airlie*, edited and arranged by Jennifer Ellis (London: Hutchinson, 1962), pp. 112–13.
6. Ibid., p. 102.
7. Windsor, *A King's Story*, p. 27.
8. Airlie, *Thatched with Gold*, p. 112.
9. Windsor, *A King's Story*, p. 24.
10. Ibid., p. 26.
11. Princess Alice, Duchess of Gloucester, *The Memoirs of Princess Alice Duchess of Gloucester* (London: Collins, 1983), p. 107.
12. Lascelles, George, Earl of Harewood, *The Tongs and the Bones: The Memoirs of Lord Harewood* (London: Weidenfeld and Nicolson, 1981), p. 14.
13. Ibid.

14. Airlie, *Thatched with Gold*, p. 113.
15. *Windsor and Eaton Express*, Saturday 2 November 1901, p. 5.
16. Carey, M.C., *Princess Mary* (London: Nisbet, 1922), p. 16.
17. Windsor, *A King's Story*, p. 14.
18. Ibid., p.15.
19. Ibid.
20. Princess Mary's Archive (1897–1965), Harewood House Trust.
21. Ibid.
22. Carey, *Princess Mary*, p. 28.
23. Wheeler-Bennett, J.W., *King George VI: His Life and Reign* (London: Macmillan, 1958), p. 26.
24. Windsor, *A King's Story*, p. 37.
25. Ibid., p. 39.
26. George VI, cited in Bradford, Sarah, *George VI* (London: Weidenfeld & Nicolson, 1989), p. 66.
27. Windsor, *A King's Story*, p. 39.
28. Carey, *Princess Mary*, p. 29.
29. *Dundee Evening Telegraph*, Friday 25 April 1913, p. 1.
30. Windsor, *A King's Story*, p. 28.
31. Ibid., p. 29.
32. Ibid., p. 33.
33. Ibid., p. 51.
34. Princess of Wales to Grand Duchess of Mecklenburg-Strelitz, 24 June 1906, cited in Pope-Hennessy, *Queen Mary*, p. 409.
35. Pope-Hennessy, *The Quest for Queen Mary*, p. 182.

# Chapter 3

1. Rose, *King George V*, p. 74.
2. Windsor, *A King's Story*, p. 72.
3. Pope-Hennessy, *Queen Mary*, p. 422.
4. Windsor, *A King's Story*, p. 76.
5. *Sevenoaks Chronicle and Kentish Advertiser*, Friday 20 May 1910, p .3.
6. Edward, Prince of Wales to Princess Mary, 22 January 1911, Princess Mary's Archive (1897–1965), Harewood House Trust.
7. *The Globe*, Thursday 22 June 1911, p. 4.
8. *Middlesex County Times*, Saturday 24 June 1911, p. 6.
9. The Bystander Wednesday 28th June 1911 p.58
10. Windsor, *A King's Story*, p. 78
11. *Daily Telegraph and Courier*, Monday 10 July 1911, p. 12.
12. *London Daily News*, Friday 14 July 1911, p. 1.
13. *Pall Mall Gazette*, Monday 17 July 1911, p. 1.
14. *Illustrated Sporting and Dramatic News*, Saturday 8 July 1911, p. 38.

# Chapter 4

1. Nicolson, Harold, *King George V: His Life and Reign* (London: Pan Books, 1967), p. 329.
2. Pope-Hennessy, *Queen Mary*, p. 476.
3. *Isle of Wight Times*, Thursday 22 August 1912, pp. 4–5.
4. Ibid.
5. Pope-Hennessy, *Queen Mary*, pp. 477–8.
6. Churchill, Alexandra, *In The Eye of The Storm: George V and the Great War* (Warwick: Helion, 2018), p. 54.
7. Nicolson, *King George V*, p. 329.
8. Princess Mary's diary, 2 August 1914, Princess Mary's Archive (1897–1965), Harewood House Trust.
9. Pope-Hennessy, *Queen Mary*, p. 490.
10. Bolitho, Hector, *King George VI* (New York: J.B. Lippincott, 1938), p. 136.
11. Ziegler, Philip, *King Edward VIII* (London: William Collins, 1990), p. 49.
12. Ibid.
13. Imperial War Museum: Private Papers of E. Silas FRSA RGS Box No: 97/37/1 Doc: 7218 A Royal Occasion 20 May 1916.
14. Windsor, *A King's Story*, p. 108.
15. *Dundee Courier*, Wednesday 23 November 1921, p. 5.
16. Carey, *Princess Mary*, p. 94.
17. *Luton Times and Advertiser*, Friday 6 November 1914, p. 5.
18. *Daily Mirror*, Monday 19 October 1914, p. 2.
19. Condell, Diana, 'A Gift For Christmas: The Story of Princess Mary's Gift Fund 1914', *Imperial War Museum Review*, No. 4 (London: The Imperial War Museum, 1989).
20. *Imperial War Museum Review*, No. 4 (London: The Imperial War Museum, 1989), p. 72.
21. The Imperial War Museum EN1/3/ORG/017.
22. Williamson, Anne, *Henry Williamson and the First World War* (Stroud: Sutton, 2004), p. 47.
23. The Royal Family on Twitter, twitter.com/royalfamily/status/1058294352206852097, 2 November 2018.
24. *Dundee Evening Telegraph*, Friday 26 February 1915, p. 4.

# Chapter 5

1. *Illustrated London News Wedding Special*, Saturday 4 March 1922, p. 17.
2. Nicolson, *King George V*, p. 403.
3. Ibid.
4. Ziegler, *King Edward VIII*, p. 80.
5. *Dundee Evening Telegraph*, Tuesday 25 April 1916, p. 2,
6. *Illustrated London News Wedding Special*, Saturday 4 March 1922, p. 26.
7. *Daily Mirror*, Tuesday 28 February 1922, p. 2.
8. *Lichfield Mercury*, Friday 16 August 1918, p. 2.

9.  Letter from the queen regarding Princess Mary, Flickr.com The British Monarchy, www.flickr.com/photos/britishmonarchy/15018686996/in/photostream/.
10. Letter from Princess Mary, 30 November 1918, Dr Rachel Crowdy Papers and Correspondence, Wichita State University, cdm15942.contentdm.oclc.org/cdm/compoundobject/collection/p15942coll166/id/107/rec/3.

# Chapter 6

1.  *Norwood News*, Friday 7 January 1927, p. 14.
2.  *Dundee Evening Telegraph*, Friday 6 December 1918, p. 4.
3.  *Irish Society*, Saturday 13 September 1919, p. 6.
4.  *Dundee Courier*, Wednesday 10 September 1919, pp. 3-4.
5.  Carey, *Princess Mary*, p. 19.
6.  *Yarmouth Independent*, Saturday 25 January 1919, p. 7.
7.  *Dundee Evening Telegraph*, Monday 20 January 1919, p. 2.
8.  Pope-Hennessy, *Queen Mary*, p. 511.
9.  *The Globe*, Monday 20 January 1919, p. 3.
10. Princess Mary's diary, 21 January 1919, Princess Mary's Archive (1897–1965), Harewood House Trust.
11. *Leeds Mercury*, Wednesday 22 January 1919, p. 7.
12. Princess Mary's diary, 22 January 1919, Princess Mary's Archive (1897–1965), Harewood House Trust.

# Chapter 7

1.  *The Common Cause*, Friday 17 February 1922, p. 5.
2.  Hampton, Janie, *How the Girl Guides Won the War* (London: Harper Collins, 2010), p. 146.
3.  Carey, *Princess Mary*, p. 147.
4.  Ibid., p. 160.
5.  Liddell, Alix, *Story of the Girl Guides 1908–1938* (London: Girl Guides Association, 1976), p. 124.
6.  Ibid., p. 62.
7.  Ibid., p. 63.

# Chapter 8

1.  *Pall Mall Gazette*, Tuesday 28 February 1922, p. 3.
2.  *Dundee Courier*, Wednesday 23 November 1921, p. 5.
3.  Airlie, *Thatched with Gold*, p. 145.
4.  Godfrey, Rupert (ed.), *Letters From a Prince: Edward Prince of Wales to Mrs Freda Dudley Ward* (London: Little Brown & Company, 1998), p. 287.
5.  Ibid., p. 286.

6. *Baltimore Sun*, Friday 3 March 1922; Marguerite E. Harrison, cited in The Esoteric Curiosa theesotericcuriosablogspot.com/2012/05/did-princess-lose-her-true-love.html.

7. Forbes, Grania, *My Darling Buffy: The Early Life of the Queen Mother* (London: Richard Cohen, 1997), p. 157.

8. Parliamentary Archives BBK/B/11 1919

9. Forbes, *My Darling Buffy*, p. 157.

10. Jenkins, Alan, *The Twenties* (New York: Universe Books, 1974), p. 54.

11. Airlie, *Thatched with Gold*, pp. 164–5.

12. Cooper, Duff, *Old Men Forget* (Suffolk: Richard Clay, 1953), p. 76.

13. Ibid.

14. Hirst, Geoffrey Frederick Robert (MBE MC), Unpublished Memoir Document 16943, Imperial War Museum, 1983.

15. Ibid.

16. Hart Davis, Duff (ed.), *In Royal Service: The Letters and Journals of Sir Alan Lascelles 1920–1936* (London: Hamish Hamilton, 1989), p. 144.

17. *Baltimore Sun*, Friday 3 March 1922; Marguerite E. Harrison, cited on The Esoteric Curiosa, theesotericcuriosablogspot.com/2012/05/did-princess-lose-her-true-love.html.

18. The Esoteric Curiosa, theesotericcuriosa.blogspot.com/2013/01/lord-lascelles-vain-attempts-to-lure.html.

19. Dennison, Matthew, *Behind the Mask: The Life of Vita Sackville-West* (London: William Collins, 2014), p. 68.

20. *Sheffield Independent*, Thursday 24 November 1921, p. 4.

21. Lascelles, *The Tongs and the Bones*, p. 26.

22. Hart Davis, *In Royal Service*, p. 7.

23. *The Graphic*, Saturday 26 November 1921, p. 10.

24. RA QM/PRIV/QMD/ 20 November 1921.

25. Ziegler, *King Edward VIII*, p. 171.

26. Kennedy, Carol, *Harewood: The Life and Times of an English Country House* (London: Hutchinson, 1982), p. 103.

27. Swingler, Sue, 'The Yorkshire Princess: Princess Mary at Harewood House', *Yorkshire Journal*, Issue 18, summer 1997, p. 9.

28. RA QM/PRIV/QMD/ 16 December 1921.

29. *Leeds Mercury*, Friday 16 December 1921, p. 1.

30. Ibid.

31. Ibid.

32. *Yorkshire Evening Post*, Friday 16 December 1921, p. 8.

33. *Illustrated Police News*, Thursday 22 December 1921, p. 3.

34. Hirst, Geoffrey Frederick Robert (MBE MC), Unpublished Memoir Document 16943, Imperial War Museum, 1983.

35. Hart Davis, *In Royal Service*, p. 8.

36. *Hartlepool Northern Daily Mail*, Tuesday 3 January 1922, p. 2.

# Chapter 9

1. *Tatler*, Wednesday 1 March 1922, p. 3.
2. *Pall Mall Gazette*, Tuesday 28 February 1922, p. 3.
3. Pope-Hennessy, *Queen Mary*, pp. 519–20.
4. Ziegler, *King Edward VIII*, p. 171.
5. International Autograph Auctions Ltd, www.autographauctions.co.uk/0107-lot-306-FRANCIS-OF-TECK-1870-1910-British-Prince-brother-of-Queen-Mary-A-more-detailed-description-for?auction_id=0&search_priority[0]=&view=lot_detail#?high_estimate=90000&low_estimate=0&sort_by=lot_number&catId=&ipp=10&cat_id=&lot_id=45843
6. Airlie, *Thatched with Gold*, p. 164.
7. Hart Davis, *In Royal Service*, p. 8.
8. Lascelles, *The Tongs and the Bones*, p. 2.
9. *Vogue*, www.vogue.co.uk/gallery/royal-weddings-in-vogue.
10. RA/QM/PRIV/QMD/1922, Tuesday 28 February 1922.
11. Ibid.
12. *Illustrated London News Wedding Special*, Saturday 4 March 1922, p. 317.
13. RA QMPRIV/QMD/1922, Tuesday 28 February 1922.
14. *Tatler*, Wednesday 1 March 1922, p. 3.
15. *Illustrated London News Wedding Special*, Saturday 4 March 1922, p. 284.
16. Princess Mary to Queen Mary, 1 March 1922, Princess Mary's Archive (1897–1965), Harewood House Trust.
17. RA QMPRIV/QMD/1922, Tuesday 28 February 1922.
18. RA QMPRIV/QMD/1922, Wednesday 1 March 1922.
19. Pope-Hennessy, *Queen Mary*, pp. 520–1.
20. Ibid.
21. Nicolson, *King George V*, p. 474.
22. *The Bystander*, Wednesday 1 March 1922, p. 22.

# Chapter 10

1. *Belfast News-Letter*, Monday 13 March 1922, p. 4.
2. *Western Mail*, Saturday 11 March 1922, p. 7.
3. *Leeds Mercury*, Thursday 13 May 1922, p. 7.
4. *Illustrated London News Wedding Special*, Saturday 4 March 1922, pp. 286–7.
5. Lascelles, *The Tongs and the Bones*, p. 5.
6. *The Scotsman*, 28 February 1922, p. 6.
7. RA/QM/PRIV/QMD/1921, 16 December 1921.
8. *Kington Times*, Saturday 21 March 1925, p. 2.
9. *Aberdeen Press and Journal*, Monday 28 August 1922, p. 4.

# Chapter 11

1. *The Sphere*, Saturday 17 February 1923, p. 4.
2. *Dundee Evening Telegraph*, Thursday 11 January 1923, p. 9.
3. Ibid.
4. The Yorkshire Film Archive, *Harewood by George: A Profile of the Seventh Earl*, Yorkshire Television 1982, www.yorkshirefilmarchive.com/film/harewood-george-profile-seventh-earl.
5. *Hartlepool Northern Daily Mail*, Monday 12 March 1923, p. 3.
6. *Aberdeen Press and Journal*, Monday 26 March 1923, p. 7.
7. Ibid.
8. *Illustrated London News Wedding Special*, Saturday 4 March 1922, p. 289
9. Ibid.
10. Lascelles, *The Tongs and the Bones*, p. 27.
11. RA/QM/PRIV/CC015/5.
12. Mackie, Mary, *Wards in the Sky: The RAF's Remarkable Nursing Service* (Stroud: History Press, 2014), p. 37.
13. *The Sphere*, Saturday 17 March 1923, p. 4.
14. Lascelles, *The Tongs and the Bones*, p. 27.
15. Imperial War Museum Misc. 44 (754), The Restoration of the Five Sisters Window, York Minster. Yorkshire Herald Newspaper Co. Ltd. York. 1925.
16. *Sheffield Daily Telegraph*, Thursday 9 June 1932, p. 7.
17. *The Bystander*, Wednesday 17 October 1928, p. 3.
18. Ibid.
19. *Western Mail*, Monday 8 October 1928, p. 11.
20. Ibid.
21. Irish Wolfhound History, www.irishwolfhounds.org/princessmary.htm.
22. Lascelles, *The Tongs and the Bones*, p. 3.
23. Richards, Phyllis, *Wakefield High School Magazine* (Wakefield: Wakefield Girls High School, 1930).

# Chapter 12

1. Lascelles, David, Diane Howse and Anna Dewsnap, *Harewood* (Harewood: Harewood House Trust, 2017), p. 1.
2. Ibid., p. 5.
3. Buckle, Richard, 7th Earl Harewood, Neville Ussher and Alfred Blades, *Harewood: A New Guide Book to the Yorkshire Seat of the Earls of Harewood* (Harewood: Harewood House Trust, 1979), p. 5.
4. Ibid., p. 20.
5. Wood, Charles H. (ed.), *Harewood House* (Harewood: Harewood House, 1960).
6. Mauchline, Mary, *Harewood House: One of the Treasure Houses of Britain* (Broughton Gifford: Cromwell Press, 1992), p. 148.
7. Lascelles, *The Tongs and the Bones*, p. 26.

8.  Hall, Geoffrey, *Fifty Years Gardening at Harewood* (Wakefield: EP Publishing, 1978), p. 14.
9.  *Belfast Telegraph*, Tuesday 9 September 1930, p. 6.
10. Hall, *Fifty Years Gardening at Harewood*, p. 17.
11. Pope-Hennessy, *The Quest for Queen Mary*, p. 182.
12. Kennedy, *Harewood*, p. 100.
13. *Yorkshire Post and Leeds Intelligencer*, Tuesday 7 July 1908, p. 6.
14. Lascelles, *The Tongs and the Bones*, p. 13.
15. Ibid., p. 7.
16. Hall, *Fifty Years Gardening at Harewood*, p. 24.
17. Ibid., p. 14.

# Chapter 13

1.  *The Scotsman*, Tuesday 21 January 1936, p.13.
2.  *Yorkshire Post and Leeds Intelligencer*, Friday 1 January 1932, p. 9.
3.  *Leeds Mercury*, Thursday 7 July 1932, p. 5.
4.  *Yorkshire Post and Leeds Intelligencer*, Thursday 7 July 1932, p. 10.
5.  Lascelles, *The Tongs and the Bones*, p. 14.
6.  *Aberdeen Press and Journal*, Monday 16 September 1935, p. 6.
7.  *Sheffield Independent*, Monday 7 August 1933, p. 5.
8.  Lascelles, *The Tongs and the Bones*, p. 91.
9.  Maxon, Jim, *Harewood: Bronze Age to Broadband* (Leicester: Troubador, 2007), p. 145.
10. Airlie, *Thatched with Gold*, p. 194.
11. The King's Jubilee 1935, YouTube, www.youtube.com/watch?v=XansRBeDRRM.
12. Pope-Hennessy, *Queen Mary*, p. 555.
13. Middlemas Keith and John Barnes, *Baldwin: A Biography* (London: Weidenfeld & Nicolson, 1969), p. 976.
14. *Daily Herald*, Saturday 18 January 1936, p. 1.
15. Windsor, *A King's Story*, p. 262.
16. Ibid., p. 263.
17. Lockhart J.G., *Cosmo Gordon Lang* (London: Hodder and Stoughton, 1949), pp. 391–2.
18. RA/QM/PRIV/QMD/1936, Monday 20 January 1936.
19. RA/QM/PRIV/QMD/1936, Monday 20 January 1936.
20. RA/QM/PRIV/QMD/1936, Monday 27 January 1936.
21. RA/QM/PRIV/QMD/1936, Tuesday 28 January 1936.
22. Princess Mary's diary, Tuesday 28 January 1936, Princess Mary's Archive (1897–1965), Harewood House Trust.

# Chapter 14

1. Letter from Princess Mary, 2 January 1937, Dr Rachel Crowdy Papers and Correspondence, Wichita State University, cdm15942.contentdm.oclc.org/digital/collection/p15942coll166/id/165/rec/32 and cdm15942.contentdm.oclc.org/cdm/compoundobject/collection/p15942coll166/id/165/rec/6.
2. RA/EDW/PRIV/MAIN/A/3167.
3. Lascelles, *The Tongs and the Bones*, p. 14.
4. Ibid., p. 17.
5. Ibid.
6. RA/EDW/PRIV/MAIN/3007.
7. *Dundee Courier*, 22 January 1936, p. 7.
8. *Nottingham Evening Post*, Tuesday 11 June 1935, p. 1.
9. *Yorkshire Post and Leeds Intelligencer*, Monday 20 April 1936, p. 4.
10. Ibid.
11. Airlie, *Thatched with Gold*, p. 198.
12. Windsor, *A King's Story*, p. 334.
13. Lascelles, *The Tongs and the Bones*, p. 26.
14. Windsor, *A King's Story*, p. 334.
15. *Daily Herald*, Friday 4 December 1936, p. 4.
16. QM/PRIV/QMD/1936, 9 December 1936.
17. Ibid.
18. Ibid.
19. Airlie, *Thatched with Gold*, p. 201.
20. Pope-Hennessy, *Queen Mary*, p. 575.
21. RA/EDW/PRIV/MAIN/A/3102.
22. *Belfast News-Letter*, Monday 8 February 1937, p. 5.
23. Bloch, Michael, *The Secret File of The Duke of Windsor* (Reading: Corgi Books, 1988), p. 58.
24. Ziegler, *King Edward VIII*, p. 343.
25. RA/EDW/PRIV/MAIN/A/3158.
26. Ziegler, *King Edward VIII*, p. 343.
27. RA/EDW/PRIV/MAIN/A/3167.
28. RA/EDW/PRIV/MAIN/A/3440.
29. Ibid.
30. Lascelles, *The Tongs and the Bones*, p. 27.
31. Hart Davis, *In Royal Service*, p. 201.
32. *Daily Herald*, Tuesday 23 November 1937, p. 8.
33. *Daily Herald*, Friday 12 November 1937, p. 5.

# Chapter 15

1. *The Scotsman*, Monday 13 November 1939, p. 4.
2. *Daily Mirror*, Monday 8 May 1939, p. 1.
3. *Daily Herald*, Tuesday 9 May 1939, p. 11.

4. Ibid.
5. *Tatler*, Wednesday 3 January 1940, p. 3.

# Chapter 16

1. *Newcastle Evening Chronicle*, Tuesday 28 October 1941, p. 5.
2. National Army Museum 9802-109-26, 10 July 1941.
3. *Nottingham Journal*, Thursday 27 June 1940, p. 1.
4. *Yorkshire Post and Leeds Intelligencer*, Monday 20 March 1950, p. 6.
5. Whateley, Leslie, *As Thoughts Survive* (London: Hutchinson, 1948), p. 7.
6. Ibid., p. 9.
7. University of Nottingham Mi4F588/1, 8 September 1941.
8. Ibid.
9. Airlie, *Thatched with Gold*, p. 195.
10. Bloch, *The Secret File of the Duke of Windsor*, p. 243.
11. Pope-Hennessy, *Queen Mary*, p. 608.

# Chapter 17

1. Lascelles, *The Tongs and the Bones*, p. 56.
2. Ibid., p. 33.
3. Ibid.
4. Ibid.
5. *Western Daily Press*, Tuesday 27 June 1944, p. 4.
6. *Hull Daily Mail*, Saturday 8 July 1944, p. 4.
7. The Earl of Harewood Obituary, *Daily Telegraph*, Monday 11 July 2011, www.telegraph.co.uk/news/obituaries/8631002/The-Earl-of-Harewood.html.
8. Letter from Princess Mary, 30 December 1944, Dr Rachel Crowdy Papers and Correspondence, Wichita State University, cdm15942.contentdm.oclc.org/cdm/compoundobject/collection/p15942coll166/id/222/rec/7.
9. *Yorkshire Post and Leeds Intelligencer*, Monday 13 August 1945, p. 2.
10. RA/QM/PRIV/CCO15/14.
11. Ibid.
12. Ibid.

# Chapter 18

1. Kennedy, *Harewood*, p. 121.
2. Lascelles, *The Tongs and the Bones*, p. 96.
3. Kennedy, *Harewood*, p. 121.
4. Ibid., p. 121.
5. *Western Daily Press*, Wednesday 28 May 1947, p. 4.

6. G92H437/1, Nottingham University.
7. Lascelles, *The Tongs and the Bones*, p. 98.
8. Ibid., p. 92.
9. *Yorkshire Post*, Saturday 24 May 1947, p. 4.
10. Hall, *Fifty Years Gardening at Harewood*, p. 37.
11. Storrs Archive Reel 20, Section VI, Box 7 Diary, 1946–1947. Palestine, 12 December 1947.
12. Ibid. Palestine, 8 January 1948.
13. The British Army Museum, 9303-1-9, 12 November 1947.
14. *The Scotsman*, Friday 5 December 1947, p. 5.
15. Ziegler, *King Edward VIII*, p. 516.
16. *Yorkshire Post and Leeds Intelligencer*, Thursday 9 March 1950, p. 2.
17. Kennedy, *Harewood*, p. 139.
18. Hall, *Fifty Years Gardening at Harewood*, p. 53.
19. Kennedy, *Harewood*, p. 139.
20. Munro, Air Vice-Marshal Sir David, *It Passed too Quickly* (London: George Routledge, 1941), p. 260.

## Chapter 19

1. *Birmingham Daily Post*, Monday 29 March 1965, p. 17.
2. *Daily Mirror*, Monday 2 June 1952, p. 12.
3. Lascelles, *The Tongs and the Bones*, p. 102.
4. Ibid.
5. Rose, Kenneth, *Who's In, Who's Out? The Journals of Kenneth Rose, vol. 1, 1944–1979* (London: Weidenfeld & Nicolson, 2018), p. 557.
6. Lascelles, *The Tongs and the Bones*, p. 96.
7. 'Marion Thorpe and Benjamin Britten: An Intimate Friendship', BBC Sounds, www.bbc.co.uk/sounds/play/p01m1v15.
8. Lascelles, *The Tongs and the Bones*, p. 118.
9. Ibid., p.18.
10. *Trove: The Australian Women's Weekly*, 2 July 1952, p. 13, trove.nla.gov.au/ newspaper/article/51595532/4876928.
11. Rose, *The Journals of*, p. 529.

## Chapter 20

1. LUA/PUB/020/A/9/1, 'Lady Elect of Royal Line', Ode for the installation of the chancellor of the University of Leeds, 9 November 1951. Words: W.R. Childe. Music: J. Denny.
2. *Coventry Evening Telegraph*, Friday 24 October 1952, p. 6.
3. *Yorkshire Post and Leeds Intelligencer*, Wednesday 11 April 1951, p. 6.
4. Ibid.

5. *The People*, Sunday 15 April 1951, p. 5.
6. *Hull Daily Mail*, Thursday 5 July 1923, p. 6.
7. LUA/PUB/020/A/9/1, *Yorkshire Post*, Friday 8 June 1951, p. 3.
8. LUA/PUB/020/A/9/1, Joyce Mather, *Yorkshire Post*, Friday 9 November 1951.
9. LUA/PUB/020/A/9/1, *Yorkshire Post*, Friday 8 June 1951, p. 3.
10. Ibid.
11. Hall, *Fifty Years Gardening at Harewood*, p. 43.
12. [missing note text]
13. *Hartlepool Northern Daily Mail*, Wednesday 2 January 1952, p. 2.
14. Ibid.
15. Ibid.

# Chapter 21

1. University of Nottingham Mi 4F589/1, 29 March 1952.
2. QM/PRIV/CC015/24, 22 April 1949.
3. University of Nottingham Mi 4F589/1, 29 March 1952.
4. Bloch, *The Secret File of the Duke of Windsor*, p. 306.
5. Ibid., p. 307.
6. *Yorkshire Post and Leeds Intelligencer*, Monday 10 February 1952, p. 2.
7. Airlie, *Thatched with Gold*, p. 235.
8. *Coventry Evening Telegraph*, Thursday 19 February 1953, p. 19.
9. Airlie, *Thatched with Gold*, p. 237.
10. Bloch, *The Secret File of the Duke of Windsor*, pp. 319–20.
11. Lascelles, *The Tongs and the Bones*, p. 258.
12. Bloch, *The Secret File of the Duke of Windsor*, p. 324.
13. Letter from Princess Mary, 9 April 1953, Dr Rachel Crowdy Papers and Correspondence, Wichita State University, cdm15942.contentdm.oclc.org/cdm/singleitem/collection/p15942coll166/id/78/rec/7.
14. Rose, Kenneth, *Who's In, Who's Out: The Journals of Kenneth Rose*, edited by D.R. Thorpe (London: Weidenfeld & Nicolson, 2018), p. 13.
15. Bloch, *The Secret File of the Duke of Windsor*, p. 329.
16. Ibid.
17. Ibid.
18. *Yorkshire Post and Leeds Intelligencer*, Thursday 22 October 1953, p. 5.
19. Ibid.
20. *Yorkshire Post and Leeds Intelligencer*, Friday 23 October 1953, p. 5.
21. *Yorkshire Post and Leeds Intelligencer*, Wednesday 11 November 1953, p. 5.
22. *Dundee Courier*, Tuesday 11 May 1954, p. 4.
23. *Yorkshire Post and Leeds Intelligencer*, Thursday 13 May 1954, p. 5.

# Chapter 22

1. *Belfast Telegraph*, Tuesday 3 January 1967, p. 1.
2. Ibid.
3. *Daily Mirror*, Tuesday 3 January 1967, p. 1.
4. Ibid.
5. Lascelles, *The Tongs and the Bones*, p. 295.
6. Ibid., p. 216.
7. Calder, John, *Pursuit: The Memoirs of John Calder* (Surrey: Calder, 2016), p. 275.
8. Lascelles, *The Tongs and the Bones*, p. 216.
9. Athol Shmith 1914–1990, National Gallery of Australia, nga.gov.au/exhibition/karshshmith/detail.cfm?IRN=66834&BioArtistIRN=12439&MnuID=1.
10. The Yorkshire Film Archive, *Harewood by George: A Profile of the Seventh Earl*, Yorkshire Television 1982, www.yorkshirefilmarchive.com/film/harewood-george-profile-seventh-earl.
11. Allison, John, 'Lord of the Opera', *Opera Magazine*, September 2011, p. 1019.

# Chapter 23

1. *Belfast Telegraph*, Wednesday 31 March 1965, p. 4.
2. *Shields Daily News*, Friday 23 September, p. 16.
3. Gladwyn, Cynthia, *The Diaries of Cynthia Gladwyn*, edited by Jebb Miles (London: Constable and Company, 1995), p. 170.
4. Ibid., p. 171.
5. *The British Medical Journal*, vol. 2, no. 505, 7 December 1957, p. 1378.
6. Nottingham University M14F 597/2.
7. *Trove: The Australian Women's Weekly*, 14 April 1965, p. 15, trove.nla.gov.au/aww/read/222256?q=PRINCESS+ROYAL&s=0&resultId=num0#page/15/mode/1up.
8. *Coventry Evening Telegraph*, Monday 15 January 1960, p. 41.
9. *Birmingham Daily Post*, Saturday 1 September 1962, p. 26.
10. The National Army Museum 9401-240-44-1, 8 July 1962.
11. Cathcart, Helen, *Anne, The Princess Royal: A Princess for Our Times* (London: W.H. Allen, 1988), p. 131.
12. *Trove: The Australian Women's Weekly*, 14 April 1965, p. 15, trove.nla.gov.au/aww/read/222256?q=PRINCESS+ROYAL&s=0&resultId=num0#page/15/mode/1up.
13. Lascelles, *The Tongs and the Bones*, p. 295.
14. Hall, *Fifty Years Gardening at Harewood*, p. 50.
15. Ibid.
16. Lascelles, *The Tongs and the Bones*, pp. 295–6.
17. *The Times*, Monday 29 March 1965, p. 10.
18. Ibid., p.14.
19. Ibid.

20. Ibid.
21. Ibid.
22. *Birmingham Daily Post*, Monday 29 March 1965, p. 6.
23. Ibid.
24. *Birmingham Daily Post*, Wednesday 31 March 1965, p. 13.
25. *Liverpool Echo*, Monday 29 March 1965, p. 10.
26. *Belfast Telegraph*, Monday 29 March 1965, p. 8.
27. Baroness Swanborough, speech in the House of Lords, 30 March 1965, Hansard HL Deb, vol. 264 cc941-6, api.parliament.uk/historic-hansard/lords/1965/mar/30/hrh-the-princess-royal.
28. Trove: The Australian Women's Weekly, 14 April 1965, p. 15, trove.nla.gov.au/aww/read/222256?q=PRINCESS+ROYAL&s=0&resultId=num0#page/15/mode/1up.

# Chapter 24

1. Baroness Swanborough, speech in the House of Lords, 30 March 1965, Hansard HL Deb, vol. 264 cc941-6, api.parliament.uk/historic-hansard/lords/1965/mar/30/hrh-the-princess-royal.
2. Swingler, Sue, 'The Yorkshire Princess: Princess Mary at Harewood House', *Yorkshire Journal*, Issue 18, summer 1997, p. 15.
3. Turton R.H. (MP for Thirsk and Malton) Speech in the House of Commons, 30 March 1965, Hansard, vol. 709, hansard.parliament.uk/commons/1965-03-30/debates/5cef0f78-7684-46fe-9210-18f056b3bdc9/HrhThePrincessRoyal.
4. Douglas-Home, Sir Alec, Speech in the House of Commons, 30 March 1965, Hansard, vol. 709, hansard.parliament.uk/commons/1965-03-30/debates/5cef0f78-7684-46fe-9210-18f056b3bdc9/HrhThePrincessRoyal.
5. *Hartlepool Northern Daily Mail*, Wednesday 2 January 1952, p. 2.

# Index